DREAM MAKERS
VOLUME II

Berkley books by Charles Platt

DREAM MAKERS: THE UNCOMMON PEOPLE
WHO WRITE SCIENCE FICTION
DREAM MAKERS VOLUME II: THE UNCOMMON MEN AND WOMEN
WHO WRITE SCIENCE FICTION

DREAM MAKERS
VOLUME II

THE UNCOMMON MEN & WOMEN WHO WRITE SCIENCE FICTION

INTERVIEWS BY CHARLES PLATT

BERKLEY BOOKS, NEW YORK

DREAM MAKERS VOLUME II: THE UNCOMMON MEN AND WOMEN WHO WRITE SCIENCE FICTION

A Berkley Book/published by arrangement with the author

PRINTING HISTORY
Berkley trade paperback edition/June 1983

For information address: Berkley Publishing Corporation, 200 Madison Avenue, New York, New York 10016.

ISBN: 0-425-05880-8

A BERKLEY BOOK ® TM 757,375
Berkley Books are published by Berkley Publishing Corporation, 200 Madison Avenue, New York, New York 10016.
The name "BERKLEY" and the stylized "B" with design are trademarks belonging to Berkley Publishing Corporation.
PRINTED IN THE UNITED STATES OF AMERICA

Acknowledgments

Compiling this book entailed asking a lot of favors. First, and most obviously, the writers whom I interviewed were generous with their time, and for this I thank them. I also want to thank Gregory and Jim Benford, for helping to arrange the Poul Anderson interview; Shawna McCarthy, for introducing me to Alice Sheldon; Betsy Mitchell, for her transcription of the Jack Vance interview; Susan Allison, without whom I might not have met Andre Norton; Brad Balfour, for bringing my work to the attention of Alvin Toffler; Forrest Ackerman and Vaughn Young, for enabling me to make indirect contact with L. Ron Hubbard; and Douglas Winter, for inviting me to participate in the interview with Stephen King.

The poem "The Head Rape" is copyright 1968 by D.M. Thomas and is reprinted in his profile with his permission.

Edited versions of the profiles of Harry Harrison, William Burroughs, Alvin Toffler, Jerry Pournelle,

Joanna Russ, James Tiptree, Jr., and Robert Anton Wilson were published in *Isaac Asimov's Science Fiction Magazine.*

The profiles of Janet Morris, Keith Laumer, Piers Anthony, and Charles Platt were first published in *Science Fiction Review.*

The profile of D.M. Thomas first appeared in *Fantasy Newsletter.*

For Douglas and Lynn,
Susan and Richard,
and others who helped me
to write this book.

Contents

Introduction

A lot of important writers were missing from the first volume of *Dream Makers,* and I think some of them were a bit miffed about it.

That book was assembled very haphazardly. At first, almost as a hobby, I did occasional interviews with friends. Then I added several well-known writers so that we would have more recognizable names to put on the cover. The selection was never intended to be balanced or definitive. I talked to whoever was most approachable, and finally stopped when my editor told me that the book was getting too long.

Volume II has been put together in a slightly more responsible fashion—but only slightly. The trouble is, I don't have the neutral outlook of a true bibliographer. I feel passionately about the work of some writers—William Burroughs, Keith Roberts, and John Sladek, for instance—and so I've included them here even though their books are far from the center of modern science fiction. By contrast, some well-known names are still missing, because I think it's very hard, and probably rather rude, to go and interview someone whose work I don't enjoy. Moreover, I have to say that the most popular writers are not always the ones who are most interesting to talk to.

So this is not an "objective" book, and I freely admit my bias—not only because I feel an obligation to own up, but because, I hope, a book with opinions may be more interesting than one that avoids presenting any particular point of view.

DISCRIMINATORY INTERVIEWING POLICIES?

I have to admit that there were very few senior citizens, disabled persons, blacks, Hispanics, Jews, teenagers, or women profiled in the first *Dream*

Makers. These inequalities didn't bother most people—except when it came to the small number of women. For this, more than one reviewer accused me of blatant sexism.

I suppose I have to try to take this subject seriously and emphasize the obvious, which is that *most well-known science-fiction writers are men*. See for yourself. Look through *The Encyclopedia of Science Fiction*. You will find, also, that the women who do write science fiction are mostly newcomers, and they tend more toward fantasy. (See "No Swords, Dragons, or Talking Rabbits," below.)

For *Dream Makers II* to be at all representative of the science-fiction field, it simply has to feature more men than women. I don't think it makes sense to try to deny reality by applying some kind of sexual quota system. To include a writer in this book simply because she is female would surely be an insult both to her and her work.

Twenty years ago, when there were hardly any women at all writing science fiction, we had an obligation to draw attention to their books and speak out against any prejudices that existed. Today, although women are still a minority in science fiction, they are not in any sense oppressed. Their work is published in profusion, often by editors who are themselves female.

If we're going to single out minority groups deserving special treatment, let's start thinking in literary terms. Let's turn our attention, for instance, to the small number of science-fiction writers capable of true human sensitivity, or subtlety, or genuine and original scientific invention. These are the oppressed literary minority; whether they happen to be male or female is irrelevant.

NO SWORDS, DRAGONS, OR TALKING RABBITS

Having dealt with one touchy subject, let me trample over another. In the 1970s, some publishers started putting out paperbacks with the word "Fantasy" on the covers in small print where "Science Fiction" used to be. Most of this "Fantasy" was descended from Tolkien or Arthurian legends, set in nonexistent worlds of primitive simplicity, and written in pseudo-medieval prose.

Today, this category of fantasy is at least as popular as science fiction, and some of its writers are becoming well known. Personally, I find it anti-rational, clumsy, and repetitive. Therefore, I am not very interested in talking to the people who write it, which is why you will not find fantasy authors profiled here. For those of you whose tastes are broader than mine, in due course, I believe, someone else will be producing a book of interviews with fantasists.

BRAVING THE BOONDOCKS

There were some people whom I couldn't face interviewing—not because of what they write, but because of where they live. Much as I love to head out into the great American heartland, in a rented car with nothing but Rand McNally and a set of scribbled directions to guide me, there's a limit to the amount of traveling a poor profiler can do on the rather modest royalties advanced to him by is publisher.

This time, I went to California, England, Connecticut, Maine, Washington, D.C., and even Florida—but Minnesota proved to be a problem, which is one reason why Gordon R. Dickson and Clifford Simak are not in this book. And I missed Elizabeth Lynn and Marta Randall the first time I was in San Francisco, and I couldn't afford to make a second trip.

Why, you ask, didn't I talk to them on the telephone, or at some science-fiction conference, or when they next happened to pass through New York? Because I don't like doing interviews that way. In a couple of cases I did settle for telephonic or hotel-room interviews, but this is a poor substitute for actually visiting a writer's workplace, assimilating all the background color, and talking at leisure, without distractions.

The original intention of *Dream Makers* was to give you the sense of visiting the writers. I have tried to stay true to that aim.

OTHER MISSING PERSONS

Some people simply didn't want to be interviewed. Ursula Le Guin told me that interviews disturb and disorient her. John Varley said he no longer gives interviews to anyone. John Norman politely explained that he is a very private person. Fred Hoyle's secretary told me he was too busy to talk about science fiction. Anthony Burgess, Stanley Kubrick, Swiss artist H. R. Geiger, and musicians David Bowie and Brian Eno never replied to my letters.

Maybe I could have snared some of these luminaries if I had been more persistent. But being persistent is not much fun—for me, or for them. I believe that anyone who really wants to be interviewed will not need to be asked more than once.

I did interview veteran avant-garde rock musician Don van Vliet, who uses the stage name Captain Beefheart. But I decided to drop that profile from the book. It didn't convey the essence of his music, in the way that a good profile of a writer can conjure up the flavor of his books. I still think of van Vliet as a "Dream Maker," though, and if this strikes you as odd, I urge you to seek out some of his records.

PUTTING WORDS IN PEOPLE'S MOUTHS

As in the first book, each profile is based on a tape-recorded conversation that lasted between one and two hours. I transcribed all but two of the tapes myself, mainly because I felt that I should take that responsibility. I then reshuffled paragraphs, and sometimes sentences, to achieve a more coherent flow than is generally possible in spoken conversation. Occasionally I had to insert an "and" or a "but" to make a statement easier to follow, and I naturally edited out the dull bits.

Bear in mind, then, that the long monologues from some of the writers in this book were originally interspersed with backtracks and digressions. You have here a kind of condensed-soup version of what was actually said. I haven't fictionalized anything, but I have used the techniques of a fiction writer in rendering dialogue so that it "sounds right" as you read it. The purpose of this is not only to trim surplus words, but to distill the essence of what was said, and also the essence of the personality.

As a check on my own accuracy, all the interviewees were shown their profiles and invited to make corrections. Some people made no changes at all; others inserted a few minor alterations; and two people chose to rewrite some of what they had said, as well as some of what I had said, in order to present what they felt was a more accurate picture.

GRANDSON OF DREAM MAKERS?

Personally, I'm sick of sequels. The science-fiction field is plagued by them, at present, as if the writers and editors are all chanting in unison, "You liked the last one, so here's some more of the same!" And fairly good novels suddenly grow into padded-out trilogies, which then grow into tetralogies, which then grow into—well, whatever comes after that. I don't know the right word, and I'm not sure I want to.

So here I am, participating in this sad state of affairs. Because, of course, the first *Dream Makers* really had to be augmented by a second volume in order to finish the job properly.

But two volumes are as far as we go. There will *not* be a *Dream Makers III*. No doubt in ten years' time some bright new writers will be on the scene, and should be profiled for posterity, or for whatever reason it is that profiles are written—even now, I am still not entirely sure. All I can say is that these bright new writers will have to find some bright new profiler when the time comes.

I've had fun being invited into the homes of strangers and asking them lots of nosy questions. I've made some friends along the way. And I hope I have supplied some insight into the real-life processes by which books are written and published.

But writing fiction will always seem more important than writing *about* fiction. And so it is that, now, to which I return.

(New York, July 1982)

DREAM MAKERS
VOLUME II

Jerry Pournelle

More than anyone else in this book, Jerry Pournelle is a man of the times. He is to the 1980s what Robert Heinlein was to the 1950s; and I'm not just talking about his talent for technological invention and sociological projection. I'm speaking of his politics.

As the tide of American liberalism recedes from its high-water mark in the late 1960s, and reveals the bedrock of conservative thinking that always lurked beneath, Jerry Pournelle's work begins to seem more and more fashionable—vogueish, even. In story after story, novel after novel, he campaigns for those traditional American traits that the nation is rediscovering, and that he's held true to all along: rugged individualism, the profit motive, deregulation, personal freedom, an armed citizenry (that most of all!) . . . plus good old Yankee Ingenuity, to save us from the low-tech, zero-growth drudgery that ecofreaks and no-nuke nitwits would wish upon the world.

Sometimes he reminds me of right-wing bumper stickers that go beyond ideology and into self-satire. Like, "Warning: I Don't Brake for Liberals!" or "More Nukes, Less Kooks!" or "Peace—Through Superior Firepower!" In fact, this last slogan is available on a T-shirt from *Soldier of Fortune* magazine, for which Jerry Pournelle is a contributing editor.

Do I exaggerate? Only a little. In Pournelle's novel *The Mercenary*, soldier-hero John Christian Falkenberg remarks, "After all, war is the normal state of affairs, isn't it? Peace is the ideal we deduce from the fact that there have been interludes between wars." (And in case you object that this is merely a fictional character talking, as opposed to Pournelle himself, check out his introduction to David Drake's story collection, *Hammer's Slammers*. Falkenberg and Pournelle share almost exactly the same phrasing.)

Or there's this quote from *Exiles to Glory*, in which an enlightened scientist is trying to recruit a reluctant student for a space-industrialization project to save mankind:

"Farrington sighed. 'You've been brought up to think somebody will take care of you. Social Security, National Health Plan, Federal Burial Insurance, Family Assistance, Food Stamps, Welfare. Union representatives to speak for you. And I'm talking about a place where it's all up to you, where you take care of yourself because nobody's going to do it for you. I guess that can be scary to modern kids. . . ."

If Jerry Pournelle had started publishing novels back in the 1960s, he might have found his market restricted to Goldwater loyalists over fifty. Young readers of that era would have dismissed him as some kind of silent-majority crackpot extremist.

Times, however, have changed. Pournelle's novels written with Larry Niven (*The Mote in God's Eye*, *Lucifer's Hammer*, *Oath of Fealty)* are among the most successful science fiction in print. Admittedly, the political angle in these collaborations is played down. But his solo-written books are becoming almost as popular, and their messages are stated so strongly that they would seem like propaganda if the ideas weren't so provocative and the stories weren't so tightly told.

Personally, I admire the solid science and careful extrapolation in his work, while I view his success with horrified fascination. By my scale of values, anyone who refers to the "inevitability" of war is helping to promote it as a self-fulfilling prophecy. And an inefficient but compassionate bureaucracy seems a lot more tolerable to me than totally uncontrolled, ruthless free enterprise. Not every individual is *capable* of being rugged; those that can't should be cared for. And military atrocities will always overshadow, in my mind, the military virtues of which Jerry Pournelle writes so often and so warmly.

So when I go to talk to him for this book, I'm not sure whether to expect an interview or a confrontation. Bearing in mind one slightly explosive encounter that he and I have already had in the past, I think he may be looking forward to our meeting now in the same sort of wary spirit as I am.

Jerry Pournelle and his wife live in a large, old, white-painted wooden house in a white-collar residential neighborhood just north of Los Angeles. Other members of the family include his three children, his research assistant, and a menacing dog that eyes me calculatingly and sniffs me carefully before I'm allowed through the front door. "Don't worry," says Jerry. "He only bites pacifists."

The office/study, where the work is done, turns out to be an unpretentiously makeshift mixture of old and new, function and ornament. A modern swivel chair stands in front of a grand old desk that dominates the center of the room. The desk is piled untidily with papers; the walls are hidden behind tall shelves crammed with books and more papers; a computer video monitor stands on a small typing table; the shades are pulled halfway down over the windows, and outside them the lush Californian foliage is dappled with sunlight.

Pournelle himself is a big man, tall and broad-shouldered. Coupled with his commanding voice, this can make him seem bombastic or even intimidating. But he welcomes me into his home with a friendly smile that allays some of my apprehensions, and he seems very ready to sit and talk at length, in an easygoing fashion, over a series of glasses of sherry.

I feel honor-bound to tackle some of the aspects of his work that bother me the most. For instance, I feel that his books suggest to young readers that complex social problems can be solved by using brute force. Does he ever worry about encouraging kids to indulge in power fantasies?

"If you are trying to tell me that I should not depict realistically the attractions of a properly run military outfit," he replies, "you're a fool. Because it can be damned attractive. Do you think I should exercise self-censorship and not let people know? In the movie version of *Faustus*, Richard Burton is on horseback in armor and he says, 'Is it not a pleasant thing to be a king and ride in triumph to Samarkand?' Should that line have been suppressed? Are you telling me that I shouldn't tell people that there *is* a share of glory? It's a damned attractive life; if it wasn't, why would so many people want it?"

I reply that it is the presentation of violence as an easy answer that bothers me most. In *The Mercenary*, for instance, a planet's deadbeats and social parasites are threatening the survival of their own society. The hero solves this problem by luring the civilians into a giant stadium, where they are massacred by mercenaries.

Pournelle, however, does not see this as advocating violence as a permanent solution. "In the stadium scene, the politician turns to the soldier and says, 'You saved our world.' But the soldier says, 'God damn you, don't say things like that, I've bought you a little time, that's all I could do, and it's up to you to do the rest, and God help you if you don't.' Now, I don't think that that is saying he has solved their problems, or anything like it. The politician may think his problems have been solved because his opposition has been temporarily eliminated. The soldier knows better.

"I think I have a realistic view of human nature. Isaac Asimov has an asinine motto, 'Violence is the last refuge of the incompetent.' I agree with it completely—if it's read properly. That is, only the incompetent wait until it's the last resort!

"If you don't believe that violence can be an effective means of changing destiny, then I invite you to ask the Carthaginians their opinion. Or the Knights Templar; they were among the most successful international corporations in the history of mankind, and were suppressed with bloody awful violence and horror. I guess what I have to tell you is that there is a terrible truth to Goering's remark that the noblest of spirits, the highest of aspirations, may be silenced if their bearer is beaten to death with a rubber truncheon. One doesn't have to like that to admit it's got a lot of truth to it."

But isn't there a danger that armed preparedness becomes a self-fulfilling prophecy? Surely, the very existence of weapons is an encouragement to use them.

"You sit here in an area which has the lowest crime rate in Los Angeles," he tells me. "Well, there may be a reason for this." He reaches under his desk. For a moment I'm not sure what to expect. Then he pulls out an enormous stainless-steel revolver, and brandishes it meaningly, at the same time taking care to keep his finger off the trigger and the gun pointed at the ceiling—for which I'm grateful.

"Probably everybody on this block can do what I just did," he continues, replacing the gun in its hiding place and relaxing back in his chair. "And yet there hasn't been a gunshot fired on this block since I've been here, and that's fifteen years. I teach my children, as soon as they're old enough, what weapons are—they all know where they are in this house, and they never touch them. There are four rules: All guns are always loaded. You must never put your finger on the trigger unless you're prepared to fire it. You never point a gun at anything you don't intend to shoot. And you never shoot anything you don't intend to kill. Now, given these rules, how could anyone get hurt, if you obey them? The people that terrify me are the *amateurs*. My kids will never shoot anyone accidentally. I don't say, however, that they will never shoot anyone.

"I have looked through history, and I've found only two periods of sustained peace, spanning generations, in the history of mankind. Do you find more? One was the Pax Romana, which was enforced essentially by the unilateral supremacy of Rome. The other was the Pax Britannica, which was enforced essentially by the unilateral supremacy of the British fleet and marines.

"Even a country like Switzerland has not had long periods of peace. Switzerland has a fairly decent record, but look at the cost—'cost' in your terms, not mine. They have universal military training, brutally enforced—do you know the penalty for refusing military service in Switzerland? The alternative is ten years in prison, or permanent exile. You don't have to guess that every Swiss household has weapons; you *know* they do. And they include not merely sporting rifles and pistols, but automatic weapons, mortars, and military equipment. And yet the Swiss crime rate is lower than ours—their violent crime rate is almost nonexistent. So I put it to you that here is a society which is not thought of as oppressive or overly violent—it is said to be dull. But it is more thoroughly armed than you can conceive of.

"My view of gun control is that we ought to implement the Swiss system in the United States. Every citizen of this country should go through at least weapons familiarity and some kind of basic training and be required to keep weapons. I don't think that anyone will invade us, after that, and we might be able to do away with some of our strategic weapons, although not all of them.

"I think the harnessing of violence, and the understanding of the price you pay if you are unwilling to participate in your own defense, is all wrapped up with my view of gun control: I prefer to reduce the agentry of the State. You know, during most of the period of the Roman republic, it had only twenty-four paid policemen: the bodyguards of the consuls. For the rest, court decisions were almost self-enforcing. Citizens were expected to aid the magistrate.

"It is very hard for the State to be oppressive when it must get such active participation of the citizenry to enforce its decisions. I think that would be much preferable to agentry—to hiring people to enforce decrees for you. Have you ever been to a cop house and talked to them, and listened to what they think of civilians?"

This sounds a fundamentally democratic kind of system—all citizens equally armed—and yet, in his fiction, Jerry Pournelle tends to portray a small group imposing its will on the masses, for their own good. And in *The Mote in God's Eye* a cyclical view of history is used to justify an eventual return to an aristocratic monarchy—which the book seems to suggest is not entirely a bad idea.

"Representative democracy is not the be-all and end-all," he replies. "In fact I don't give a damn if the political system is monarchical or elective, so long as it has large areas in which it leaves me alone. And my suspicion is, by the way, that a king has less power over me than a president. Read your Rousseau on the subject: his theory of the general will. The general will is the will of all, and thus if you oppose what the government says, you are really opposing your own will, and therefore *you may be forced to be free*, hm? That strikes me as being the ultimate rationale for something even worse than fascism, because fascism at least understood that there are differences between people and said, basically, 'You are going to compromise your differences and work together.' I'm talking about Italian fascism, not German national socialism, which is an entirely different matter and was not based on any rational view of anything.

"The communist system is based on Rousseau's idea of the general will. The Marxists say that we'll just eliminate all the classes but one. So I still think that fascists are considerably less enemies to traditional Western civilization than communists, so long as we clearly distinguish between German national socialism and Ibero-Italian fascism. Mussolini not only made the railroads run on time, he *built* them. Whatever you want to say, Italy would probably be better off under him than it is under whatever the hell it has now.

"I don't know, I'm not an Italian, and in many respects I have no right to an opinion on the subject; but I just look at their economic development pattern in the 1920s, starting with a much lower base than they have now. And I find that the Italian anti-fascist writers do not have the verve of the German anti-Nazi writers; they find it harder to find something to hate. I mean, the guy who makes you drink castor oil is certainly not being very nice to you, but that's entirely different from his putting you in a goddamn camp, or cutting your balls off, or making a lamp shade out of you.

"I think it is very possible that Mussolini could have made a different decision and become an ally of the West. He almost was; he kept Austria from being absorbed by Germany for many years, and could to this day be a hero. After all, Stalin is still thought of in some heroic terms, and yet that son of a bitch managed to knock off more people than Hitler ever did, and I'm not talking about during the Second World War, I mean in the phony famine in the Ukraine, and all the rest of it. He racked up a score that Genghis Khan would envy."

I break in here, to object that there can't be many people who admire Stalin any more.

"What about most professors of philosophy over age fifty?" he responds. "After all, don't we still think of Marcuse as a legitimate philosopher? And yet what is he but a Stalinist apologist? He takes Erich Fromm's theory of alienation, and uses it to become an apologist for the worst excesses of the Stalinist regime. Do you find that rational? Do you find his book *readable*, for that matter? Yet he was a tenured professor at a California university supported by the taxpayers.

"You know, I don't find this country in terrible danger of losing all its freedoms, when it will pay a man as *dull* as Marcuse to be a professor at one of its leading universities." He smiles wickedly.

Still on politics—since so much of his writing is political, and since Jerry Pournelle himself obviously loves a political debate—I can't resist mentioning that I heard he was, at one time, a member of the Communist Party.

He pauses and looks not so much embarrassed as rueful and abashed. "That was a long time ago. After I got out of the Korean war, and came back and was an undergraduate. I fell into the hands of those who kept telling us that Marxism was within the Western tradition, and so forth. I was also victim of the snigger-theory of philosophy, which is that if you admire anyone other than a leftist then you're barely tolerated in the university department, and they laugh at you. I had been through a pretty miserable war; the communists promised to do something, and it didn't look to me as if anyone else was going to do anything." He shrugs. "Misplaced idealism.

"Being a communist was a matter of selective blindness. You adopt a system of looking at things, and if you interpret what you see in those terms, and in no other way, it's easy to delude yourself. You cut yourself off from almost everyone else, your only close friends are people who are part of that movement. If you try to quit they throw you out in such a way that people who used to be your best friends will cross the street to avoid you.

"I've studied formal philosophy, and quite a lot of it. I wasn't converted to the materialist view of things for some time; I found it unsatisfactory. On the other hand, communism didn't give me an incentive for doing anything. To march in step with the flywheel of history is about the only inducement that Marx gives you for being loyal to his cause. 'What is going to be, is inevitable; and therefore you ought to be for it, because that's what's good.' That seems to me nothing but the rather contemptible worship of power. And yet, the modern American intellectual finds communism more acceptable than fascism."

Unlike many science-fiction writers who dabble in future social history and interstellar empires, Jerry Pournelle has some first-hand experience of that on which he speculates. Prior to becoming a full-time freelance writer in the early 1970s, he worked for local city government: "I was director of research for the City of Los Angeles, which was a political plum in some respects—I wrote the Mayor's speeches for him, that was the one thing I really *had* to do."

And before that, he spent many years in the aerospace industry: "I had a very senior position for someone my age, in North American Aviation, which at that time was the outfit that was building Apollo. I was a Space Scientist; my position was to find things within the company that I thought I could contribute to, and go work on them. The last professional assignment I had was to work on the experimental design for Apollo 21. But there wasn't going to be any Apollo 21, it became fairly obvious, and at the same time the management said, 'We've got to trim the number of people who are senior scientists.' They offered me a position with actually a raise in salary, as a manager in the operations research department, which is what I'm supposed to know most about, in scientific disciplines. But I would have been supervising two-hundred-and-something employees, which would have been a disaster. I have never been a supervisor of any large group."

And so, after moving into the political work and various other activities, he chose to become a writer: a job in which one manages—and answers to—no one but oneself.

Pournelle remains active in real-world politics, however, particularly where the space program is involved. "Very early on, when I was managing the human factors laboratories at Boeing, it had become obvious to me that the space program wasn't really going anywhere. Kennedy's announcement just committed us to a specific goal; it was not a program of designing fundamental building blocks to exploit the space medium. We have yet to do that.

"There were, and are, no *technical* problems in doing what it seemed then, and seems now, so very obvious that we ought to be doing. The problems were all political. So, already possessing a doctorate in psychology, I went out and got another one in political science, to study politics and learn how to manipulate those levers.

"This, I suppose, is one reason why I'm now a writer; I can reach considerably more people. I'm not conceited enough to think that I was that good in the systems analysis business; I have no great illusions that my value to the space program in a professional capacity would be that much greater now than, perhaps, my son, who has more recently been to the universities. So I prefer to get my message across by having a lot of readers."

At the same time, he is secretary of the L5 Society—a privately funded group advocating space colonies along the lines suggested by Gerard O'Neill—and he is co-founder of The Citizens' Advisory Council on National Space Policy. This latter group has hosted meetings of notables including aerospace engineers, company presidents, the Administrator of NASA, and the Presidential Science Advisor, and has submitted its recommendations to the government.

But his main interest—and a formidable source of income—is still his writing.

"The best way I know, to be persuasive, is to be read by a very large number of people. They pay you lots of money for being read by a large number of people. I call it doing well by doing good. I certainly do well; it's up to you as to whether I do good. I think I'm being fairly effective.

"*Lucifer's Hammer*, for example, put across a stronger pro-technology message than you might think. It said that civilization is fragile, and it's worth keeping, which is a relevant message in these times when a large number of people seem to think that the benefits of civilization come free-flowing from heaven with no work on anyone's part. People have about as much understanding of where these benefits come from as my dog has of where the canned dogfood comes from. I think that's tragic.

"The book put forth a legitimate message, and it did it without any of its characters, save one, knowing what the message was. I think that's the right way to write ideological fiction, if you want to call it that. I don't think the characters ought to know what the message is. That's my quarrel with Ayn Rand, other than that I don't agree with her message anyway."

Since his collaborations with Larry Niven have become true best sellers, I ask Jerry Pournelle if he doesn't worry that this "blockbuster" system in publishing draws resources away from other, less-commercial books by new authors—who may find it increasingly difficult to get published, as a result.

"I completely agree," he says. "But what am I to do?"

Does it bother him when the money that his books earn, or the books themselves, attract criticism?

"I can get in the mail twelve favorable reviews in major publications, and one bad review in an amateur magazine that is circulated to twenty-six people, nine of whom don't read it . . . and I will brood over that bad review all day." He smiles and shrugs; and I get the impression that he is indeed sensitive to criticism—yet it will take more than bad reviews to deflect him from his sense of purpose.

I ask if, as a writer of scientifically accurate, predictive fiction, he disapproves of the trend toward fantasy.

"I know very little about fantasy. If I ever wrote it, I would have to come up with a very self-consistent mythology in which to place the story. I would be cheating my readers if I did not give them what they expect: a fairly ruthless internal consistency.

"I'll tell you that, of twentieth century authors, I probably admire C. S. Lewis more than any other, and I suppose in a sense *The Great Divorce* is one of my favorite works—which we stole from outrageously for *Inferno*, by the way. Lewis did it better than we did, I'll be the first to admit, although we made it maybe a little more exciting. So I like good fantasy, but I have not been willing to work hard enough to come up with an epic book. I guess I would have to do an epic-proportioned fantasy; I don't know how to do little tales.

"Some fantasy is unutterably trivial. You know, you may criticize

The Mercenary, but what about John Norman?" (Author of numerous slightly erotic fantasy novels featuring male barbarian warriors with female slaves.) "I think my wife would not even be civil to Mr. Norman if she were to meet him at a cocktail party. I've been married to the most liberated woman you've ever met, for twenty-something years. She is in the top one percent of salaried women in the country, she is an expert at what she does, she may be the world's best at what she does. She teaches reading to jailed teenagers. Her students are all illiterate, over thirteen years old. She has not yet failed to teach one to read, though she gets them with documentation and tests from psychologists proving it's impossible. So you see I have a different view of women than in the John Norman novels, which I find fairly boring. Norman—like Marcuse—is both ethically horrifying and *dull*. In the first place, to be quite blunt about it, the idea of sex with a woman confined in a rape-rack does not appeal to me enormously. I guess that was almost the first thing that struck me in reading those books, how little fun that would be." He hesitates for a moment. "I'm not sure I want that quoted... but maybe I do."

Leaving aside fantasy, what of science fiction? Does he feel that, despite the vast increase in the quantity of books, innovation in the field is declining?

"In some respects science fiction is becoming bankrupt; we're not studying much science, and most writers are way out of date on what's going on.

"But isn't part of the problem also that at least a portion of the field takes it literally that works have to be depressing in order to be good? As in Vonnegut's view of life, which is that inevitably you get stepped on. I don't find that to be historically true, and I don't find it to be true of my own life.

"I admire Brian Aldiss greatly, but I have never heard a more outrageous statement than his defense of giving the first Campbell Award—the one then given by Harry Harrison and his groupies—to Barry Malzberg for *Beyond Apollo*, which is probably the one novel which you could be absolutely certain that John W. Campbell would never have bought or have read more than ten pages of. Aldiss said that the book recognizes the fallen state of man and the tragic view of life which is essential to all literature. I simply cannot buy that; I cannot agree that literature must be tragic or that man's fallen state has to be the central thesis. It's the central thesis of Christianity, but the Christian sects that I find most admirable dwell upon that less than they do upon the idea of *redemption*.

"I prefer to think that mankind has a 100-billion-year future, and I try to write in such a way as to help bring that about. Can you believe that we are no more than a million years old—if that—and we have ahead of us 100 billion years? Hell, ours may be the last generation not to be immortal! So how can you be depressed? We have this whole universe, with trillions of stars in it, to conquer. It's all ours, as far as we can tell.

"I am absolutely certain that if you'd let me invest in the kind of future that I want to bring about, then I can give you whatever you want, even a little enclave in which you make your living literally by the sweat of your brow, and putter in your garden and have your own vine and your own fig tree—the biblical recipe for happiness. I guess what I am trying to say is, what *do* you want?

"Suppose that life is meaningless in that we really are merely the dance of the atoms—which I find an enormously improbable thing to believe; you can't calculate the odds against it. But even if this is so, don't you find it exciting that there are 100 billion years ahead of us, and we've just started? Who knows what we can build? Maybe what we're doing is creating God."

I comment that, to the writer or the reader weighed down with everyday woes, taking the long view is not always easy.

"But how can you have anything *but* a long view? Perhaps you can't understand what it was like to grow up in a town in which the ice man really came around in a horse and buggy. I literally went from riding horses and jumping over fences, supervising tenant farmers in cotton fields, who were only a degree removed from slavery...to seeing people land on the moon. Now, that's a transition. We live in a marvelous time, and it's getting better. So people have to invent reasons for being unhappy. Well, if you're trying to tell me that you see no purpose to life, then I can only tell you that you haven't looked very hard."

I notice that he has been referring increasingly to theological concepts; and this prompts me to suggest that the strength with which he holds and defends his views reflects a quality that some find in short supply these days: faith.

"I've read the book of common prayer, and was brought up around it. I attend church—Church of England. Our boys go to church schools, if that means anything. And they're respectful, they're polite, they do not seem to be particularly unhappy or rebellious, and they don't sit around and brood and stare at their navels. My daughter is an officer in the paratroops, and was, by the way, the first in her class, which ain't too bad." With quiet pride he points to a picture of her, in her uniform, on the wall.

"People tell me ways I ought to live," he goes on, referring perhaps to criticism that he has received because of his political views or his apparent intractability. "But I look at them, and they don't seem to be as content as I am—or to have as many reasons to be content as I do."

This may sound complacent, but I think it reflects a sincere belief in his values—and a real concern for the future.

I can't say that my visit with Jerry Pournelle has remade me as a member of the Right. But anyone should be impressed, I think, by some of the points he makes, either in person or in print. He demonstrates beyond debate the benefits that technology can bring. He argues from a broader historical perspective than most of us maintain. And he is, in the end, an idealist. He seems to feel no equivocation; there is right, and there is wrong, and you defend your principles with all the physical and mental resources that you possess.

The core of it, I think, is his sense of community. Again and again, throughout his work, a small, cohesive unit looks after its own with great compassion, while arming itself against outsiders, who are always viewed with suspicion.

The small, cohesive unit may be a bunch of colonists on an alien planet, or (in the super-city of *Oath of Fealty)* a vast gathering of American families. Most often, though, the unit that looks after its own is a military unit. Near the beginning of *The Mercenary*, when Falkenberg is a young recruit who has just joined the space marines, he's rescued from the clutches of a corrupt bureaucrat by a petty officer. Pournelle writes:

"The petty officer was twice his age, and no one ever called John 'sir' before. It gave John Falkenberg a sense of belonging, a sense of having found something he had searched for all his life."

This, I think, is the very human yearning behind the nationalism and the rugged rhetoric. And it's a yearning which Jerry Pournelle's fiction itself satisfies, among alienated young readers all across America. His books offer a sense of belonging: to an ethos, or a vision of the future. And that is something that transcends politics.

BIBLIOGRAPHICAL NOTES

Of Jerry Pournelle's solo-written novels, *The Mercenary* (1977) remains central. Thrown out of Earth's space navy because he wouldn't toe the bureaucratic line, Colonel John Christian Falkenberg balances self-interest with expediency as he brings armed peace to various colonized alien worlds. Might tends to make right, as in the notorious stadium massacre, portrayed as a final solution to deadbeats who threaten the survival of their own society. The future-history scenario of this book recurs in *The Mote in God's Eye* (1974), the highly successful epic written with Larry Niven.

For younger readers, *High Justice* (1977) and *Exiles to Glory* (1978) mix hard science and conservative politics to produce a healthy antidote to liberalism, or an outrageously unfair caricature of humanistic social policies, according to your outlook. Either way, the narratives are swift and the ideas are compelling.

Jerry Pournelle's lively and persuasive nonfiction about the future, focusing on space industrialization in particular, has been collected in *A Step Farther Out* (1979).

Written with Niven, *Inferno* (1975) shows that Jerry Pournelle has a sense of humor, too, describing a science-fiction writer in Dante's Hell, befriended by a sadder, wiser, and rather noble Benito Mussolini.

PHOTO BY MICHAEL VILAIN

Larry Niven

"I would say that we're the most successful collaboration in science-fiction history," Larry Niven remarks of his partnership with Jerry Pournelle. "Frederik Pohl and C.M. Kornbluth were good; they did as well as was possible in the science-fiction field of their time. But today is different. Today you can sell to an audience a hundred times as large. And that means, incidentally, you can spend more time on each piece of work."

He speaks decisively, leaving no doubt that he knows exactly what he's talking about. At the same time, he's very relaxed, almost bored, as if he wouldn't bother to argue if anybody started disagreeing with him. He has the bland equanimity of someone from a wealthy family who has gone on to make his own small fortune on top of theirs. If nothing seems to bother Larry Niven very much, these days, that's hardly surprising.

"When I first started writing there seemed zero chance that I would make serious money out of it. I was doing it as a hobby; my real profession was counting the money in the trust funds I inherited. I wrote science fiction because it just happened that that was where my ideas were coming. All I wanted out of it was a Hugo Award. What I achieved was way beyond my ambitions.

"Even now, I'm not in this for the money; we'd be living in a smaller, less comfortable house without it, but I mainly use the money to keep score of how many people I've reached. I'm talking to a lot of people—my audience is over a million. And I'd like to talk to a lot more."

Perhaps this sounds self-satisfied. Perhaps, if you're a struggling, starving author measuring out your dinner of boiled beans in your crumbling cold-water tenement, Niven's attitude is the sort of thing that makes you more than a little angry. From your point of view, times are tough; the American publishing industry is no healthier than any other industry at this time of economic recession, so it's even harder to sell your work than it used to be, and even when a publisher does buy one of your novels, not much money changes hands.

The truth is that, on the whole, this has always been a low-paying field. A typical novel only earns its writer $5,000 or so, and many writers bitterly refer to science fiction as a literary ghetto.

So how is it that Larry Niven has come to be rewarded so highly, and read so widely, while most others struggle to get by?

For a start, Niven rejects defeatist talk about the so-called ghetto.

"I dislike that phrase. I suggest you adopt the phrase 'science-fiction country club' and see where we get.

"Look at the parameters of a country club. It's expensive to be there, but it does have certain advantages. One is the company of your peers, and another is the chance to make business deals conveniently. All of this is true of science fiction.

"The expense of being a member is—well, the royalty advances are low, science fiction receives a limited amount of critical acclaim, and very little publicity. This does cost you money.

"But the company of your peers? Damned straight. And the opportunities to make business deals are very real. All you've got to do is go to a science-fiction convention, and you'll meet all the people you want to deal with. To the new writer, that's a godsend.

"It's utterly true that the new writer won't make a million dollars on his first novel in science fiction. But the science-fiction label guarantees that he'll sell a minimum of, let's say, 40,000 to 100,000 copies. People will buy it just because it's science fiction.

"Here's the real advantage. You can always step outside the science-fiction country club to make a little money, once you've gotten yourself established. John D. MacDonald did it right. He started in science fiction, made a name for himself, enough money to keep going, and presently went to the mainstream.

"Niven and Pournelle did the same thing, except that they didn't stop writing science fiction. They just started selling to the mainstream audience as well."

He says this as if nothing could have been simpler. And the way he talks about himself in the third person accentuates his air of serene detachment.

He agrees, however, that there was a little luck involved in his early success.

"I got started in the heart of the 'new wave' period, in the late 1960s. This was one of the best pieces of good fortune that I could have asked for. In that period, the 'new wave' looked really good to all the new writers, who were interested in experimenting and getting away from old-style science fiction. The only new writer who didn't go along with that, and stuck with solid stories of the Poul Anderson model, was Larry Niven.

"Algis Budrys was the first guy to notice Larry Niven as a good thing in the field. He said something like, 'Larry Niven makes you feel as if it's important whether the main character gets killed.' Nobody else was doing that.

"Some of the critics of that time, of course, did not like what I was doing. I had to wonder hard whether these critics were right. But when Damon Knight turned down 'Inconstant Moon' for *Orbit*, in exactly the form in which it went on to win a Hugo award—I knew Damon was wrong before the awards came up. I knew how valuable that story was. I knew how well I'd written it. And I stopped taking Damon seriously as a critic.

"Okay, that's for Damon Knight. As regards James Blish, I do not give great weight to his comments on *Ringworld*, which were that it would probably win a Hugo but it shouldn't.

"I admit, I felt picked on by the critics. Or rather—I felt ignored, and that's worse. And what I told myself then I guess I still tell myself now: If I need a critic to explain a story for me to the reader, then there's something wrong with the way I wrote it."

Like other writers I've met who have become very commercially successful, Larry Niven shows more respect for his readers than his critics.

"I'm very keenly aware of the obligation I owe to anyone who buys one of my books. When I was fifteen, I spent a month with my dad and some other people in Carmel. The TV set got only one channel, and it wasn't very interesting, so I tried being a storyteller. And it was glorious. But I could see it was easy to lose the attention of all those other fifteen-year-olds.

"Okay, now I'm expecting people to pay me honest-to-god money for my storytelling. I'm still keenly aware of how easy it is to lose that audience.

"I grew up among mundanes. When I say 'mundanes' it's not pejorative, it's a short way of saying 'people who never look to the sky for anything other than to tell the time.' And sometimes not even that.

"The whole world I knew was like that when I was in my teens. The people who think like science-fiction fans, in terms of a future that's different from the present, have grown in numbers by leaps and bounds since then. It's been a series of jumps: Sputnik, the Russian men in space, the American men in space, *2001: A Space Odyssey*, the moon program, *Star Trek*, *Star Wars*—each of these caused a surge in the number of people willing to listen to ideas such as the ones that I use.

"I have profited enormously, but so has the rest of the world, because we do now think in terms of projecting problems, finding solutions, looking for the ideas that can create the technology that can solve the problems.

"There still are the mundanes, of course. Most of the populace still doesn't bother with this kind of stuff. They expect, and would feel more comfortable in, a future which is just like the present. But I am not talking to those people. I am trying to talk to the people who are ready to know that the future will be different from the present.

"When I decide to write a story, I can get a feel for what kind of audience it will call for. A novel like *Protector* includes enormously complex games played with sociology, anthropology, and space travel. The audience for that one is small, has a very high I.Q. and a very good education. Okay, that's who I was writing to in that one, and I can resist making concessions with the language, for such people, and I can skip over some ideas that they already know. They have the education or they wouldn't be reading the book.

"With *Lucifer's Hammer* it was different. A very simple idea, here; there's nothing really complex about the description of a comet hitting the earth. With that simple an idea, I've got a potentially very large audience. And I have to explain even the simplest concepts to them, or I'm not doing them justice."

I ask him how he made the transition from writing mainly short stories, solo, to writing best-selling collaborative epics.

"My collaboration with Jerry began like this. We had met a few times at social events, because Jerry has been a science-fiction fan longer than I have, back when he was working on the space program, essentially creating the field of space medicine, wiring astronauts with all kinds of instruments.

"He and I got talking one time after a science-fiction convention, and he started talking about collaboration.

"I'd done a collaborative novel with David Gerrold and enjoyed myself a lot. 'Let's try it again,' I said to myself; but what I was really saying was, 'Let's keep talking about it,' because talk is cheap and talk is recreation.

"We set up a date for Jerry to come over one night after dinner. I dug something out of my files: an alien I'd been calling 'Cross-hatcher,' designed for a novel that fell apart two-thirds of the way through.

"One of the first things Jerry said was, 'This book can't be in Known Space. I can't believe in Known Space, it doesn't follow sociological principles that I know are valid.'

"I said okay—I didn't want him in Known Space, anyway. I don't let anybody into Known Space. It's my private domain.

"He told me about his future-history, the empire he'd been working in. He'd published some stories in it; 'The Mercenary' was one, I think. I could see he had a fully human empire, with no alien intelligences. This struck me as pretty dull.

"I realized I could put an alien planet in the middle of his empire. I tossed the alien into the pot. And we had a hell of a night. I introduced him to brandy and coffee, which gets you drunk without putting you to sleep, and we drank brandy and coffee all night, and by the time we finished we had elaborated and extrapolated and made vast amounts of notes, and we set to work."

And from this, of course, came *The Mote in God's Eye*, which was more successful for Niven than any of his other work had been.

Since then, however, he's proved that his own fiction can be just as successful. *The Ringworld Engineers* was a recent example.

"I was mightily surprised by the success of *Ringworld Engineers*. Sequels to successful books are generally not as good as the original, and maybe they don't sell as many copies, total, because their real audience is restricted to people who remember reading the first one.

But what does happen is that the sequel to a successful book sells in one lump. So *Ringworld Engineers* was on the paperback best seller list for a month, in mainstream."

This was classic hard-science, high-tech Niven—the kind of problem-solving fiction for which he's famous. He has written fantasy novels too, however. As a serious advocate of science and space technology, I can't help wondering how he can produce fantasies that could actually encourage people to reject science and turn away from real-life problems.

"If the fantasy weren't there those people would be reading *nothing*, and watching television, and I think that would be mildly worse. Fantasy does show a world that is different from our world, and it does stretch people's imaginations. So I'm not against it. I'm not even against the kind of sword-and-sorcery which is very popular now. There are vast numbers of people out there taking approaches that I wouldn't take, but I'm reluctant to stop them. I wouldn't even stop Ralph Nader. Nader has done a great deal of damage to America's ability to become power-sufficient. He's against the building of any kind of atomic power stations anywhere, apparently. And he is a mighty voice; he is listened to. But I got hit from behind while my car was at a stoplight, a while back. I got out, and here is this woman cringing in her driver's seat, and a McDonald's hamburger on the floor. She had tried to save it from sliding off the seat at a point when she should have been stopping. Wham! Her car hit me fairly hard. But I've got a headrest, right? So I'm not whiplashed. And there was no damage to my car, because of the shock-absorbing bumpers. I have Ralph Nader to thank for that."

But I thought Niven was a conservative, in favor of Reagan-style deregulation.

"Yes, I'm certainly more in accord with them than with Ralph Nader. But I think they should both keep talking."

Is this a free-for-all libertarian outlook?

"No. Libertarianism is a form of anarchy, and they can put up some pretty good arguments, but it turns out that I can shoot holes in their arguments most of the time."

And to prove his point, as in the previous example, he argues from something that happened to him personally. I get the feeling that whereas Jerry Pournelle reaches conclusions by examining the big sweep of history, Larry Niven works on a much more direct, day-to-day basis.

"I was in Houston, Texas, in a restaurant near the center of town, in a bad neighborhood, with Marilyn in a fur coat, both of us looking expensive. It was getting late, and we kept trying to call taxis to take us back to our hotel, but the taxis never showed up, and we finally got a taxi company to admit that they just wouldn't send a cab to where we were. Period. So you can guess now that I have no real confidence in the libertarian method. If a taxi driver can choose not to go to a certain part of town, that perfectly fits the libertarian philosophy, but it leaves me in a hell of a lot of trouble. So I want a certain amount of regulation, simply to protect my own interests."

Is this a kind of law-and-order outlook?

"Yes it is. The people who call themselves law-and-order advocates want a great deal more regulation than I do, but I see where regulations make things easier. Licensing taxis is good. Traffic lights are good. The Food and Drug Administration is good, if they'll do their job, which includes getting useful drugs on the market."

What about regulations that legislate equality?

"I would think 'equal before the law' is as much equality as we would want to legislate. After all, someone who has obeyed the law should not be equal to someone who has not obeyed the law, in the eyes of the law. That's what the law is for; it's set up to *create* inequalities, to some extent."

To what extent should rewards be unequal?

"Put it this way. The administration seems to be returning tax breaks to the people who actually pay the taxes. And there is a lot of yelling from people who seem to think that this is a new and radical and dangerous idea. Well—I'm for it!"

This leads him into a little lecture on economics—with space industrialization as the lesson to be learned.

"The way we're handling currency problems now creates inflation. That leads, in the end, to poverty. There are two ways to deal with this. One is a hell of a lot work: You stop printing more money, and mean it. Japan took that route, and the result of course was a decade of not much money. And then they got used to the idea that the government really meant what they said. That is easier for a Japanese to grasp than it is for an American—Americans are less likely to believe what their government tells them—so if we take this route, we can expect a couple of decades of real horror. It'd be fourteen dollars for a steak, and nobody would have the fourteen dollars, until the butcher finally decided that the government really meant it, and would not print any more money, at which point he would lower the price of steak to seven dollars. That would end inflation.

"The other approach is to create actual new wealth. If you do that, then you can keep up with the new money that's being printed.

"This sounds kind of vague and nebulous, so let me get concrete. I bring an asteroid into near orbit around the earth. I mine it for all the metals, and I ship them down. I sell the metals. Now the inflationary spiral isn't doing anyone any harm.

"Not long ago, the Citizens' Advisory Council on National Space Policy met at this house under Jerry Pournelle's guidance. About thirty-odd of us, including three science-fiction writers. Our purpose was to carve out a detailed space program for the United States, and present it. We have no authority, of course, but at least we had guarantees that certain people would listen.

"We pushed for a total tax break for products brought back from space, until the year 2000—that's obvious. Not so obvious is rewriting the laws regarding what happens to money plowed into space. These regulations are a little fuzzy, a little vague. A corporation lawyer trying to tell a corporation president what will be the result if he does thus-and-so is in a hell of a bind if the laws are vague. And there's no cost to the taxpayer in making these laws hard and rigid, using unambiguous language. So we pushed that idea very hard.

"Then there are the space treaties. Not just the moon treaty, which hasn't been signed, but earlier treaties that were signed. They all seem designed to keep free enterprise out of space. We have got to get out of those.

"Our basic aims are very simple. In the near term, we want to save civilization and make a little money. In the far term, we want all the pollution-producing factories out in space, and the earth made into one great park."

He sounds just as definite, talking about this, as he sounded when he was talking about the science-fiction country club. It's hard to imagine Larry Niven expressing self-doubt or misgivings, just as it's hard to imagine him getting very agitated over anything.

After we have talked for ninety minutes or so, he shows me around his home. He and his wife live in the hills above Tarzana, northwest of Los Angeles. It's a quiet location, surrounded with lush vegetation, and not too many neighbors.

The house is dramatically modern, a series of huge spaces linked by big archways offset from one another so that the perspectives keep changing as you move from room to room. The living room, where the taping took place, has big windows of tinted-brown glass, a long, soft, ample couch, and a ceiling two stories high. We walk through a central dining area, like a modernist baronial hall, where eight high-backed chairs stand around a long glass-topped table. He leads me up to his office, where there are the usual writer's bookshelves, a photocopying machine, and a comfortably upholstered chrome swivel chair in front of a word-processing system. Niven prints out a copy of his bibliography for me while I look out at the swimming pool and patio at the rear of the house.

Before I leave, he talks a little more about his own role in science fiction.

"I continue to benefit from the growing audience of people who think that the future will be different from the present, and who think that this is a good thing," he says.

I mention that New York publishers seem to think that the readership for science fiction is diminishing at present, rather than expanding.

"That is true. What happened is that the field pulsed wide open, and then contracted. A lot of the *Star Wars* audience went out looking for books to give them more of the same, but then they found—oh, my book *Protector*, and it was too complicated for them, or Barry Malzberg, and it was a critical treatise being sold as a novel, or Samuel Delany, and it wasn't comprehensible. You can expect that two-thirds of them, at least, got turned off by whatever it was they came across.

"When the field contracts, the new writer is in a hell of a bad shape. But you see, those writers who are at the *top* of the field, in terms of money and audience, aren't hurt at all." He smiles cheerfully, and puffs on his pipe, as unruffled as ever.

BIBLIOGRAPHICAL NOTES

Many of Larry Niven's short stories take place in "Known Space," a future history best documented in *Tales of Known Space* (1975). The stories in *Neutron Star* (1968) and *Inconstant Moon* (1973) share this scenario, as does his best-known novel *Ringworld* (1970), postulating a world in the form of a belt, as opposed to a planet, orbiting its parent star.

Niven is known not only for the science content of his work but for the whimsical yet realistically described and colorful alien life forms that populate his universe.

With Jerry Pournelle, Niven has written *The Mote in God's Eye* (1974) and *Lucifer's Hammer* (1977), the latter a near-future catastrophe novel describing the collision of a comet with the earth, and the subsequent social devolution.

Most recently, *Oath of Fealty* is a collaborative novel developing in meticulous detail the sociopolitical structure of an arcology, or self-contained city-in-a-giant-building, of the type proposed by architect Paolo Soleri.

PHOTO BY JERRY BAUER

Christopher Priest

Forget, for a moment, million-dollar success stories of best-selling novelists. They are a fortunate, tiny minority. As I implied in Larry Niven's profile, most writers live on the edge. Many of them have to take part-time work to support themselves. Door-to-door encyclopedia salesman, typist, bartender, deckhand, short-order cook—almost any writer's bio is littered with jobs like these, done not for fun, or even for research, but out of necessity.

Some shun manual labor and earn quick cash, instead, by doing "hack work." A "hack," or hackney, was originally a horse that was rented out for menial farm labor. Applied to a writer, it means much the same thing: a lowly scribe laboring in the least fertile fields of literature. Pornographic novels are hack work (and I have written my share). True-confessions stories, horoscopes, comic books, movie novelizations—the next book-of-the-film you happen to pick up may well have been hammered out with desperate expediency, in one hasty, uncorrected draft, by some hungry author impatient to get back to the serious writing he really cares for.

A few writers—a select and lucky few—can survive by writing solid, serious novels and nothing else. Throughout the 1970s, Christopher Priest was one of them. But even such a successful and well-established author enjoys no such thing as job security. He is still dependent on the publishing industry for his income—and publishers can be quixotic, to say the least. Consider this scenario:

Scenting a boom in a new fiction category, publishers up their output. Editors scramble to find extra manuscripts to fill the enlarged monthly quota. Good books are not instantly available—so they sign up bad ones, and hope readers won't notice the difference.

The market becomes flooded with mediocrity. And so . . . sales slump! Editors panic! *My God, what happened?* Those damnably fickle readers—first they wanted this stuff, and then, when we gave it to them, they decided they didn't like it after all!

So the publishers cut back their lists, and plant a new literary tombstone on which is engraved: "No Further Demand for This Type of Book."

Perhaps that sounds too silly or simplistic to be true. But it is precisely what happened to historical romances in America in the mid-1970s. That category was established by a few editors who published sagas so rich in romantic melodrama that they became best sellers. Smelling easy profits, other publishers scrambled to copy the formula. They flooded the market with feeble imitations, disillusioned their readers, and so killed the whole category.

Science fiction used to be untouched by this bandwagon mentality. Most novels sold between 30,000 and 60,000 copies, which was just enough to be profitable but not enough to draw any attention from management, who let editors do more or less what they wanted. Many editors were therefore able to buy some unconventional, ambitious, "literary" books, without any interference. Those books didn't do terribly well, but then, science fiction in general didn't do terribly well.

No more. After *Star Wars*, publishers such as Del Rey Books discovered that modern marketing and promotion could be successfully applied to science fiction. *Dune* and a few others became genuine best sellers. And the conglomerates that had bought up most of the independent American publishing companies during the 1970s expected *every* book to make a profit.

Today, commercial considerations counsel a quick killing via movie tie-ins, sequels, or clones of Conan, and our category has become as vulnerable as any other to sudden fads and reversals. For instance, we may see the collapse of sword-and-sorcery in a few years, if that area continues to be cynically exploited, as historical romances were once exploited.

None of this has been good news for writers of serious or "difficult" science fiction. Many of them are British: that literary climate was always more tolerant of slow, thoughtful work. But to survive, most British writers need to sell their work not only at home, but abroad. And this has become increasingly difficult—for Christopher Priest, in particular.

"My game plan," he says, "was to write work that I wanted to write, which would fit into the science-fiction idiom, and slowly build an audience. Having built that audience, I hoped to take it with me where I wanted to go.

"What's gone wrong with my plan is that, as of this year, it's no longer possible for me to make a living doing that. The market has vanished for me. And I'm not alone. Last year, Keith Roberts couldn't sell his new novel in the States, Brian Aldiss, John Sladek, and Robert Holdstock had great difficulty, Ian Watson couldn't sell his, J. G. Ballard couldn't sell his. And these are all writers who had no trouble selling their books previously.

"Meanwhile, look at Barry Longyear, for instance. Barry Longyear is a *joke* in literary terms. He's even a joke in science-fiction terms. His writing is like a bad dream, it's so awful. But publishers want his work, he gets a lot of money for it, *and* he won a Hugo, a Nebula, and the John W. Campbell award!

"If you take that statement in isolation, it sounds like sour grapes. But the reality is that any one of those writers I just named can write the underpants off somebody like Longyear. I mean, Longyear *can't write*. It's not his personal fault that he's being hyped; it's the environment in which he works, which has become corrupt, which allows him to rise so high.

"I don't read science fiction anymore. No, I haven't renounced it—it has renounced me! Actually, I think what finally broke my back, and put me off it, was reading it for a publisher for six years. I mean, for example, I actually became the British expert on Piers Anthony. As of a few years ago, I had read every fucking word that Piers Anthony had ever written. This is something which actually burns brains out!"

He laughs, but without any malice, or even much resentment. He has a self-effacing style, and maintains a very British sense of the absurd and the ridiculous, even at times of real difficulty.

He's a tall, angular man of thirty-nine whose novels tend to be more sober and straight-faced than he is in person. As a writer of careful, thoughtful literature, he received high critical praise in the 1970s, from the likes of John Fowles and *The New York Times*. But by the end of the decade it became clear that the "literary" direction of Priest's work was not the direction that American science fiction was taking. And Priest has since developed comprehensive theories explaining this split.

"I feel that the current definition of science fiction is wrong. The British writers I've already mentioned, and Ursula Le Guin, Gene Wolfe, or Tom Disch, in the U.S., have suddenly become 'difficult' writers. Five or ten years ago, the idiom was sufficiently liberal that we could all be accepted as science-fiction writers. But now we're not.

"Science fiction is now going in the direction of Silverberg's *Lord Valentine's Castle*. In other words, it's becoming more of a genre for blockbusters. Larry Niven gets almost a million dollars for some garbage he turns out in three weeks, or three months, whatever it is. Same thing with *God Emperor of Dune*, or the new Clarke novel, or the new Asimov novel. That's just one or two books per publisher per year. The average working writer won't be part of it.

"On my most recent trip to America, editors were saying to me that they were looking for quality writing. And I think they meant it. But I don't know whether the sort of editor who buys science fiction has sufficient clout anymore, within his firm, to carry that off.

"The other day I was in a science-fiction bookshop and saw the books of a publisher I'd rather not name, but which you would hope to be a fairly liberal publisher. And he's churning out all this garbage, all this sword-and-sorcery stuff. Like *The Saga of Thod the Thug: Tome I*, and that kind of thing. You expect better than this from an editor who supposedly knows the difference between good writers and bad. Perhaps he just hopes to make money so that he can also publish good stuff. But the junk becomes an end in itself. Suppose you have a best-selling fantasy series which goes into the hundred-thousand sales figures; that establishes a sort of tide-mark for your turnover. If you don't equal that the following year, because you haven't got a similar book, then your job's on the line. So you have to keep coming up with bigger and bigger products. It's a self-defeating process.

"I had always felt that science fiction in the commercial paperback form had something over the rest of paperback fiction. You could put a Philip K. Dick novel into print, and it would subscribe quite badly, but five years later you'd still be selling 2,000 copies a month, whereas the new Judith Krantz, you'd sell five million in the first month but six months later you wouldn't sell any.

"You can go for the quick buck or the slow cent. It seems to me the quest for the quick sale in the science-fiction category is self-defeating because if you do get a quick sale, you've got to follow it with another one, quicker and bigger, and that takes attention off the long-term sale, and it also creates the conditions where the long-term sale can never happen. If you've got 20,000 books in a warehouse for five years, they'll accrete a lot of overhead, which publishers now say they can't afford—they've seen how quickly they could move the new Judith Krantz, so they want more books like that. So people's expectations of books are changed by their own practices.

"It seems to me that science fiction is being marketed in such a way that it looks intriguing to the casual reader, who picks it up looking for a cheap thrill, reads it, might or might not get the cheap thrill, and is just as likely to go back to reading books in other categories which also supply cheap thrills. I think that science fiction should supply much more than cheap thrills. It should supply the intelligent reader with a kind of thinking he can't get anywhere else. Readers are being sold extremely short."

If this sounds a radical outlook, consider Christopher Priest's origins. He started out as one of those young British writers of the 1960s who sold their first work to *New Worlds*, the slightly avant-garde magazine that spawned science fiction's "new wave" of that period. Back then, it looked as if the new movement was nudging science fiction toward becoming the kind of literature that Priest feels is being squeezed out of existence today. What happened?

"By my definition of it, the new wave was a shared feeling, a revolution, a total rejection of Poul Anderson, Isaac Asimov, and Robert Heinlein. But it wasn't just a negative movement, to overthrow the boring old farts. We shared the positive idea that science fiction could really be very good; that it had been written very badly thus far, but we could start doing it right.

"What happened to the new wave was that it became assimilated. It was made into a sort of Uncle Tom. People like David Gerrold and Stephen Goldin got hold of it, and became 'new-wave writers.' It was reduced to just another idiot genre within a genre, represented by a particular kind of bad writing—a 'type' of story containing, let's say, typographical tricks, some sexual references, an introspective tone, an ambiguous ending. Just another formula.

"The new wave in *that* sense is dead—and thank God. What I would like to see now is some kids coming up to overthrow *us*."

By "us" Priest seems to be identifying himself with the British status quo. There's some justification for this; during the 1970s, he trod a steady path out of the slime of "sci-fi" into that supremely civilized retreat, the British literary establishment.

This was a formidable achievement for someone who came from what he describes as an "anti-literary background."

"I used to be a closet writer. I was in fear of ridicule from my family and friends. I once said to my girlfriend that I wanted to be a writer, and she laughed so much she literally fell off her chair." He shakes his head ruefully. "I never mentioned *that* again, I'll tell you.

"As a teenager, I was given the chance of becoming an accountant, so I took it, through total indifference. I believe I had a bad education—it, too, was anti-literary. Novels were taught as textbooks, and you had to read a chapter every week, so that I left school with a very profound dislike of fiction. The only thing I ever read for pleasure was nonfiction. I started reading science fiction purely for the ideas, then got interested in fiction as a form, got interested in the style of fiction, and then started writing."

I'm talking to him in his living room in Harrow, at the north edge of London. It's a spacious flat in the basement of a large, solid Edwardian mansion. Outside the bay window is a neatly trimmed lawn, with beds of flowers. On the other side of the house, across the road, is a cricket pitch; beyond that, a hill that's golden-brown with autumn foliage, a church spire peeking out above the trees.

As a suburb, it's idyllic. To Priest, however, it's a relatively dull urban area compared with his second residence, a cottage in Devon. He bought that not long ago with the accumulated earnings from his books of the 1970s, and has been spending most of his time out there in the country with his wife, Lisa Tuttle, herself a science-fiction writer.

But now it seems as if the Devon retreat may have to be sold, because his first novel of the 1980s, *The Affirmation*, has not done well in Britain and never did find a paperback publisher in America.

"In *The Affirmation*," he says, "I was writing a novel I had always wanted to write, about the creative process and how close it is to madness. I've had the reaction from a lot of people that it's a jolly good complicated novel, clever and cerebral, not very exciting or readable. I don't understand this—I actually intended it to be, well, a *good yarn*."

I suggest that the book is rather complex and introspective, and makes more demands on readers than most science fiction.

"That sounds as if you're saying, 'Your books are very hard to read, Mr. Priest. Do you mean them to be hard to read?' No, I don't think being hard to read is good at all; I think books should be easy to read. In many ways my favorite novelist is John Fowles, and the sort of novels he writes are instantly comprehensible on one level. The style is clear, the descriptions are good, you know who the characters are and what they represent to each other. But as you go along, the implications of what you are reading build up in your mind, so that you get extremely involved on an additional level. And that's what I try to do in my own work.

"*The Affirmation* can simply be read as a science fiction story about a man who becomes an immortal; there's no question that that's in there. But the implications were what interested me.

"I wouldn't want anyone to think, 'I've got this book, and I know it's going to be good, but I have to wait until I've got five hours when I can concentrate and the phone won't ring.' I wrote the book in the real world and it's supposed to be read in the real world."

His comments and opinions are voiced to me in short, sudden bursts separated by awkward pauses. Now and then he breaks off and laughs at what he has been saying, especially if he senses it might have sounded pretentious or self-serving, and it's important to him to maintain a wry perspective on himself.

At the same time, he's obviously very serious about everything he is telling me, and feels it intensely. He sighs, scowls, gestures despairingly, and a couple of times stands up and paces to and fro, as if he can't contain his agitation.

From his British perspective, science fiction has forsaken what he thinks should have been its central subject matter and style.

"In a way, science fiction, as a category, backed the wrong horse. I feel that originally, Wells and a few others—not very many—were doing the right thing. What then happened was that an opportunistic American magazine publisher, Hugo Gernsback, rationalized the whole thing in the late 1920s and made it into a category. After that, the Wells tradition was neglected, and we went off along the Gernsback tradition, which has been slowly improved, but has always refused to admit many influences from outside. Rather, it feeds on itself.

"Anything which excludes something is wrong. One's doctrine should be to *include* things. The very word 'mainstream' is an excluding word, used by science-fiction writers to refer to anything which isn't part of 'us,' whether it's a novel or an algebra textbook. I think that's a very sad ghetto mentality. They're frightened of what's outside. I don't say necessarily that what's outside is better; I just think it's very stupid not to go and find out.

"People in the science-fiction world talk about George Orwell or Aldous Huxley or Olaf Stapledon as though they're 'outsiders' who once wrote a little science fiction. But actually those are the people who wrote the real stuff; all the Heinlein stuff is a pure confection, all air, like the stuff you put on top of apple pie. So I feel, now, that nobody is writing real science fiction. All we have is a caricature of what it might have been.

"For a while, in the late 1960s, there was some hope that this was changing, and the barriers were going down. At that time, which was when I started writing myself, science fiction was broad enough to include people like Sladek and Ballard.

"Now, however, publishers are creating an environment in which expectations are anti-literary. Just today I had lunch with an editor whom I have a genuine respect for, and he was saying to me, 'Look, if you're hard up, why don't you write a wham-bam space adventure but put some ideas into it so that it's intellectually respectable?' And that simply misunderstands how people write books. To me *the ideas make the novel*; it's not a case of writing something and putting ideas in afterward."

I sit and talk with Priest some more, about individual editors, what they want, what they can no longer accept, and what he plans to do next. He seems to be contemplating some sort of commercial novel, just to stay alive: "I've got to write something else, or I'm going to go bankrupt."

Personally I believe that Christopher Priest will ultimately find a way to continue doing the serious work that interests him—although such work will be harder to sell in the 1980s than it was in the 1970s. And yet, as publishing has changed in the past, it will change again, possibly in unexpected directions. Priest's situation could be quite different by the time this profile appears in print.

For now, however, his outlook is single-mindedly gloomy—to the point where, despite all his vehement opinions, he makes jokes about his own judgment. "My feeling this year is that, no matter how sincere

I am about all this, I must be wrong." He shrugs uncomfortably and gives me a funny grin. "I'm going out of business because I'm wrong."

BIBLIOGRAPHICAL NOTES

Christopher Priest's *Fugue for a Darkening Island* (1972) remains one of his best-known novels, grimly and graphically picturing a near-future Britain torn by civil strife when it becomes overrun by black immigrants fleeing an Africa made uninhabitable by nuclear war.

Inverted World (1974) is a surreal parable in which the earth has been transformed from a sphere to a saddle-shaped surface of negative curvature, on which a giant city must be hauled across the landscape in order to stay in a zone of normal space-time. Remembered mainly for its totally original central concept, this novel is also notable for its concern with solipsism and the creative process, themes recurring in *A Dream of Wessex* (1977) and in *The Affirmation* (1981), the latter being a playful yet ominous duet between two characters writing books about each other, in two alternate worlds.

PHOTO BY JERRY BAUER

William S. Burroughs

It is William Burroughs I'm concerned with here. Not Edgar Rice Burroughs, who created Tarzan and wrote all those well-loved science-fiction adventures about John Carter of Mars. No, *William* Burroughs, whose surreal, drug-obsessed book *The Naked Lunch* was tried for obscenity, and whose most recent novel, *Cities of the Red Night*, perpetuates his preoccupation with perverse fantasies and paranormal science. If it seems illogical for a book about science-fiction writers to focus on this Burroughs rather than the other one, bear in mind where our definitions of science fiction come from.

Before World War II there were a lot of American magazines publishing short stories in categories such as detective fiction, Westerns, and romances. Each category used its simple storytelling formulas: the hard-boiled detective with a beautiful dame for a client, the rowdy cowhand ambling into a sleazy saloon, the small-town sweetheart tempted into the arms of a promiscuous playboy, and so on.

In 1926 Hugo Gernsback invented the science-fiction category, which had not existed before. As Christopher Priest has pointed out in the preceding profile, Gernsback's writers didn't follow the literary traditions laid down by H. G. Wells and Jules Verne. Instead, they used storytelling formulas just as simple as those in the other popular American magazines of the time. And so science fiction built a reputation as the category of mad scientists, flaming rockets, radium, ray-guns, and slimy aliens threatening everything from planet Earth to the whole universe.

Since the 1920s, of course, the literature has matured somewhat. But still, when we intuitively decide what is science fiction and what is not, we've got those old magazine formulas in mind. And that is a severe limitation, since they exclude a writer such as William Burroughs, even though his novels speculate about science and pseudoscience, and are full of surprises—which, surely, were what drew many of us to science fiction in the first place.

Burroughs is an innovator, not only in concepts but in writing technique. His "cut-up" system of scrambling text has earned him a reputation as a difficult avant-garde author. At the same time, the obscenity trial of *The Naked Lunch* gave him a lasting image as a "pornographic" writer, even though the book was judged not obscene and is not shocking by today's standards.

In fact, Burroughs's recent books are not difficult to read and he is not concerned with sex or drugs in themselves but with fantasy and interpersonal control, in various forms dramatized via surreal or science-fictional images. Of his novel *The Soft Machine*, he has said, "The book takes place, to a large extent, in a mythical area which bears some resemblance to South America and also to the planet Venus. It concerns, I should say, a struggle between controllers and those who are endeavoring to throw off control. . . . [Venus] has been a theme in science fiction for some time. And most writers have equated it with something like South America: a lush tropical scene teeming with poisonous, exotic life forms. . . ."

Similarly, his novel *Nova Express* describes aliens infiltrating Earth, their invasion symbolizing all attempts by powerful groups to impose corrupt systems of oppression. "The purpose of my writing is to expose and arrest Nova Criminals," Burroughs writes metaphorically. "I show who they are and what they are doing and what they will do if they are not arrested."

While planning to visit Burroughs at his New York City home, I prepare myself by reading *With William Burroughs*, a collection of taped conversations with personalities ranging from Lou Reed to Susan Sontag. In all these dialogues Burroughs seems very reserved or withdrawn, and my own interview begins to seem an ominous prospect. Maurice Girodias, who first published *The Naked Lunch*, recalls: "Burroughs was very hard to talk to because he didn't say anything. . . . At this time he was living with Brion Gysin and Gysin would do all the talking. . . . All three of us would sit on the bed—because there were no chairs—and try to make conversation. It was really funny. The man just didn't say anything. . . . I never had much editorial conversation with him, actually none. He'd just bring in the manuscript. . . . I think he was doing it to pay the rent. He really needed the money."

At that time, in Paris in the 1950s, William Burroughs had little to live on. Though the giant Burroughs business equipment corporation grew from an adding machine invented by his grandfather, the family had long since sold out all its interest in the company. And twenty-five years after *The Naked Lunch*, Burroughs is still by no means wealthy; he earns only small royalties from his work and lives modestly on the Bowery.

The Bowery at Houston Street: a classic New York scene. Ragged old men stagger up to cars at the stop light and panhandle for spare change, their faces reddened by chill wind and cheap wine. Old newspapers and cigarette packs tumble in the wind. Kids smash bottles, set fire to a trash barrel, and run away hollering. Trucks roar-rattle-crash down the street, trailing clouds of dust and diesel fumes. It's a derelict zone of burned-out tenements, subsiding storefronts behind rusty window gates, welfare hotels, and a couple of missions serving soup from God.

CBGB, the club where New York punk-rock began, is located near here, mainly because punk ethos dictated an ostentatiously "honest" low-rent locale. Some brave, starving artists have moved here since nearby Soho became unaffordably chic. But it'll be years yet before gentrification alleviates the poverty of this part of town.

Until then the Bowery's only retail trade is in second-hand restaurant equipment, sold out of run-down specialty stores offering everything from pizza ovens to napkin dispensers. Burroughs himself lives above a place that deals in old-fashioned vinyl-padded diner chairs. The owner of the store, a fat man in a torn T-shirt, sits outside atop a stack of these chairs chewing a cigar and holding a can of Colt 45 wrapped in the remains of a brown paper bag.

Burroughs emerges from a large painted steel door adjacent to the store. His complexion is ghostly pale; he peers out into daylight like the caretaker from a mausoleum. He gestures for me to come inside, and leads me slowly up a flight of dusty wooden stairs, into the place he refers to dryly as "The Bunker," which is his home.

The floor is of concrete, painted white. Likewise the ceiling. And the walls, also. There's only one window, and that's been boarded up. Fluorescent tubes cast a pallid light. This vast, empty place was once an athletic club's changing room. All the lockers have been stripped out and hardly any furniture has been substituted.

Burroughs leads me to a kitchen area. Our footsteps echo across the concrete floor as though we are walking through a huge cellar. We sit at the table near a sink unit which has been installed in makeshift fashion. From this vantage point the rest of the space recedes into the distance. The only other furniture that I can see is a gray steel desk on which stands an old gray office typewriter, over against the far wall.

Burroughs turns out to be almost as difficult to talk to as I had feared. He is very polite and seems willing to tolerate my presence for as long as I wish to stay, but many of my questions bore him. He smokes a succession of Player's Navy Cut cigarettes, moves his hands and arms in awkward nervous mannerisms, fidgets in his chair, and several times gets up, walks to and fro, then sits back down again while he continues talking. He's nearing seventy and the years show in the lines on his face, but he has a powerful, assertive voice. Typically he makes a brief, categorical statement, then stops and regards me with his pale eyes as if waiting to see if I really intend to ask any more dumb questions.

I begin with science fiction. He has clearly used aspects of it in his work; does he read much of it? Does he enjoy any of it?

"Writing science fiction is very difficult. Very few writers ever manage to convince you that this or that ever could have happened. Usually you'll find just a few paragraphs; if you find a good chapter, that's a very good science-fiction book."

I ask him for an example.

"Henry Kuttner's *Fury*—which is out of print, and Henry Kuttner's dead, and they reprinted all his work except the one good thing that he did." Burroughs pauses. "Eric Frank Russell is pretty good. A lot of science-fiction writers, you know, produce just a few good sentences. . . . Fred Saberhagen is very good on sword and sorcery. But he's just written another one that I can't read—I couldn't read beyond the first page." Another long pause. "H. G. Wells's stuff still stands up pretty well."

If this seems a peculiar mix of rather old-fashioned authors it's because Burroughs uses science fiction for his own purposes, to feed his special obsessions. He describes Eric Frank Russell's *Three to Conquer*, for instance, as "One of the better 'virus' books." Burroughs has a special interest in viruses as a form of quasi-life that invades a person much as heroin takes over the metabolism of an addict, or totalitarianism takes over the mind of a citizen. In Burroughs's world, viruses are a metaphor for psychological or physiological control.

In *Nova Express*, for example: "Without hesitation K9 gave the order: 'Release Silence Virus—Blanket area'—So The Silence Sickness flashed round the world. . . ."

Or, earlier in the novel, in one of its laconic, comic scenes: "So I walk in on this Pleasantville croaker and tell him I have contracted this Venusian virus and subject to dissolve myself in poison juices and assimilate the passers-by unless I get my medicine and get it regular—So I walk in on this old party smelling like a compost heap and steaming demurely and he snaps at me, 'What's *your* trouble?'

"'The Venusian Gook Rot, doctor.'"

This kind of ironic and multi-leveled writing is a long way from conventional science fiction, which must be one reason that Burroughs is so out of sympathy with much of it, even though he draws upon its ideas.

Another less obvious reason is that he has little interest in conventional space travel. "All they're contemplating, and all they have accomplished, is traveling in an aqualung," he says, cryptically and dismissively.

I ask if he's against the space program.

"No, it's practically the only expenditure I don't begrudge the government. Even to have gotten out there in an aqualung was a great accomplishment. But to my way of thinking, the only possible hope for the human species is to get into space and accommodate themselves to space conditions."

Is he implying we should adapt ourselves to live in space without life-support systems?

"Absolutely. It's quite as drastic a step as leaving water for land. Whether it'll be made or not is another question, but if it isn't made, that's it. Any species comes to an end; they've got certain potential, to carry them so far, and then there comes a point to mutate or die. We've reached that point. I think a lot of our sociological chaos really is reflecting a biological crisis, the fact that we're near the end of the line. But you see, if you've got creatures living in water, looking up, they can't of course imagine clearly what it's like to be up there, to be out of the water, in a different dimension. There are going to be whole new fears—the fear of falling, for instance, has no meaning for a fish, but as soon as he gets up on land, it will.

"Just as a fish must have air-breathing potential before it can move, so to my way of thinking space research should be directed towards effecting biological alterations in the human structure that would make it more suited to space conditions. That's the first step."

I object that we've got to have oxygen in some form.

"Well, that's what we say, but there's no prerequisite."

In that case, he's talking about rather substantial modifications.

"Oh, absolutely. Very drastic modifications."

And psychological modifications, too.

"Everything is both biological and psychological; everything is both instinctive and emotional. There's no line there at all. That's one of the errors of Western thought, this 'either/or' thinking. Korzybski [originator of General Semantics] points that out, and really should be required reading for everyone. All these 'either/or' lines are completely erroneous. Like internal and external: all phenomena are both internal and external.

"Of course, you've read Monroe's book, *Journeys Out of the Body*? That's a step in the direction of adaptation. You see, one of the most important limitations is weight. Weight, and then on top of that, having to transport the whole environment, around something that's fairly heavy to begin with—the human body. Well, we have, here, a model body that's much lighter, perhaps pretty nearly weightless, and that's the astral body, the dream body, and Monroe's done quite a lot of research along these lines. He has some machines to facilitate leaving the body."

In Burroughs's books he has a penchant for dry, almost deadpan humor; but talking about astral bodies, he seems quite serious. I ask him if he really believes that out-of-body experiences happen.

"Of course, it happens all the time. It happens every night, for example, in dreams. We now know that dreams are a biologic necessity. They're showing us the direction in which we're going, and some hints as to how to get there."

But—taking this seriously—if space travel were to be done by "astral bodies," no biological adaptation would be necessary. The physical body could stay back home and sustain itself.

"Yes. But there comes a time when it doesn't. So Monroe's done a lot of work with dying people. So it won't be such a shock. He gets them accustomed to living outside of the body."

I decide to try to bring things back to a more material level. Does Burroughs like the idea of space colonies?

"Sure, why not? It'd be a step in the right direction." He shrugs.

Would space colonies, in his view of things, revitalize the human spirit?

"Undoubtedly. Eventually people will have to think in these terms—if they have time."

He seems to have lost interest in the subject. I decide to try a different tack altogether. Has he been troubled, over the years, by readers complaining that his books are hard to understand, or difficult?

"They have to tell me what they think is 'difficult' and why," he says flatly. "What it means is what's there. Salvador Dali, when asked what his pictures mean, just points to his pictures. I do the same thing. It means what is there, that's all. If it doesn't mean anything to you, then it just doesn't mean anything to you, that's all. You can't tell anybody if they don't know already."

This prompts me to ask about the "cut-up" system, which Burroughs used in many of his earlier books in response to a suggestion from artist Brion Gysin. In the "cut-up" method a writer takes a normal, coherent piece of prose—a page of his own manuscript, or a paragraph of someone else's work, or both—and chops the text arbitrarily into pieces a few words long. These pieces are then reassembled at random, resulting in prose such as: "Explosive fragrance—Love between light and shadow—The few who lived cross the wounded galaxies—Love?—Five years I grew muttering in the ice—Dead sun reached flesh with its wandering dream—" (from *Nova Express*).

"It's closer to the actual facts of perception," Burroughs explains, referring to the scrambled way in which our thoughts actually occur, hopscotching from everyday experiences to fragments of childhood memory to speculations on what may happen tomorrow, and back again. "I'm talking about how things are actually perceived by the brain. When Cezanne's pictures were first exhibited people didn't even realize that this was a lemon or a fish seen from a certain angle in a certain light; they didn't even see it. Now any child will see what it is. So the function of art and creative thought, I think, is to make people aware of what they know, but don't yet know that they know. And this always upsets a certain number of people; they don't want to be made aware, but then over a period of time, of course, it becomes common knowledge, and the expansion of awareness is accepted."

This sounds optimistic, yet I feel that public receptiveness for experimental fiction has diminished over the years.

"That depends, of course. Certainly best sellers are usually written in the old nineteenth-century novel tradition, which has nothing to do with the facts of perception. The omniscient author, and all that, is a form quite as arbitrary as the sonnet. And it's still very widespread. But I mean, good heavens, we've had Joyce, Gertrude Stein—all these verbal innovators have certainly had an effect.

"Just the same thing has happened in painting. Painters had their whole representational position knocked out from under them by photography. One of the first things they did was the equivalent of the cut-up in painting: the collage, the montage. And then they've gone further and further than that, very far from representational painting indeed."

Large parts of Burroughs's most recent novel, *Cities of the Red Night*, are written in totally conventional prose that apes the private-detective idiom. Does this indicate a break with his earlier work?

"No. There's passages written in much the same way in *The Naked Lunch*. Clem Snide is one of my old characters." He pauses. "And then the Health Officer is unmistakably written in the style of Graham Greene. There's also quite a lot of Conrad in there."

Has Burroughs ever been tempted to try writing a book with real mass appeal? A best seller?

He shakes his head. "All best sellers are written up to the limit of the man's ability. Something that people will immediately sense is that they're being written down to. You cannot do it. It isn't that I have any scruples, it's just that it doesn't work. I know how best sellers are written; there are two main formulas. One is 'The Menace.' Challenge posed by the menace, removal of the menace. Like *Jaws*. It can be an epidemic, an alien invasion, nuclear holocaust, whatever. The other is 'Something that People Know Something About, and Want to Know More About.' *The Godfather*, Inside Madison Avenue, Inside the Cosmetic Industry, etc., etc., etc. Those are the two main formulas.

"I think *Cities of the Red Night* has sold quite well. I think it will be as financially successful as *The Naked Lunch*. A lot of my books didn't do anything financially. *The Job* was a complete financial failure."

Was that hard to take, over the years?

"Well no, I mean you have to adjust yourself. I managed to get by, and when I came back to America [in the 1970s] I started doing a lot of readings, and that has carried me; about half of my income comes from that source. I couldn't live on books alone—at least, I haven't been able to, up to now. But I hope that I will be able to, because I want to give all of my time now to writing. I'm getting tired of performing."

Cities of the Red Night is to some extent an alternate-universe novel, in which the Americas are settled by utopian colonists in small communes allowing total equality and liberty. Burroughs explains in his introduction that the idea comes from "Libertatia," a real colony established by a pirate captain in the eighteenth century. "There were other such colonies in Central and South America, but they were not able to maintain themselves, since they were not sufficiently populous to withstand attack. Had they been able to do so, the history of the world could have been altered. . . . Imagine such a movement on a world-wide scale. Faced by the actual practice of freedom, the French and American revolutions would be forced to stand by their words."

The book thus dramatizes realistically Burroughs's continuing concern for liberty versus oppression.

"In *Cities of the Red Night* I'm writing principally about getting rid of the Catholic influence," he explains. "While the Spanish were in a sense displaced from South America by the liberal revolutions of 1848, their whole way of doing things remained in effect. The language, the whole Spanish bureaucracy, and the Catholic Church. So there weren't any very basic changes. If they wanted to make such changes, the first thing to do would be to change the calendar. Very important, because Catholicism is very much dependent on the Saint calendar. Change the calendar, change the language, change the whole way of doing things. The bureaucracy."

I ask his views about contemporary U.S. politics. Is he pessimistic about the Reagan administration?

"Pessimism is a word which doesn't do much for me. Pessimism and optimism are really meaningless words. I mean, if the captain says the ship is sinking, is he a pessimist? Well, if it isn't sinking, perhaps. You see, I'm not concerned with politics at all. I feel when things get on a political level, it's all really pretty hopeless. I'm not interested in politics at all, or political solutions."

The other main theme in *Cities of the Red Night* draws upon the work of Wilhelm Reich.

"I think Reich's cancer theory is extremely valid and has in fact been stated word for word by a doctor connected with the space program, with no acknowledgment to Reich. If you have a cell with a high electrical potential at the surface, it's a noncancerous cell. When the electrical charge at the surface gets below a certain level, then the cell is suffocating and you get a precancerous condition. That's exactly what Reich said, and the orgone accumulator was an attempt to raise the electrical potential of the cell at the surface, and could probably be carried much further with magnetic iron. Doctors have said that cancer can't exist in a strong magnetic field. So there is a lot of very valid material there, which nobody has ever used."

Burroughs himself has owned and used an "orgone accumulator," a box designed by Reich to gather "orgone energy" from the cosmos and focus it on the user sitting inside.

"I think it does have some effect on cancer, and anything that's anti-cancerous will tone up the system in general. Pyramid-shaped accumulators, magnetism, I think there are many possibilities there."

I remark that I find it hard to believe in pyramid power.

"I don't find it difficult to believe that energy can be concentrated by shapes, and particularly in magnetic fields, because in a sense what animates the human body *is* a magnetic field, and I think there's a strong possibility the whole answer to cancer is right there. But there's no experiment going on, certainly not in any conventional cancer research. Innovation is stifled by the way large organizations are set up. The more expensive your project, the better, from the scientist's point of view. The way in which appropriations are assigned militates against finding a cure. They may think they are looking for a cure, but actually they are not; they are looking for a way to perpetuate themselves and their particular department, whether it's accomplishing anything or not."

Most science-fiction authors play with concepts (such as UFOs) that in real life they do not take very seriously. Burroughs, however, seems absolutely serious about all the concepts in his work. As he says, he sees no divisions—no "either/or"—and is so open-minded as to seem gullible to those of us who reject "crank" theories.

But Burroughs's open mind is a large part of his genius. His imagery and metaphor are so vivid, his grasp of psychological and social forces is so acute, because of his sensitivity. Just as he is probably the only author to have contrived fine prose via the use of drugs, he is one of the few to have synthesized a coherent message from weird ideas about altered states of consciousness and orgone energy. As he puts it, in his afterword to *The Naked Lunch*: "There is only one thing a writer can write about: *what is in front of his senses at the moment of writing*. . . . I am a recording instrument. . . . I do not presume to impose 'story' 'plot' 'continuity'. . . . In sofaras I succeed in *Direct* recording of certain areas of psychic process I may have limited function. . . . I am not an entertainer."

Nor did he ever set out to be a writer. "I didn't write anything till I was thirty-five. Then, when *Junky* was published, that gave me encouragement, and I went on from there. The writing of *The Naked Lunch* took place over a period of five or six years or more, as a series of sketches. Maurice Girodias in Paris wanted to publish it, I had to get it ready in about three weeks, and there were about six or seven hundred pages of notes, some material which was finished and some of it partially finished, so I just made a sort of an arbitrary selection, and that was the book.

"Almost always, I will change the concept at some point during the writing of a book. I have some general idea of the way it's going, but not specifically."

He mentions that his next novel will deal with guerrilla warfare. Before I leave, he shows me back issues of *Guns and Ammo* magazine that he's been reading for research, and a modern, sophisticated blowpipe and darts, for "silent assassination." On one of the concrete walls of the Bunker are life-size posters of enemy agents. The posters have been used as targets in handgun practice. They've been shot full of large bullet holes.

I ask him if he has any parting message for science-fiction writers. "Well, it's up to them what they do, I can't dictate. It has seemed to be an area where they had far-out ideas, but the way in which they developed the ideas was pretty conventional.

"Dreams and fantasies are quite as real as what we see around us—simply a different level of reality. As we now know, dreams are as necessary to us as food. We die without them."

On this note I depart, leaving him alone in the Bunker, his strange, echoing, windowless retreat where the dreams are made.

BIBLIOGRAPHICAL NOTES

The Naked Lunch (1959) was not Burroughs's first novel (it was preceded by *Junky* (1953), under the pseudonym William Lee), but it remains the one for which he is best known, and it established the obsessions that have recurred ever since: addiction, mind control, black humor, and paranoid fantasies of social and sexual distortion.

Nova Express (1964) is probably the most science fictional of Burroughs's work, and contains large chunks of fairly conventional narrative. His most recent novel, *Cities of the Red Night* (1981), contains sociological speculation, ESP, and some science-fictional ideas, narrated largely in a deadpan detective-story style. It uses none of the cut-ups or impressionistic techniques that made earlier works such as *The Soft Machine* (1962) and *The Ticket that Exploded* (1962) so densely packed with imagery, and consequently difficult for some readers to tackle.

PHOTO BY CHARLES ADAMS

Arthur C. Clarke

It's a fresh springtime morning. Seen from the windows of the fifteenth floor, the buildings of Manhattan are a sun-and-shadow masonry mosaic under the bright blue sky.

I'm looking out onto this panorama from a comfortable swivel chair, behind a big desk, in the ample office of an editor who's away for the day, in the headquarters of my publishers on Madison Avenue. It's a setting to inspire power fantasies and delusions of grandeur ("Hello? Scott? Yes, we're willing to go up to 1.5 million on Arthur's new one, if we can get ten percent of Book Club . . ."). But the truth is, I'm just here to make a free phone call.

I tried to tell my publishers that there was only one way to do this job properly. I should be sent to Arthur Clarke's tropical retreat in Sri Lanka, to meet the man in person. Think of all the background color, I said. Face to face with this legendary seer of the space age in his colonial mansion, chatting in the Trophy Room over a dish of curry and a few cups of locally grown tea, while the houseboys fan us with palm fronds, the monsoon rains patter into the rice paddies, parakeets squawk in the coconut palms, and monkeys chase tarantulas in the front yard—what a profile this would make!

But, as my publishers put it, we had to be *realistic*. And in the end it turned out that a half-hour international telephone call was as realistic as they were prepared to be.

Well, a phone call would be appropriate in a way: The conversation would be conveyed to Sri Lanka by satellite, and Clarke was the man who invented communications satellites in the first place.

No one took him very seriously, of course, when he wrote that first article about "extraterrestrial relays" for *Wireless World* in 1945. Even *he* didn't take himself very seriously: He didn't try to patent his invention, because he didn't imagine it would be built in his lifetime.

It's hard to remember, now, that in the late 1940s and early 1950s space travel of any kind was nothing more than a vague, wistful fantasy. Most people, including many respectable scientists, openly laughed at the notion. Even the tiny minority who took it seriously, including visionaries such as Clarke in the British Interplanetary Society, tended to assume that it wouldn't happen until decades or even centuries had passed.

But the move into space gathered momentum exponentially. And with it, so did Clarke's career.

His success has been like a space shot. First, the dull groundwork prior to launch, building his own telescopes as a kid (he couldn't afford professional equipment) and publishing his first stories in amateur magazines. Next, lift-off, in which early work consumed large amounts of energy for small initial gains. Then, as his trajectory lifted him to greater altitudes in the science-fiction medium, he encountered a fast-moving body of high mass, in the form of Stanley Kubrick. And this fly-by was the last boost that Clarke needed to accelerate him to escape velocity. Suddenly he was free—forever free!—from the gravity-well of category fiction. His mission, now, was to boldly go where no science-fiction writer had gone before, into a rarefied realm of luminaries and macrocosmic events: science prizes, best seller lists, international conferences, congressional speeches, prestigious awards. And he's been coasting in free-fall ever since.

By the 1970s, Clarke found less and less to tempt him away from Sri Lanka (formerly the British colony Ceylon), where he had relocated originally because of a chance meeting in a London pub with an old friend who got him interested in scuba diving—the nearest thing to zero gravity available on planet Earth.

Finally, in 1980, Clarke renounced writing altogether and retired into permanent tropical hedonism. Interviewed in *Science Digest*, he said he was following the example of the composer Sibelius, who "locked himself up in his study . . . and said 'I am writing my great work,' and all he did was enjoy himself and drink a bottle of brandy a day and do no work at all. And I admire that."

But Clarke's claims proved premature. Moved by his New York literary agent's heartfelt cry ("You owe it to your readers, Arthur!"), and moved perhaps still further by a million-dollar offer from Del Rey Books, he sat down and wrote what he'd always said could not be written: the sequel to *2001: A Space Odyssey*.

On the date of my phone call, Clarke is doing the final revisions to this sequel. It's nine-thirty A.M., New York time, as I wire my tape recorder to my publisher's telephone and direct-dial Clarke's number halfway around the world. It's ten-and-a-half hours later in Sri Lanka, and he should just be finishing his day's work.

Distant relays click. Impulses leap from one repeater to the next, then take that big stride 22,300 miles up to a communications satellite and down again. Of course, this is just one routine international call out of thousands made every hour; yet still the technology seems impressive. Maybe I'm naive to feel this way, but Clarke himself seems never to have lost his wide-eyed wonder at science and technology, no matter how much it becomes a part of everyday life.

He answers the phone, sounding very British. "Ah. Hang on a second," he says. "I'll just switch off the word processor."

There's a pause, and then he's back on the line, ready to talk. He sounds close and clear; the only clue that this is an international call is the echo I hear of my own voice, delayed by half a second from having traveled 50,000 miles to Sri Lanka via satellite, and 50,000 miles back again.

Since I'm stuck in New York, unable to witness with my own eyes the Sri Lankan parrots, monkeys, tarantulas, and so forth, I ask Clarke to describe his surroundings.

"I'm sitting in a long room," he says. "What I call the 'ego chamber,' where I work." (His British pronunciation rhymes "ego" with "echo.") "At one end there is a TV set with two video recorders. Then there is an 8 mm and 16 mm projector, and a 35 mm slide projector, and a lot of bookshelves. A door leads through to the lav.—on that door there are instructions for using a zero-gravity toilet. From *2001*, I expect you remember.

"Where I am at the moment, at the other end of the room, I'm surrounded by my word processor and printer, and telephones. There are windows along one wall, and trees outside. We're near the center of Columbo. This house is quite modern, about twenty years old—one of the last that was built without any concern for expense."

He speaks in quick, precise sentences that end abruptly, as if he doesn't like wasting words. His matter-of-factness reminds me of his writing, which seldom attempts to be stylized, and even now sometimes falls into the idioms of old British boys' adventure fiction. In *2010*, for example, a character exclaims "Phew!" after a moment of danger—an expression I hadn't seen in print since I read *Biggles* novels twenty years ago.

I'm interested that Clarke has stayed so faithful to his original writing style and intentions, unlike some of the other elder statesmen of science fiction who started out when he did.

"You mean people like H. G. Wells?" he jokes.

But I'm thinking of, say, Pohl, whose style has changed considerably over the years, or Heinlein, who has experimented with all kinds of different themes and methods.

"I guess I'm just an old conservative," Clarke replies. "Although, really, if I have stayed true to the original form of my writing that's simply because I have a constant commitment to science."

A commitment that still entails that almost childlike quality of wonder?

"Yes, very much," he agrees immediately. "And I'm proud of that. I regard it as something of an achievement not to have become cynical."

Or pessimistic; he seems to retain perpetual faith in the future.

"One must obviously be very worried about all sorts of things," he says. "Right now, the Falkland Islands, for example." (At the time of this interview, the British had just landed.) "And of course the ecological and other well-known possible disasters. The unavoidable ones, as well as avoidable ones like nuclear war. But I do remain an optimist, especially in my fiction, because I hope it may operate as a self-fulfilling prophecy."

The ending of his novel *The Fountains of Paradise* seems a slight exception to this, in that it has a wistful quality, as if Clarke is regretting a far future of space exploration that he will never live to see.

"If the ending of that book does seem wistful, that's only because, at the time I wrote it, for a number of reasons I thought it was my last book. Actually, as regards the space program, I never dreamed I would see this much. I have no gripes, no complaints at all. I never dreamed, for instance, that I would ever know what Jupiter looks like. From a purely personal viewpoint I'm not too bothered by the present lull in the space program. We need time, in a way, to make sense of what we've already learned. On the other hand, I have friends in the program who are suffering now because of the cutbacks in funding."

The new novel, *2010*, depicts manned exploration of Jupiter's moons less than thirty years from now.

"But that's just a continuation of the future we visualized in *2001*," he explains, "and of course it has already become an impossible future. When we wrote *2001* in 1964, 1965, and 1966, it did not seem unreasonable to imagine that by the end of this century there would be these giant space stations." (Necessary in order to build manned ships to explore interplanetary space.) "But Vietnam and Watergate and all the other things that happened in America changed all that. It will all still happen one day—but not on that time scale.

"I've never attempted to predict the future, and am not interested in doing so, *in my fiction*. Only in my nonfiction.

"Conceiving *2010* was actually rather difficult, because I'd painted myself into a corner in so many ways in *2001*. I think some people were expecting me to bring back Bowman [the astronaut from the first story] in white robes, or something, but I wanted to avoid any cliche of that type. For a long time I didn't see how I could write any kind of a sequel at all."

The new novel is dedicated to two Russians: one a cosmonaut, the other a scientist. Clarke has always expressed idealistic yearnings for world peace and cooperation; I ask if he deliberately includes this kind of message.

"As far as putting messages in my fiction is concerned, I'm always fond of quoting Sam Goldwyn, who said, 'If you've got a message, use Western Union!' But of course there is an *implicit* message. No writer can avoid it if he's worth anything at all."

Is there going to be any more of the *2001* saga? Dare one ask—does *2020* come next?

"As a matter of fact, the joke's already going around. Not *2020*, though—it's supposed to be *20001*."

But he's not serious.

"No—except that now I've got this word processor, anything might happen, in five or ten years. I've just started writing articles again, believe it or not. I just sent off a long piece—well, long for me—to my agent, which may cause a lot of controversy. 'The Menace of Creationism.' I've even hinted it might be a communist plot. That's tongue-in-cheek, of course, but I wanted to make people think."

I ask him if he still reads any science fiction. But, like so many of the best-known authors in the field, it seems he feels no need to.

"I gave up the magazines years ago, just as a matter of necessity—I didn't have enough time. In fact, I hardly read any fiction these days."

Is it simply a matter of his finding no science fiction now that he feels is worth reading?

"That is indeed a possibility," he says dryly.

The vast amount of money paid for world rights to *2010* is, of course, symptomatic of modern publishing: the blockbuster system, which robs attention and money from more minor novels—especially those by new writers.

"I suppose that may be true," he says, as though he hadn't thought too much about this. "I don't know. From my own point of view, I'd naturally prefer to live in a penthouse than a garret."

He's achieved so much, at this point, I can't help wondering whether he can possibly have any ambitions left to fulfill.

"Hardly any. I say half jokingly that I'd like to go in the space shuttle, but I think that's not very probable. Actually, my only remaining ambition which I could fulfill is learning to play the piano. I can play a scale now, which is more than I used to be able to do. Then I have two computers in the house, now, and I'm spending a lot of time learning to use them.

"And of course it's a full-time job just trying to decide how to spend all this money!"

I suppose I should end there. According to the Alfred Bester method, an article should always end with the Best Anecdote, and that one-liner seems to be it.

But that wouldn't be quite fair. Clarke cannot be casually characterized as someone whose main concern is making money. He's delighted by his own successes—in fact, he tends to talk about them at every opportunity. But his intentions as a writer and as a futurist have always been idealistic. Back at the beginning of the 1960s, in his classic nonfiction book *Profiles of the Future*, he wrote:

"Whatever the eventual outcome of our exploration of space, we can be reasonably certain of some immediate benefits—and I am deliberately ignoring such 'practical' returns as the multi-billion dollar improvements in weather forecasting and communications. . . . The creation of wealth is certainly not to be despised, but in the long run the only human activities really worthwhile are the search for knowledge, and the creation of beauty. This is beyond argument; the only point of debate is which comes first."

In the same book, he predicted that communications satellites could foster global unity via totally free, international, educational television.

And so, to Clarke, space exploration was not merely a power fantasy, or escapism, or a profitable investment, or a form of heroism. Rather, it was something through which we could transcend ourselves; something so big that it could eclipse petty differences and unite us all. He has come back to this theme again and again, not only in his nonfiction but in almost all his novels.

Prelude to Space, revised in 1954 but mostly written in the bleak post-war Britain of 1947, includes a lyrical vision of what the first manned lunar landing might mean to humanity:

"Out of the fears and miseries of the Second Dark Age, drawing free—oh, might it be forever!—from the shadows of Belsen and Hiroshima, the world was moving towards its most splendid sunrise. After five hundred years, the Renaissance had come again."

It didn't work out that way, of course, and his sentiments now seem naive. But as Clarke says himself, he is proud not to have become a cynic. If the idealism in his fiction has turned out untrue-to-life, I cannot see this as a failing on his part. I prefer to blame the world leaders whose lack of imagination and spirit molded our real-life future, falling so far short of Clarke's grand vision of how things could have been.

BIBLIOGRAPHICAL NOTES

Like Bradbury or Asimov, Clarke remains best known for his earliest work, even though his recent novels have been more capably told. His classic *Childhood's End* (1953) describes collective impotence, followed ultimately by transcendence, as humanity is first dominated by benevolent aliens, then welcomed by them to a kind of cosmic fulfillment (a message similar to that in *2001*). Similarly, *The City and the Stars* (1956) romantically portrays a young person's discontent with his unchanging far-future utopia and his search for an end to human stasis.

More recently, *Rendezvous with Rama* (1973) describes an expedition to a giant alien construct passing planet Earth; *Imperial Earth* (1975) is the travelogue of a young space-born man touring Earth for the first time in 2276; and *The Fountains of Paradise* (1979) describes the construction of a "space elevator"—a cable stretching from Earth's surface to an orbiting satellite. In all these novels Clarke shows awe for science and the universe, and longings for a future of peaceful cooperation. These themes persist in *2010: The Odyssey Continues* (1982), the sequel to *2001*.

PHOTO BY CHARLES PLATT

Alvin Toffler

He's not a science-fiction writer by any definition. In fact, so far as I know, he has never published any fiction at all.

But he is, very definitely, a "Dream Maker."

His best-known books, *Future Shock* and *The Third Wave*, encourage readers to ponder the possibilities of technological progress. Toffler describes worlds that may lie forty or fifty years ahead; he extends trends and tries to imagine their impact on society and on human behavior.

This, of course, is the technique used by writers such as Clarke, Heinlein, and Pohl. The difference is that Toffler presents his prognoses as fact, rather than dressing them up as fiction.

He's quick to acknowledge the comparison between what he does and what science-fiction writers do, and the practical role that science fiction can play.

"Science fiction is a very valuable tool. For creating future consciousness, for allowing young people to entertain alternative images of reality. I view science fiction as a treasury of models—of alternative political, social systems, sexual relationships, forms of technology, and so on. The more alternative models of which we are aware, the more flexible our responses can be to present-day situations.

"I have read a fair amount of it. I like John Brunner, I like Bob

Sheckley. There are many, from time to time, whom I've enjoyed. I read *Man Plus* by Frederik Pohl; I thought that was a very fine book."

I'm talking with Toffler in his apartment on the Upper East Side of Manhattan. It's a sprawling, sparsely-furnished expanse of white walls and gray carpeting. The decor is restrained—almost austere—like a modern art gallery waiting for paintings to be installed. There are built-in, leather-covered couches, modern marble-topped tables. Few ornaments; no clutter; and nothing, anywhere, out of place.

In his books Toffler comes across with pulpit-thumping fervor, stressing the One True Way of socio-technological fulfillment. He's been criticized for his brash, breezy style, which summarizes social subtleties in jargonized prose reminiscent of marriage manuals and diet guides. "Blip Reading," scoffed *The New York Times*, which went on to ridicule Toffler's "titillating but slipshod analysis."

In person Alvin Toffler is very different. He is not at all a wide-eyed prophet preaching some simplistic hot-gospel of high-tech. A middle-aged, slightly balding, amiable man dressed conservatively in gray suit, white shirt, and dark tie, he speaks quietly, patiently, making frequent thoughtful references to social studies and statistics. He reminds me of a psychiatrist, with the world as his patient: he gently examines its condition and offers his diagnosis in a manner that is neutral and detached yet full of compassion. Clearly, he is more than a little concerned about the future.

"Things are going to be *much* worse," he says, when I ask about the next ten or twenty years—a period *The Third Wave* tends to skip over as "transitional" along the way to a decentralized utopia. "I think there is a good likelihood of severe economic conflict," he goes on. "In the U.S. we're going through a precarious and almost sinister lull in the political mood. But I don't think that the present administration is going to continue to be unopposed. And the forms of opposition and conflict are liable to be quite different from those of the past.

"We're not going to go through a classical depression or classical inflation. What we're seeing is the emergence of a differentiated society. While some people are eating dogfood, there's money to burn in other communities—the sharp contrast between a Second-Wave community like Youngstown or Detroit, and embryonic Third-Wave communities like Dallas, Houston, or Silicon Valley, makes this plain. We no longer have a uniform national economy, and the problems can't be addressed using the blunderbuss tools that were developed for uniform systems. So I look forward to a great deal of economic difficulty, of a new kind."

He is referring, here, to his belief that a split is developing between "Second-Wave" communities (wedded to big government, heavy industry, and traditional values) and communities evolving toward his "Third-Wave" vision of loose-knit, diverse, untraditional citizens whose allegiance is more to scattered special-interest groups than to the nation as a whole, and who are starting to use technology for their own individualistic ends rather than remain passive consumers dependent on the products of large corporations. It's almost a libertarian vision, putting great faith in the potential of the individual, whom Toffler seems to trust far more than our contemporary organizations and institutions:

"The peculiar position we find ourselves in today challenges the old political assumptions that have been made by radicals of both Right and Left, that an elite is running things for its own advantage, against our best interests. That presupposes that the decisions being taken by an elite will actually bring about the results which they anticipate. A far greater danger to us lies not in the anticipated consequences of policies taken by elites but in the unanticipated consequences. In a time when an elite understands its society and knows how to play the game to its own advantage, then it makes sense to say 'they' are doing us in deliberately for their own self-interest. Now the best you can say is they may do us in by mistake. Because they don't understand the system that they're allegedly managing.

"Some of our best-known leaders in business and industry are actually very intelligent people, but they make very unintelligent decisions. I think the explanation of this paradox lies in the decision-making institutions. I believe that our instititions are stupid, because they're obsolete, and you could put teams of geniuses to work in those institutions and the results would still be stupid."

Future Shock was a study of damaging side-effects of technology, and a plea to humanize progress. As Toffler's comments indicate here, his ideas in *The Third Wave* go much further. He is now concerned not so much with improving our ability to live with change as with regearing the whole system. *The Third Wave* even proposes a new Constitution, to enable direct democratic representation of the electorate by means of votes cast from personal home-computer terminals.

I comment that, regardless of whether his vision is desirable, it sounds implausible, since it would entail dismantling very large organizations that wield a great deal of power. His response, however, is that the process has already begun.

"Industries that seem extremely powerful today are going to die, no matter how the managers of those industries try to hang onto their seats of power. I have actually had an oil company president say to me, 'We're finished. We're going to be as dead as the railroads. We're going to be replaced by solar photovoltaics, by hydrogen, by a thousand new ways of producing energy.' So that's one member of the elite who isn't going to wait around for change to overtake him.

"Systems do change, and institutions do collapse and die, and new ones spring up. One way that this happens is by internal restructuring—in a coup d'etat, the young turks take over from the old turks. Usually this is in response to great external pressures on the system. Another possibility is that outsiders simply topple the institution and create a new one. But the most common way in which changes occur is when the old institution stays in place, and we continue to pay lip-service to it, while at the same time new institutions spring up almost unnoticed and take on the real business of society. Pretty soon what you have is the shell or husk of the old institution still intact—a monarchy is a good example—while the real decisions and activities take place somewhere else.

"I think we're going to see something like that happen in many areas. Take education: the factory-like school in my view was a Second-Wave phenomenon. We may not wipe out the school, but more and more kids are going to be educated at home, on the job, in summer camps, in computer stores on Main Street, and in a dozen other places. The school may continue to crank out a routinized education but that's not where things will actually happen."

I comment that one place where his ideas for a Third-Wave society could be brought to life without the need for displacing an existing system would be in a space colony. Does he believe this will ever be possible?

"I hope so. I like the idea of our adventure in space. However, most of our images of cultures in space are highly unimaginative derivatives of terrestrial cultures. For example, the movie *Outland* pictured a mining operation on one of Jupiter's moons, but the social structure was a classical industrial-style society and culture, and I think the notion that you can take a Second-Wave industrial form of management and transfer that into space at a time in the future is simply inane. I think we're going to invent new forms of management and industrial relations, and it's not going to be the 1890s or 1930s factory reproduced in outer space.

"The second thing to be said about space colonies is that I fear they represent a form of escapism. I like the idea of a human thrust into space, but I think there is a kind of blind wish on the part of the most enthusiastic space advocates that all of our present social and political problems would somehow go away; that if we could make that fresh start out there it wouldn't matter that millions of people are starving to death on earth, or that people are killing themselves, or that riots are bloodying the streets."

Despite Toffler's obviously comfortable lifestyle, he often refers to everyday problems and hardships in a manner implying first-hand experience. When I ask him about his background it turns out that, although he always knew he wanted to be a writer, he spent a lot of time doing manual labor.

"I went to New York University at the very end of World War II. I met my wife in as clicheed a fashion as possible, on a park bench in Washington Square. As soon as I finished at the university we decided to leave New York and go to the Midwest to work in factories. At that time I couldn't get a job writing, anyway; and we wanted to get away from the sheltered middle-class environment in which I'd grown up; and I wanted to help organize unions. For more than five years I worked as a millwright in a steel foundry, as a punch-press operator, on an auto assembly line, I used a jackhammer to break concrete, I drove a truck, I became a welder. . . . My wife worked in a steel foundry, a lightbulb factory, and she became a shop steward.

"Drawing on my experience, I went to work for a trade-union newspaper, my first job as a journalist, covering strikes and political meetings. From there I went to Washington as a correspondent for a small Pennsylvania newspaper, and then I began writing for popular magazines."

Toffler has been self-employed ever since, with the exception of a two-year stint as managing editor of *Fortune* magazine. He has taught at The New School in New York ("it may have been the first course on the future, in 1965"), has lectured widely, and has done other academic work. He has also served as a consultant to various organizations, most notably AT&T, for whom he spent two years writing a report that was initially suppressed because of its unpopular recommendations but has recently been exhumed by management and may have been influential in recent reorganization. Of this experience, Toffler remarks, "I'm proud of the fact that they did not initially get what they wanted. My income has never depended on selling contract services. Unlike a think-tank, which operates from corporate consulting fees, I'm an institutionally unaffiliated individual. I can say what I want."

I ask him if he has plans to go out and implement the changes he describes theoretically in his books. His answer is emphatically negative:

"I have long ago assessed my own strengths and weaknesses and I am not an organizer. I don't get any creative satisfaction out of administrative or organizational activity, and I'm not very good at it. My role is to communicate, to encourage, to help in any way I can, short of taking a direct organizing role. I do not see myself as a guru or as the leader of a mass movement. Not only would my own happiness be impaired, but I think whatever value I have as a creative contributor to this process would be diminished.

"I don't believe everything I've written in *Future Shock* or *The Third Wave* will happen, or can happen. I don't believe that the 'solutions' I present to our deepest problems are necessarily workable.

"For instance, I've spent the last ten or fifteen years trying to argue that we need more and better technology, and we need to be far more highly selective about it, and these decisions can no longer be left to scientific, business, or political elites. The risks and the gains in powerful technologies are too important to be left to those elites. Now, it is easy to *say* that, but very hard to come up with practical procedures for giving people a voice in the selection of tomorrow's technologies. But if you do not give people that voice, you are not giving them a voice in the selection of their own future. If major technological decisions continue to be made in the way they have been made in the past, it's a living hypocrisy, and a dangerous one.

"When I write about this, or about, for example, the introduction of random sampling into the political process, or ways of linking referenda to representation, I don't think somebody's necessarily going to run out and do it. I present these ideas very often because I think they will stimulate other people to invent alternative ways. I want to open up the reader's mind to other ways of conceptualizing our political and social structures. I think that that helps people adapt; and to have a repertoire of alternatives is necessary.

"Imagination is the resource that's in shortest supply; we have run out of imagination long before we've run out of oil, and I think that that's a result of child-parent relationships as well as the entire Second-Wave education system, which operates, as I think is now understood by most people, to eliminate imaginative decision-making by children. I place an extremely high value on imagination and on the ability to dream and to visualize new possibilities."

If we look again at Toffler's books, bearing this attitude in mind, and trying to ignore the occasional excesses of his prose (which he himself describes as "passionate"), the text makes much better sense: not as literal-minded prescriptions for immediate action, but as notes for unwritten science-fiction novels, devised to stimulate the imagination.

His division of modern history into "Second Wave" and "Third Wave" may not be as all-embracing as he would like to believe. His plans for a truly democratic process do not seem very practical. And I think, perhaps, his own need to be an independent, unaffiliated individual makes him overrate other people's desires in that direction.

But Alvin Toffler has developed a totally original perspective, and he has written about it in such a way as to reach vast numbers of people who might otherwise not think so much about the promise and potential of the future. And this, surely, is what any dream maker most hopes to achieve.

BIBLIOGRAPHICAL NOTES

Alvin Toffler's two most influential books have been *Future Shock* (1970), arguing for a more humanized relationship with technology; and *The Third Wave* (1980), identifying trends that Toffler suggests could create an entirely new social structure incorporating utopian elements.

He has edited two notable collections of essays: *The Futurists* (1972), featuring writers such as Arthur C. Clarke, Buckminster Fuller, and Marshall McLuhan, writing about the future; and *Learning for Tomorrow* (1973), a symposium arguing strongly for educational reform.

More relevant to a science-fiction perspective is *The Eco-Spasm Report*, in which Toffler contributes some near-future disaster scenarios, any one of which could have been written as science fiction.

PHOTO BY CHARLES PLATT

John Sladek

To me, something vital is missing from Arthur Clarke's visions of science and human destiny, or Alvin Toffler's ideas about the promise of technology. What's missing is a sense of humor.

So I turn now to John Sladek, our shyest, slyest satirist, unable to take anything seriously for long, up to and including his own career. He's veered playfully from one literary joke to another—all the way from science-fiction parodies to a book that revealed the "missing" thirteenth sign of the zodiac, so convincingly that it even fooled some professional astrologers.

Sladek is deadly serious about our microchip future—just as serious as Alvin Toffler or any other futurist. But he sees it mismanaged, messed up, and malfunctioning. He sees corporations obsessed with idiot objectives, fail-safe systems that do fail and aren't safe, and machines that misunderstand their masters and refuse to turn themselves off.

His recent trilogy, *Roderick*, is a clever, funny parable about the world's first human-like robot, built secretly with embezzled NASA funds on the whim of an eccentric bureaucrat. Abandoned by his makers when the money runs out, Roderick wanders into the world like a mutant Horatio Alger, with nothing but a set of Boolean-algebra truth-tables and a thorough knowledge of TV soap operas to help him understand human behavior. The result is more than whimsy, much more than farce. It raises some awkward questions about what we're going to do with our computerized future, where the dividing line lies between human and machine intelligence, and why we seem so interested in making gadgets that imitate us in the first place.

For the most part, Sladek's humor overshadows these serious messages. And yet they are the point of the book, so far as he's concerned, and he seems happy to start our interview with a little lecture on this subject (the laughs come later).

"It's clear that we're very uneasy about humanoid machines. We either relegate them to jokes, or to horror stories. There doesn't seem to be any ground in between, where we feel comfortable with the idea. And yet we're very certainly going to build the corny, classic robots that go clanking around in science fiction.

"Artificial intelligence researchers say we're *not* going to build them, because it wouldn't be practical—there's no rational reason to fit an artificial brain with arms and legs and have it behave like a human being. But rational reasons have nothing to do with it. We're going to build robots because we *like* the idea of building robots.

"The idea of the robot is much more deeply embedded in our culture than people realize. The notion of machines that look or act like people has been a guiding esthetic principle for inventions going back to Greek times. Greek mythology is full of robot stories—Prometheus making a clay man and someone else criticizing it and saying he should have left a window in the chest so people could see what it was thinking, for instance. The Chinese were building very elaborate puppet theater, automatic orchestras and so on, about 300 A.D. There are also stories about statues coming to life—Pygmalion is the classic example—and the sexual side of robots was pretty evident in that story. There were also stories of robot soldiers, guards, or defenders—such as Talos, the bronze man who was supposed to fire himself up to glowing heat and then embrace people to kill them. Then there was plenty of building of clockwork automatons at various times throughout Eastern and Western culture, as soon as clockwork had been invented.

"It seems to me that there must be some reason that people are endlessly fascinated with imitations of the human form. Since we're primed psychologically to recognize other individuals and distinguish them as separate from the rest of the world, the notion of artificial people calls that whole distinction into question. If they're artificial, how can they be people? If they act like people, how can they be separate from humanity? I think that these questions are going to get much more interesting in the next few years, as all the predictions that we're not going to have robots don't come true. I think robots are going to be built in large numbers, as servants, playmates, teachers, sex objects, and just for company.

"When I started thinking about all this, it seemed to me that it hadn't ever been dealt with properly in science fiction. It seemed to me that robots had been," he chuckles, "*badly treated* in science fiction. People keep talking about, you know, Isaac Asimov's three laws of robotics, but that's not the way it's going to be at all. Those laws are supposed to be logic laws, but really they're just legal laws. They depend on interpretation. The first law says a robot may not harm a human being or allow a person to come to harm; well, in that case, a robot's got to know what a human being is, so it's got to have built into it a whole lot of the stuff that we've got built into us, to be able to identify another human being. So it's going to be a very good imitation of us, in which case it may well have a lot of trouble telling the difference between human beings and other robots, built like itself.

"Asimov's first law is unrealistic, anyway. If a millionaire builds a robot, his first thought will be to protect his investment. So the robot's first law will be to protect itself—not other people. And since a principal interest in building robots is likely to be military, those robots are certainly going to harm human beings as much as they can. So I would say that, when and if robots are built, they're going to be much more like Philip K. Dick's imaginations than Isaac Asimov's."

And this brings him to the Roderick books.

"I set out to make Roderick a learning machine, whose job is to learn how to be human. If you wanted to make a very human-like robot, that would be the way to go about it, rather than by pre-programming.

"But I found that the book was turning into something else as I wrote it. I found myself contrasting the machine-like lives of the people with the rather human life of the robot." He grins, enjoying the irony.

So his serious novel turned into a surreal situation comedy, a blend of black humor and playfulness, as if by Franz Kafka under the influence of nitrous oxide.

In Sladek's next novel, he plans to make more of the darker implications, and hold back the humor, while still dealing with the same subject.

"It's provisionally titled *Tik-Tok*, set about fifty years from now, when people have recreational, home-use robots and they give them awful-cute names like 'Tik-Tok.' Tik-Tok begins by committing a hideous murder in the first chapter, and then. . . ." Sladek shakes his head with fatherly regret. "I'm sorry to say, he goes downhill from then on. You see, I really can't imagine robots being incapable of wrongdoing; it's so built into our conception of what it means to be human. Even people who dote on animals prefer just those animals that will naturally tend to disobey them, and have to be trained like children. I mean, not many people dote on *worms*, or *insects*, you know?

"I do mean eventually to stop writing about robots. But the whole field of computer science is so important, and people are so ignorant of it generally, there's a lot of material that needs to be dealt with. Right now most people seem to think that microchip technology is just a good way of building videogames, as if videogames were the end product. And of course they're just the beginning."

Sladek lives in London, and has been there for fourteen years. But he was born in Minnesota, in 1937. He looks back on his American childhood with a mixture of laughter and loathing, and still uses the mid-American cultural wasteland to pathetic and ludicrous effect in his comic novels.

He first started writing with the encouragement of fellow Midwesterner Thomas M. Disch.

"Tom and I collaborated on a few short stories, in the first instance. Then I wrote some of my own, and sold the first to Harlan Ellison for *Dangerous Visions*. Tom and I collaborated on *Black Alice* [a modern murder mystery] and on a terrible gothic novel, and I wrote another gothic myself, under a pseudonym. Then we went traveling, and while Tom was writing *Camp Concentration*, I wrote *The Reproductive System*."

This book pits a mob of earnest, dedicated, small-town buffoons against the totally ruthless Dr. Smilax, maddest of all mad scientists, whose favorite relaxation is to sit in his custom-built dentist chair and drill and fill his own teeth. Smilax plans to rule the world via his "reproductive system": intelligent machines that build replicas of themselves and adapt to any challenge or contingency. The plot grows ever more complex, and manages to ridicule, with some affection, every science-fictional cliche ever invented.

"I've never specifically wanted to write science fiction," Sladek recalls. "I just wanted to write stuff, get it published, and make a living out of it. Science fiction did seem to be a good way of starting out; and I suppose I ended up a science-fiction writer because what I write won't fit anywhere else. It's a more tolerant genre than the others."

He arrived in England just when science fiction's "new wave" was emerging in the British magazine *New Worlds*. A lot of his work began appearing there, though he never felt part of the movement.

"I've never really understood schools of writing and literary categories. I just liked the idea that there was this fantastic magazine, the most experimental publishing venture around, I guess, taking all my stories. I read everybody else's work in it, but I can't say I identified with any of it. Not even Ballard, though he was and is one of my favorite writers."

It was in *New Worlds* that Sladek published his classic novelette "Masterson and the Clerks," a surreal fantasy about small-time businesses with delusions of grandeur that entice them further and further from sanity. Since then, Sladek has repeatedly satirized the corporate mentality.

"I actually worked at various jobs for small companies like that, with maniac bosses. Lots of things in 'Masterson and the Clerks' really happened. I got interested in the way companies and people in them set about dehumanizing themselves, in this idiotic rearrangement of human lives, this curtailment of human sensibilities, just for the purposes of some silly organization. I suppose this sounds depressing, but comedy is always the other side of tragedy. Not that any of my stuff approaches tragedy—I'm mainly concerned with *pathos*, I suppose. With *wasted lives*." He laughs happily. "Wasted lives can be wonderfully funny—if they're appearing in fiction."

After *The Reproductive System*, Sladek's next seriously satirical novel was *The Muller-Fokker Effect*, which he says "vanished without trace." Perhaps because he felt disillusioned by this failure, he spent the next ten years following whatever literary whim came into his head, with total disregard for building any kind of coherent career.

First he devoted two-and-a-half years to researching *The New Apocrypha*, a nonfiction source-book that methodically debunks every possible pseudoscience, crank cult, and mystical belief, from parapsychology to perpetual motion. "I kind of suspected that book wouldn't be too successful," he says, "because people don't really like books which tell them things *aren't* true.

"So after it was published, and it didn't do very well, I decided that if I couldn't sell books by telling people the facts as I saw them, I would try—well, *lying* to people! I picked the most outrageous lie I could imagine, which was that there are thirteen signs in the zodiac. I figured out all kinds of evidence to prove that the thirteenth sign had once existed, and had been suppressed. I called it Arachne, the sign of the spider."

He published this as *Arachne Rising*, by "James Vogh," a secret identity that has not been revealed until now.

"It certainly did better than *The New Apocrypha*. It was a good exercise, actually, in finding out what believing this nonsense is like, because I had to convince myself it was true, so that while I was writing the book I was completely caught up in the notion. It gave me some insight into what makes lunatics write lunatic books.

"It's not at all different from the kind of belief that I think scientists have in their ideas and theories. The only difference is that pseudoscientists drop all pretense at criticizing their own work and at trying to make it fit reality. They simply promote what they're doing.

"And it's really kind of fun being obsessed in this way. If there were nothing else in my life, and I'd come up with this one idea that there was a thirteenth sign in the zodiac, I suppose I would go on promoting it for the rest of my life.

"I fooled quite a few astrologers. Stan Gooch, he's a writer on astrology and the paranormal. And several British newspaper astrologers. They wrote to me, and I met a couple of them—as James Vogh."

Friends of Sladek, who were in on the joke, told him this was all good fun, but a long way from the serious fiction he should be working on. Sladek responded to this helpful advice by writing, of all things, an old-fashioned British murder mystery.

"I had written a short mystery story for a contest in *The Times*, and won the contest. So"—he chuckles at the absurdity of it—"I got a contract to do a full-length detective novel. I wrote that, and enjoyed it, so I did *another* one. But by this time, even if publishers had been thinking of reviving the detective novel, they changed their minds. It wasn't going to take off.

"So I decided finally to get down to work, and *Roderick* was the next project. That represents what I ought to be doing."

But he still has a wayward, obsessive intelligence that gets hung up on almost any kind of distraction, from Rubik's Cube to the Rosetta Stone. Games, codes, and logic problems can lure him into a single-minded state that lasts for days or months. Partly because of this, he often seems withdrawn. Receiving visitors, he stops for a moment with a momentary blank look, as if some kind of recognition system is being powered up; and then—"Oh, hi," he says, with a shy smile, emerging (part way) from whatever conundrum he's been mulling over. The visitors are invited in, and he's friendly and funny, but still not entirely present, as if he's running a mental program labeled "Polite social conversation," while most of his mind is busily thinking: "Maybe if we substitute *X* for *A* and invert the matrix, and then. . . ."

He lives with his British wife and young daughter in an anonymous, system-built housing development on the northeast edge of London.

"Just lately I've been realizing," he says, as if with a sense of revelation, "how my horizons have shrunk. You know, the United States disappeared a few years ago, then the rest of Britain disappeared and I was left with London, and now during the last year most of London has gone, and I'm just down to Tottenham, and during the last week or so—well, I've hardly left the house! I guess I have gotten more and more reclusive. I suppose I'm alienated from the everyday world; after all, I've chosen to live in a foreign country. But I don't know what effect it has on my work. I don't trust analogies from my life to my work. I like to think of my work as being just invention. Anyway," he shrugs it all off, "I'm not that self-analytical.

"I'm certainly alienated from the science-fiction field. I was looking over the first volume of *Dream Makers*, and out of twenty-nine writers I had only read anything at all by nineteen of them, and of those there were only about three that I'd read in any depth at all.

"I'm perfectly happy for my work to be published as science fiction, if people will buy it and read it. But I don't know if it is science fiction. I suppose if I had to define it, I'd say I'm writing 'class' science fiction." He laughs at the idea. "It's good quality, no shoddy materials, the workmanship is all there to be seen. Something like that.

"A lot of science fiction does strike me as junk-food writing. I think Isaac Asimov is a very good example, and Robert Heinlein is another, and Ray Bradbury. The old clan there. Of those three, Bradbury is the only one who ever *could* write, really. I suppose Heinlein did one or two things which I'd have to say I liked a lot. But even his good stuff is really marred by bad writing. And Isaac Asimov, I don't think, ever cared to do anything else but pulp writing, and would probably be perfectly pleased to be known as a bad pulp writer. Wouldn't he? It's his ideas that he's interested in, I suppose, so he probably figures that he doesn't mind how he gets them across."

Does Sladek like modern fantasy any better?

"It's just a matter of taking a background of Grimm's fairy tales, plus Arthurian legends, and cranking out adventure stories. At least, the stuff I've seen looks like that. It seems to me very much like the Western; the rules are very restrictive. More so than science fiction. I guess it'll be popular for a while, and then die out."

So what does he like?

"John Barth, William Gaddis—I think Gaddis is very important. His novels deal with large ideas. I can't lump together all the books I like, except to say that they're not conventional novels. I think the conventional novel must be dead by now; I can't imagine anyone sitting down and writing a conventional novel and making anything important out of it."

If he prefers to read non-category fiction, does he mind having his own work categorized?

"The fact that 'science fiction' is stamped on a book cover will probably guarantee a certain sale. That's to my benefit. But I'm really sorry that people feel it necessary to be told the books are science fiction before they'll buy them—or that other people will *avoid* books because they're science fiction. Probably a lot of my stuff isn't taken seriously enough by non-science-fiction people because it has that label on it. That doesn't bother me too much; it would be nice if it weren't so, but I don't see the categories breaking down."

He sounds uncomfortable, as if he finds it hard to deal with this kind of businesslike topic, and would much rather be talking about abstractions—like computer programming, or mathematical games, or (of course) robots. I get the impression that he prefers to avoid practicalities altogether. Did he, in fact, ever have any realistic plans about where his writing would lead?

"No." There is a long silence. He laughs. "I bet you like helpful answers like that! But I guess I'm not terribly ambitious. Everybody who writes would love to be lionized, to be a famous writer, to be at the top of whatever pyramid it is, and of course I would too. But I'm not very good at gauging where I am. I know I'm not at the very bottom, and I certainly know I'm not at the very top. I don't have any idea about the levels in between and I don't indulge too much in charting my career. I just decide what I'm going to do next—and do it."

BIBLIOGRAPHICAL NOTES

John Sladek's first science-fiction novel, *The Reproductive System* (1968, titled *Mechasm* in its first U.S. edition), can be considered self-satirical adventure fiction; it pits a cast of comic-cliche characters against the onslaught of self-replicating machines—which ultimately usher in a utopia.

The Muller-Fokker Effect (1970) forsakes conventional science fiction even for satirical purposes; it is more a novel of contemporary social comment, implicit in the alternatingly comic and inhumane events that result when tapes, on which a human being's entire personality has been recorded, fall into the wrong hands.

Roderick (1981), the saga of an experimental robot wandering through contemporary America, explores the man-machine relationship and the rituals of suburban life in greater depth than the earlier novels. Like all of Sladek's work, it is rich with "detail" humor—puns, riddles, and other word-play—besides presenting clever situation comedy with an ultimately serious message.

The New Apocrypha (1973) is a rigorously skeptical reference guide to the entire spectrum of mystic, paranormal, and pseudoscientific beliefs.

Sladek's short stories are collected in *The Steam-Driven Boy* (1973), *Keep the Giraffe Burning* and *Alien Accounts* (1977 and 1982, both British collections), and *The Best of John Sladek* (1981, a U.S. collection).

PHOTO BY JOYCE RAVID

D.M. Thomas

"Of course," I said to the students in my science-fiction class, "you've all heard of D.M. Thomas."

Twelve blank faces looked back at me.

"D.M. Thomas, author of *The White Hotel*."

The faces remained blank.

"But it's been at the top of *The New York Times* best seller list for months," I protested. "It's just been brought out in paperback, in a first printing of a million copies. You must have seen it. You all read books, you go to bookstores. There are big displays of D.M. Thomas at the front of every store."

"When I go to a bookstore," one fellow spoke up, "I usually head for the science-fiction section at the back."

Of course. And this is the point that I'm making here: Fiction is divided into categories, now, and categories are crippling our reading habits.

Fifty years ago, there was no "science-fiction section" to go to, because books weren't segregated that way. There was no science fiction, and there were no horror, suspense, westerns, detective, or romance novels, either. There was *fiction*, plain and simple, and you browsed through it for something that might happen to appeal to you.

Putting books in categories was an American idea to make life easier for salesmen and store managers, who need to know what they're selling without actually reading it. And from categories grew the idea of the "package"—the whole assembly of cover art, title, and blurb, which American publishers hope will push mental buttons in book-browsers, and provoke instinctive responses. For instance, anyone who sees a fat numeral "1" in the top-center of the cover knows without thinking that this book is a "best seller." Likewise, a title printed in colored metal foil suggests that this book is being promoted heavily and is in some way "special." Blood-dripping fangs or ominous black silhouettes mean it's a horror novel. A woman in the foreground, with a man standing behind her and nuzzling her neck (or some other part of her anatomy), means that this is a romance for women. And so on.

Publishers say that the system makes it easier for readers to find what they want. But, of course, it helps the publishers, too. By simplifying books to the point where they can be packaged like TV dinners, the books become easier to merchandise. If *Night Thing*, with its title in green metal foil above the silhouette of a huge bat, sells 300,000 copies, *Dark Creature*, with its title in red metal foil above the silhouette of a huge spider, should do equally well. All the quirks and surprises have been minimized—and with them, the financial risks. The publisher knows how many books to print, and salesmen and store managers know what they've got without ever needing to open a copy.

This is bad news for books that can't be summed up in a few words of blurb and a simple cover picture. People such as Christopher Priest, John Sladek, or Keith Roberts, who write novels that actually have to be *read* before you understand what they're really about, are in trouble (see their profiles, in this book). Publishers hate dealing with novels that can't be categorized, because salesmen and bookstore managers don't know where to put them. Readers, too, have gotten accustomed to thinking in categories—even science-fiction readers, such as those in my New York class, whose tastes, incidentally, are probably more adventurous than most.

But not adventurous enough to discover D.M. Thomas, who is in fact a fantasist in the truest sense, and has also written science fiction. If you doubt this claim, I offer you the following poem as proof.

THE HEAD-RAPE
by D.M. Thomas

Chastity veil: *Universal headdress, often highly ornamental, con-*

sisting of telepathy blocks (usually in the form of jewels) fixed to the critical points of the skull. (First used c. 2800.)
—from the *Revised Anglamerican Dictionary.*

He raped her. Ripped the filaments from her skull.
She pleaded, by their home, their children, but
he tore the jewels off, mad with desire
to know her, to entirely penetrate,
like some Europa-storming bull.

A topaz—and he was in her in a flash;
he saw his bulging eyes leer down, smelt
the beastly courage he had drunk, he heard
blood pounding at her eardrums, felt
mind cleaving open as the stones

went . . . diamond—and he flinched at her
emotions . . . onyx
—and one hammer-thought—HE'LL KILL ME . . .
sapphire—and vestigial memory
rushed into him—a girl beneath her father,

on a blue quilt; with the more terrible
revelations of the times she'd lifted jewels
willingly . . . which horned an urge to kill
in earnest this wombed softness he
screamed in; and since he had come nude,

and she could not help but see, he re-
re-felt his lust, being carboned in her brain,
she re-re-felt the hysteria
that he re-felt, so he re-re-re-felt— .
Their bedroom infinite: two facing mirrors.

Blood and black hairs on the ripped veil.

Thomas wrote a series of such science-fictional poems in the late 1960s, deriving some of them from short stories by well-known writers in the field. He took their adventure-story prose and turned it into a subtler kind of art.

"It struck me that no poet, really, had dealt with this material. It seemed to me that science-fiction writers were creating future myths, dealing with deep-rooted terrors and apprehensions about how life was going to be. I felt there were only perhaps half-a-dozen subjects—possession, organ transplant, technology, and so on—and they were all threats to one's identity. So I wrote poems about them, which at the time was a release in that it enabled me to write narrative, which I hadn't really done before.

"I wasn't looking at science-fiction stories as examples of good prose writing. In a way, almost, the cruder they were, the more emphasis there was on the myth content that I was interested in. It was the actual story, the plot, that interested me."

He recalls a Tom Godwin story, "The Cold Equations," whose theme he adapted for a long poem. "Simply the idea of having a spaceship where weight limits meant that you couldn't allow a stow-away to stay, and you had to eject her, seemed to me a very pure myth about abortion in our time, the conflict of the need to limit population, and yet the continual tragedy of killing something. It was the pure myth element that I responded to.

"But then I started to feel uneasy about the poems, because it's not quite so easy, in poetry, to use the artifices of science fiction—names of planets, strange names of characters, and so on. There is something about poetry which is more to do with the here-and-now, and resists being taken into the future."

So his writing went more into areas that happened to coincide, to some extent, with what "new wave" science-fiction writers were doing in *New Worlds* magazine in the late 1960s.

"It's interesting that writers such as Moorcock and Aldiss had moved away from the early, crude science fiction; it looks as though better writers, maybe, are always pushed toward greater sophistication after a while, and prefer to approach the world as it is now.

"But of course we're living in science fiction already; technological advance is so swift, you almost don't have to go to the future anymore. Transplants and genetic engineering are already here."

—And were used as images by Thomas in a later series that he wrote: "Computer 70: Dreams and Lovepoems." He also began to write more about internal landscapes of the psyche, and developed a deepening interest in psychoanalysis and insanity, expressed in his work up to and including *The White Hotel*.

"Those of us who are relatively sane have had to come to terms with hypocrisies; we create our own fog which makes life bearable. But of course the psychologically disturbed patient hasn't got that fog, and sees everything with a kind of piercing vision. Of course, writers have always had this feeling—King Lear saw more clearly when he was mad, for instance. It's also more poetic, to have someone who is not constrained by the normal decencies, who just comes out with what he thinks. And I was interested by the interplay of the supposedly sane mind and the supposedly insane mind. Sometimes it seems to me that in a way the therapist is madder than the patient."

By this time, D.M. Thomas had become a well-known modern British poet—which is a polite way of saying that not many people had heard of him. However, in the late 1970s, a series of transitions occurred that changed all that.

"I was a lecturer at Hereford college, teaching English, until 1978, when I was given the sack because the government closed the place. During the last three years of the college there were fewer students, I had more time, and this enabled me to start writing novels. I wrote *Birthstone* and *The Flute Player* [his first two novels] and then went to Oxford, ostensibly to take another degree. I was going to do a thesis on the problems of translating Russian poetry, but that turned eventually into my translation of Pushkin—a book rather than a degree. And I also wrote *The White Hotel*.

"I think it was psychologically the right time for me to start novels, when I was about forty. Till then, I'd had no thought of writing anything but poetry."

Following a brief prologue, *The White Hotel* commences with a long poem-fantasy from the viewpoint of a mentally disturbed woman confessing to Sigmund Freud that she has had an affair with his son. The first section of this poem originally appeared in *New Worlds* magazine in 1979; Thomas felt in some way that it was unfinished, and put it aside for almost two years.

"Then I read Kuznetsov's *Babi Yar*, and suddenly thought Babi Yar would be the end of a novel and the poem would be the beginning of it, so that it would relate psychoanalysis and the holocaust. After that, the various sections seemed quite logical, expanding the poem and literalizing its images to build up a serial story, enabling Freud, in the third section, to get some material to work on—and, incidentally, enabling me to find out something about the woman."

Did he have any idea that this would attract an immensely larger audience than his earlier work?

"No, none whatever. I do think my work generally has moved toward more clarity over the last few years; and I hope that, without ever cheapening the book, I made the reader as welcome as I could in *The White Hotel*. Why not? Books are to be read.

"I was quite pleased with the initial English response. There were a few enthusiastic reviews, and the book was selling in the usual steady way—oh, one or two thousand copies. I thought it had done pretty well.

"Then the American thing took me overwhelmingly by surprise. Reviews started coming out all over America, before publication—there was a kind of a race to review it. And they were all enthusiastic.

"Viking, the American hardback publishers, had had no thoughts that it would sell widely. They warned me that it probably wouldn't get a paperback sale at all! Two paperback publishers in England had already turned it down, so the omens weren't good."

But the reviews, spearheaded by a front-page paean of praise in *The New York Times* Sunday book review section, catalyzed *The White Hotel* to best seller status, with American paperback rights selling for several hundred thousand dollars, and plans to make a movie.

Thomas, of course, was astonished and delighted. Some of his British colleagues were not.

"Many critics in England had originally complained that the book was obscure, and difficult. They implied that if you knew your Freud well, you might tackle it—'Go to the bookshop but take your A-level certificate with you,' that was the kind of approach.

"But then, when the book started selling widely, some of these same people started saying the book was opportunistic, almost as though I had planned to write a best seller. I found that abhorrent.

"You can always see, later on, why a particular book has caught on in a popular way. You can say, 'Oh, this book has got violence, the holocaust, sex, and Freud.' You can make it sound almost as though it was a packaged book. But of course, no one in his right mind would ever predict beforehand that such a book would catch on. With a twelve-page poem at the beginning, and then some highly sexual fantasy, and then a rather complex Freudian analysis—you'd say, 'No, that's incredible, it won't work.'

"So I feel rather angry with people who talk after the event.

"In this country, particularly, there is still a very strong 'rump,' as I call them, who really detest my book. Some of them take any chance to say so. They were absolutely delighted when the Booker Prize was being contested, and I didn't get it."

And the backlash has gone further. At the time of my interview with him, Thomas is under attack in the London *Times Literary Supplement* letter column, accused of plagiarism.

"I had made it abundantly clear that I had used the historic testament from *Babi Yar*, yet for some reason someone was outraged that there was a similarity at the climax. And of course if you print the actual texts together—which he did—at the place where I intended the voice to be not my own but that of history, it sounds as though Thomas just pinched it from Kuznetsov.

"And that was a chance for others to plow in. One elderly British poet wrote in saying 'Of course, Thomas acknowledges this, but it reminded me of five poems he wrote, based on science-fiction short stories.' He was referring to the poems I wrote fourteen years ago, where I had acknowledged using myths from Ray Bradbury and Tom Godwin. Five tiny poems, and Griegson found them."

Meanwhile, in the U.S., Thomas's new literary fame brought him a different kind of problem altogether. It was not a matter of too much criticism; more a matter of too much praise.

"I was invited to be a visiting professor in Washington, D.C., earlier this year. At the time they asked me, about May or June last year, I was still a bit worried that I was unemployed and I didn't know whether I'd have enough money to get by, so I thought that if I could do odd semesters in America it would be very nice.

"But when I got there I felt the terrific pressure of people's expectations. They wanted me to be a kind of guru. I was getting so many requests, too, to appear here and there, with a sort of unnatural deference and respect. And everyone was talking about *The White Hotel*, which was all very nice, but I got sort of fed up with it. I was on my new book, and you don't want to keep talking about the old one. I felt uncomfortable, and I knew I wouldn't be able to write while I was there.

"So I woke up one morning realizing that I was going to get out. It was a kind of overnight decision. Pure self-preservation. I felt immediately so happy, and yet also horrified at what I was doing. I remember getting quite drunk on whiskey that the university had bought for me.

I finished the bottle and typed out some very elegant letters of apology, and I remember at one point wanting to say, 'Thank you for your kindness,' and I typed 'mindless' instead of 'kindness,' saw what I'd done, and sort of rolled around in hilarity.

"So I disappeared."

In an article he wrote later for *The New York Times Magazine*, he freely admits having enjoyed, for a while, the best-selling author's "small vanities of success." But he adds that, in the end, "reality is where the blank sheet rests in the typewriter, where the new novel or poem is as great a struggle as ever."

One reviewer has suggested that Thomas can never write anything else as powerful as *The White Hotel*, because he has used up his three main obsessions—"Cornwall, Russia, and Freud"—in his first three novels. I show this review to Thomas, who looks amused but also thoughtful.

"That's quite perceptive in a way, except that Freud isn't an obsession—Freud is really the mouthpiece of an obsession with Eros. I say 'Eros' rather than 'sex' because it suggests something slightly larger and more mysterious.

"I've just finished a fourth novel, so whether it will disprove the reviewer or not remains to be seen. This one uses the cold war as a metaphor for the divided self. The hero, or anti-hero, is a contemporary Soviet poet who tries to be liberal enough to get across to America occasionally, but Marxist enough to please his masters in Russia. So he walks a tightrope between the two. I think it's a rather more poetic novel than *The White Hotel*; it veers between the present day and the age of Pushkin, fifty years ago." (Thomas has a special interest in Russian poets. Having learned Russian by chance while doing his "national service" in the British army, he has refined his skills to the point of publishing several books of translations.)

"I'm now in a state where I simply don't know what I shall be writing next. I've really got no ideas in my head, so it's just a matter of waiting to see what comes. I don't think that it's in any way inevitable that my next book will be a novel.

"In a way I'm quite pleased to have this time of wondering, but also a little bit wary, a bit uneasy—will I write anything else, you know?"

He still has the small semi-detached house where he lived while he was teaching, in Hereford, near the border between England and Wales. Thomas's quiet little back street looks very like a London suburb, with

1940s houses of brick and pastel-painted stucco, and neat little walls and fences around every neat little front garden. It's pure conformist middle-class Britain—a long way from the wild psychic terrain of White Hotels. The only sign of flamboyance about Thomas's house is a new red Ford Capri in the driveway.

His working room is in an extension built at the back of the house, looking onto a small, totally nondescript garden. A modern electric Smith-Corona stands upon a modern office desk, facing this view, which he describes as "pleasant but undistracting." The room also contains a couch, where I sit during the interview, and a few shelves of carefully selected books, including the Russian poets and some classics.

He talks very quietly, and moves quietly, too, with precision, as if his choice of mannerisms is as careful as his choice of words in a poem. He seems shrewd and thoughtful, and quietly ambitious: undoubtedly a romantic, but an analytical one. He seems extremely private and protective about anything to do with the creative process; unlike many writers, he shows his work-in-progress to no one, until after he has sent the manuscript to his agent.

The White Hotel is a long way from the early science-fictional poems that attracted me to D.M. Thomas's work more than a decade ago. And yet the old work and the new have one thing in common: they are non-representational. By this I mean that Thomas isn't interested in describing reality as it is. As a "dream maker," he writes, instead, about imaginary landscapes, which is why his style was so easily adaptable to science fiction. Even now, he can still be termed a fantasist.

"I would be bored stiff writing prose which simply held a mirror up to nature. Others can do it so much better than I can. I'm not particularly observant. I don't remember things. My contribution is to strike through that and get a kind of poetic sense of things. My novels are, for me, poems in another form.

"They are fantasies, but I hate the word 'fantasy.' It was in some ways a pity, I thought, that when *The Flute Player* and *Birthstone* first came out in England they were labeled 'Fantasy.'

"I hate labels. For me 'fantasy' has overtones of Tolkien, a kind of rather twee Englishness with gnomes and things, and for me there is nothing more boring than gnomes.

"I cannot write books as escapism in the way that I think Tolkien did. I'm interested in the opposite of escaping—actually plunging deeper into the world, into the *psychic* reality."

Thomas can continue to do this, now, following his own path, in the knowledge that whatever he writes will be widely read—at least during the aftermath of the success of *The White Hotel*, and perhaps for much longer.

His sudden, amazing leap from being a relatively unknown poet to having a million copies of his book in print in America has convinced him that publishers have been guilty of underestimating the public. "The success of my book, and of several other serious novels in the last couple of years, shows that there is a craving for real, honest books," he has written. "The bookshops are stuffed with mass-produced fodder, and it is assumed that people want nothing else. Rather—I suspect—the hungry sheep look up and are not fed."

Thomas's success story is not the only one of its kind. Kurt Vonnegut, for instance, finally made it with *Slaughterhouse Five* after ten years of being categorized as a relatively unknown science-fiction writer.

But for every Thomas or Vonnegut, hundreds of others remain stuck in obscurity, mainly because they aren't easy to categorize. The only way these writers can survive, and the only way that the system of categories can be resisted, is if readers take the time to browse more widely and have the courage to buy unusual books.

I've already suggested that William Burroughs could be considered a science-fiction writer if our preconceptions about that category weren't so rooted in cliches dating back to the 1930s. D.M. Thomas could likewise be thought of as a fantasy author, if our definition of that category could shake off the flavor of Tolkien and his imitators. The whole point of science fiction and fantasy, it seems to me, is to reject limits, and allow imagination as much room as possible.

BIBLIOGRAPHICAL NOTES

Despite his having reached best-selling status, much of D.M. Thomas's work remains out of print. His *Two Voices* (1968) collection of early poems contains some science fiction, including the long title poem in which technology eloquently and elegantly merges with eroticism.

By contrast, Thomas's recent collection of poems, *Dreaming in Bronze* (1981), is much more naturalistic in flavor. His interest in "high-tech verse" seems to have died.

The Flute Player (1979), his second novel, is an intense and evocative tribute to human spirit surviving successive purges in a mythic totalitarian state—an imaginary dystopia with obvious parallels to Eastern Europe.

The White Hotel (1981) opens with the surreal sexual fantasies of a young woman, described poetically. This material is literalized in subsequent chapters of prose, offering us Freudian analysis and other objective perspectives on the woman's subsequent life—leading up to a documented episode from the Jewish holocaust, which ties the element of fantasy to grim historical fact.

PHOTO BY CHARLES PLATT

Keith Roberts

Keith Roberts stares balefully out of his window at the moss-covered tiles on the roof of a centuries-old building across the street. "It's a dump of a town, Henley-on-Thames—a sort of *ingrown toenail* of a town. I'm from Northamptonshire originally; I only came here to work for a firm that was doing cartoon animation."

He refills his pipe and sits down on a high stool in front of his drawing board. He sounds vaguely discontented about the circumstances that have led him to live here and do what he does.

"I was trained as an artist, originally, you see. I did four years of art college. If I hadn't had the art training, I would never have developed the outlook that I did.

"At art school the system was very simple: any self-satisfaction you might have had as a 'draw-er' was absolutely hammered out of you. I had been there for about six months and rather thought of myself as a young lion because I could draw well, and my tutor was being critical of one of the little paintings I had done, and I was foolish enough to say, 'I don't agree.' So he said, 'Look, Keith, how can I make my point more fully to you?' And he threw this thing down on the floor and stamped on it, and continued to stamp on it till it was in fragments. Then he walked out and slammed the door.

"I was almost in tears, and if he hadn't been so big I would probably have hit him. For a week I sulked, and then I realized that maybe he was right, and it was really just a *bad little picture*.

"This is a gigantic shift of attitude, away from self, towards an awareness of what art really is. Unless you've gone through that strange training, I think people don't know what art is and what an artist is. It's an awareness of absolutes—and this relates deeply to writing."

It relates to Keith Roberts's writing in two ways. First, his stories are breathtakingly visual. Whether he's describing the atrocities of the Catholic church in a barbaric alternate future (*Pavane*), or giant alien wasps (*The Furies*), or post-holocaust Britain (*The Chalk Giants*), the scenery is more than graphic—you can smell the damp earth and feel the texture of every rock.

Secondly, although his writing is eloquent, it is always modest, never self-satisfied. He writes with a minimum of affectations; he chooses each word with strict attention to function. He shows a kind of deferential respect for literature itself, and the largeness of the landscapes that he describes. His characters can seem relatively powerless against these big panoramas and the forces of history; their lives tend to be governed by circumstance, which is how Roberts sometimes talks of himself, especially as regards the circumstances of book publishing.

Some of his books have been too grim to be very popular. Most of them have fallen somewhere in that awkward area that lies outside the everyday world of modern literature, not quite in the technological territory of science fiction, but beyond the pure wish-fulfillment of modern fantasy. He's critically acclaimed: "A challenging thesis in a beautiful, lyrical work too long unrecognized," says the sober reference guide *Anatomy of Wonder* of his novel *Pavane*. But he remains almost unknown in America, where *Pavane* is currently his only book in print.

Keith Roberts tries to take this philosophically, but he says he does feel the need for an audience, and it bothers him that he isn't published as widely as he used to be.

"I certainly couldn't ever write just for myself. I need to communicate, and hence the slight depression about having a fairly small readership. But I've always considered British hardback publication to be The Thing—it gets me into the libraries, and then I can also sell to France, Japan, and Germany. I still do very well over there."

He doesn't have to worry about making a good living from his books, because he still works as a graphic artist from his home in Henley, fifty miles or so west of London. However, he says that art doesn't fulfill him as much as writing.

"I think the only ambition I ever had was to write books. The first one was *The Furies*, in obvious homage to John Wyndham. Wyndham had done life from under the sea, he'd done telepathy very well indeed, and the biological menace, the Triffids, was probably his best. So I decided that the only thing he hadn't done was thundering great insects.

"I think Arthur Clarke once spelled out to me the old idea of writing a story: You're given one impossibility, and the name of the game is producing logical structures from that impossibility. Well, in *The Furies*, the impossibility was bloody great four-foot wasps.

"But there was a colder reason for writing it, in addition to paying homage to Wyndham. If you want to communicate, you're going to be categorized, so you've got to choose a category. What are the categories? Women's fiction, crime, horror, westerns—but all these genres tie you down so tightly. If you're J. T. Edson, for instance, you can write about anybody you like as long as they're cowboys. This is intolerably limiting.

"Of the categories, science fiction is broadest. When I started in the field it was in a boom situation, so I had a much better chance to get a book out which was categorized as science fiction than if I'd tried a mainstream novel.

"Since then I've obviously wondered if I really should have categorized myself as a science-fiction writer. A lot of people have this complaint, of course. They jump up and down and shout 'I'm not a science-fiction writer!' and it's a sort of arrogance. So I rather tend not to say it, to avoid being seen that way. All the same, I can't help wondering. If I'd gone into the main list, I might have done better. I suggested this to my agent, but he said if I hadn't been categorized as a science-fiction writer, I might not have sold anything at all!

"I suppose one must have categories, but the danger is that a publisher starts to say, 'I know what fantasy is,' or, 'I know what science fiction is, it's like such-and-such a book, which we published last August, and that did well, so we want another one like it.' So the tail begins to wag the dog, and you get a crazy situation where a new book is not read for its own sake, it's read with regard to—'What category can we put this in?' And this becomes the first thought, not the last. The first thought *should* be, 'Is this a good book, is it interesting, and does it hold the reader's attention?'

"Incidentally, the classic English mainstream novel is the most circumscribed 'category' of all—there are many things you cannot do in it. Imagination, for instance, is rather unacceptable in the classic English social novel which the literati go for, the snobs, whatever. When Golding's *Lord of the Flies* appeared on the scene, one critic at the time wrote that 'This novel is an earthquake in the petrified forest of the English novel.' But any good science-fiction book, had it found itself in the mainstream list by some accident instead of remaining hidden in the science-fiction shelves, would have provided just as powerful an earthquake. That kind of imagination is just not part of the English novel.

"Edmund Crispin once said that the standard short story is a head-and-shoulders portrait, while science fiction gives a disquieting image of figures in a landscape. The focus is not on the traditional human level. It is somewhere else."

The landscape that recurs throughout Roberts's stories and novels is as British as a Turner painting or a Wordsworth poem—but transliterated, usually, into a mutant future, or the sinister grip of barbaric political repression. Roberts uses the richness of British scenery as other fantasists use alien planets. And he mixes the past with the future, as if history is just as real to him as the present-day world.

"I think there are two ways you can perceive things: intellectually and emotionally. I know the first time I went to Corfe Castle I was almost physically shattered, it had such a profound effect. Hell, I know what we all know, that the Normans invaded Britain in 1066, they did this and that, they built castles. But to go there and be hit between the eyes quite unexpectedly with this stupendous image! I thought, 'My God, they were *here*.' That place spoke so much of cruelty, oppression, and terror. I thought, 'These were jack-booted *thugs*.' This sort of emotional awareness is far more powerful than intellectual awareness.

"The only other time this happened to me, I went with a friend to a Roman villa at Chadworth. I'd always known that the Romans invaded Britain in 410, but I had the same sensation in this very lovely place, that they were *here*. It's at the head of a little coombe; the Romano-British knew how to site the great houses. They're always sheltered, and obviously there's a spring, which they promptly built a little nymphaeum over, so you've got your little temple, and then, being Romans, the stream next runs through the kitchens, and finishes up going through the latrines. Again, I was absolutely overwhelmed by this image, as I realized that all this had actually happened, it wasn't something on the pages of a book."

After transposing these landscapes into alternate futures of magic or medievalism, Roberts populates them with hauntingly memorable characters. Many of his stories have featured young, forceful females—so much so that everyone asks him why he always writes about teenage girls.

"But of course I don't. I actually write half the time about men, half the time about women. But it seems science fiction is still a very male-orientated field, so equality of the sexes seems unusual.

"Perhaps this has something to do with why I've always had a lot of female readers. You know, I've never allowed my picture to appear on a book flap. I felt that it would spoil the image, for my readership. Exactly why women like my work, I don't know; maybe because I try to treat them as human beings. I still think there's a tremendous lot of male chauvinism in science fiction. Women still tend to be portrayed either as demons or angels. Bradbury is obviously the classic illustration of this, though I feel he was doing it consciously and quite deliberately in *The Silver Locusts*. It was what he wanted. But a lot of writers don't seem to be able to handle it.

"There's a serious side to my 'Anita' stories." (He is referring to a fantasy series featuring an especially strong-willed, rebellious young woman.) "I've always been very annoyed by the present-day concept of morality. When people talk about morality, what they're really talking about is sex. You can be the biggest bastard un-hung, but if you don't do 'it,' or if you're not caught *in flagrante*, then okay, you're deemed to be moral. Morality is a euphemism for sex.

"But Anita's morality is shifted sideways from this. She's always bedding the local farm boys; but in one of the early stories, where she makes friends with a human girl, she's horrified that they don't grow things in the garden, and says 'How immoral!' So she has a very strict morality, but it's not sex-based; it's sideways to it.

"I think Anita is now modern. I think that what I was saying in those stories, in the 1960s, has actually come to pass. The center of morality has shifted away from sex, while, at the same time, real morality is stronger than when I was a kid. For instance, back then, things like Vietnam were going on, but I don't think there was any idea that we could or should voice a moral protest against it."

Roberts talks in a low-key, matter-of-fact tone. Dressed in an oversized old sweater, fiddling with his pipe, he seems studious, inoffensive, and shy. It's a misleading image, of course; his books are full of intense emotion, and violence that is frightening—not because it is melodramatic but because it is drawn so truly to life. One broken finger, in a Roberts story, can be a lot more horrifying than a dozen disembowelments in a run-of-the-mill sword-and-sorcery novel.

The only time he shows any actual angry passions, himself, is when he talks about his critics.

"Some fellow in a literary magazine called me a 'Middle-class Prospero,'" he says, reflectively. "I thought I ought to rearrange the gentleman's features for him. Not out of revenge, you understand, but to concentrate his mind a little.

"Then I was attacked violently by one young lass in *Books and Bookmen* for my story 'Our Lady of Desperation,' which is a black comedy with farcical overtones, about civil servants being attached on a one-to-one basis to socially suspect people. I wasn't seriously believing this could come about; it's farcical. But she attacked my 'shaky economic theories.' So sober! Critics condemn books by measuring them against their own yardsticks, which may not have anything to do with what the writer set out to achieve. They look for what they feel should be there, and then raise the roof because it's not.

"I now seem to have got a weird reputation for being, as people call it, 'heavy.' What is 'heavy'? I've never understood this. And someone whose name I won't mention, who has made a lot of money as an adroit ripper-off, tagged me when *The Furies* came out as a 'pastiche writer.' The book wasn't a pastiche; it's an act of deliberate and careful homage to Wyndham.

"When I wrote *Pavane*, I derived a lot of the feeling in that from a fine historical writer named Alfred Duggan, who wrote *Leopards and Lilies*, about the internecine warfare between the Normans and the other lot after the conquest. But everyone praised me for *originality* in that book—which is a wonderful illustration of the narrow reading of most science-fiction buffs. They could pick up the homage to Wyndham, no problem. But anything outside of that field. . . ." He shrugs.

Today, Roberts seems almost as baffled as he is angry, when confronted with his critics and the state of science fiction. I ask him if he's ever tried to deal with it by giving people what he thinks they really want.

"Yes, to an extent, but I found that the things that I started along those lines seldom got finished. Unless I believe in what I'm writing, the sheer process of mechanically typing it is too much for me.

"I don't think you *can* second-guess the public, anyway. The whole area has become very difficult indeed, for me, now. I didn't get English paperback publication for my last novel and short story collection. The whole trade is in such a weird state; 'Middle-of-the-road books,' as they call them, just aren't getting published anymore. Everyone wants to do a 'Major Novel,' a best seller. But personally, I wouldn't be in the shoes of some of these people who are hyped so highly. They get a tremendous amount of money, and have to go out and live in the Canary Islands as tax exiles before their books are even published. Really, I'd rather keep going the way I am, sort of plodding on. I've been doing more and more artwork; that's always the other string to my bow."

BIBLIOGRAPHICAL NOTES

Keith Roberts's "Anita" stories, chronicling the adventures of one of science fiction's most spirited female protagonists, are collected in *Anita* (1970).

His *The Furies* (1966) is a classic British disaster novel. Being more homage to John Wyndham than pure Roberts, it lacks the more vivid emotional power of his subsequent work, especially *Pavane* (1968), in which there is a grim struggle to revive progress in the face of oppressive Catholicism in an alternate future.

The Chalk Giants (1974) is a complex blend of post-holocaust imagery and romantic and sexual fantasies of a lonely male anti-hero (who was partially edited out of the American edition). In some ways it is Roberts's most complicated and ambitious book.

Molly Zero (1980) describes a future Britain where socialism has decayed into totalitarianism, seen from the gradually maturing viewpoint of a young woman. This book has yet to find a publisher in the U.S.

A SWING THROUGH THE SOUTH

Journey with me now to the appendix of America. A land of gator-tail sandwiches, pink motels, dancing dolphins, and drag-racing farm tractors. That long, thin peninsula full of short, fat senior citizens, a flatland of sunshine and stasis, a sanctuary for those who want to get away from mainland hassles and *not be bothered*.

Four important science-fiction writers live in Florida: Andre Norton, Piers Anthony, Keith Laumer, and Joe Haldeman. To meet them, I took an automobile safari into that surreal backwater of giant mosquitoes, moon rockets, and Mickey Mouse; and, viewed through these urban eyes, the local residents seemed at least as exotic as the land where they have chosen to live.

Andre Norton

The sluggish tide of automobiles surges from one stoplight to the next, through a landscape of giant signs: Pizza Hut, Burger King, Hungry Man Restaurant, Puppies and Guppies, Pantry Pride, Kentucky Fried Chicken, International House of Pancakes, Bicycle Castle, Bob's Pool Service, Majik Market, McDonald's, Wendy's Hamburger, The Sun Bank (Open 24 Hours), Denny's, the Fill-em-Fast gas station, Sundance Apartments ("If You Lived Here, You'd Be Home By Now!")....

It's a concrete wasteland encircling Orlando, Florida, and it seems endless. But after ten miles or so, I reach Winter Park, a quiet, small town embedded in the suburban sprawl. The buildings are older here, and the scale is more appropriate to people than to automobiles. In fact, some citizens have actually shed their cars and are strolling down the sidewalks. A lawn sprinkler spreads rainbows; lizards bask in the sun; pastel pink, blue, and green ranch-style houses stand dappled in shade from oak trees, maples, palms, firs, and exotic frondy Florida trees that are strange to me. Andre Norton's house is on this street.

Once, long ago, she was Alice Norton. But when she started selling stories in the 1930s, it simply Wasn't Done for a woman to write fast-paced action-adventure, and so she chose Andre as a suitably ambiguous pseudonym.

She's a gray-haired, rather reserved lady in her late sixties. She very seldom gives interviews; she values her privacy, never travels, and never allows photographs, either, because they would conflict with the image she projects in her novels. As she greets me at her front door and politely invites me in, I suddenly feel as if I'm visiting my aunt.

Her living room is large and shadowy. There are endless shelves of ornaments and pictures and miniatures, and everything is scrupulously neat and tidy. She has already decided who should sit where; she directs me to the couch and settles herself into a well-preserved straight-backed arm chair, facing me. Two cats come wandering across and sniff me as I set up the microphone. Another cat sits on the dining table, looking inscrutable. Two more are lurking in other parts of the room, and another two are outside in a big cage that has been improvised at the back of the house, to allow the felines to enjoy the Florida sun without danger from traffic on the street.

Since I imagine that Andre Norton might be unaccustomed to talking about herself to a stranger, I begin by asking her about the simple facts of her career.

"I've been writing since 1934," she tells me. "I'll have ninety-eight books published by the end of this year. In addition, I have done seven anthologies, and have collaborated on six books with other people.

"I wrote my first book in high school, but I didn't sell it. I sold my second book, when I was twenty-one. Then I went back and rewrote the first one, and sold that too.

"I always enjoyed science fiction, reading Wells, Verne, Merritt, and some of the other pioneers. But when I began writing, there was no market in America for book-length science fiction. It was strictly a short-story form, and I find it very hard to write short stories. I've only done about twelve in my whole career.

"So I started out writing in other fields. I had always preferred, myself, adventure stories. Talbot Mundy, Haggard, and that type of thing, so that is what I wrote, into the early 1950s, while I was a children's librarian in my home town of Cleveland, Ohio, for twenty years, long before I moved to Florida.

"My mother was from an old Ohio pioneer family." Now she makes herself more comfortable in her chair, and she relaxes a little, as if she'd rather talk about her family than her fiction. "My mother's people got their land as bounty land. Now, you probably don't know what that means."

I admit that I don't.

"Well, the men who served in the Revolutionary War, instead of being paid off in money at the end of the war, when the country was broke, were given western lands, if they chose. The state of Ohio was largely settled by bounty-land men.

"One ancestor of hers, who had served in the Maryland line, took bounty land, and married an Indian. And this was in the 1780s. As a result of his settling there, mother had a great deal of background of early Ohio. When she reached her seventies she started to write the story of her life as a child, which was back in the 1870s. When she died, she left half of the book in her papers. I was able to finish it, to give a picture of childhood and life in a small town in farming country in Ohio in about 1878. The book was titled *Bertie and May*; mother's name was Bertha, and her sister was May.

"My mother started to read to me when I was very, very young—poetry, at first. She had learned reams of poetry. So I got a feeling for words even before I knew what they meant. By the time I was five, she was reading *Little Women* to me.

"Mother also had a fascinating library of Victorian novels, which were what got me started on writing my one nonfiction book, which, incidentally, has never been published. It is a history of five women writers in the United States who, from 1840 to 1870, were the very best sellers—they outsold all the men, being the ones that Nathaniel Hawthorne referred to as the 'Damned scribbling women,' because they sold when he didn't!

"Three of these women wrote books that are just as readable today as they were then. They knew how to plot and to tell a story. Mary-Jane Holmes, Maria Cummings, and Elizabeth Wetherall. If you want to know how the pioneer people in New York lived in about 1840, all you have to do is read Elizabeth Wetherall. She describes the daily life of the people.

"When I wrote my own Victorian novel, *Velvet Shadows*, I did intensive research into the Victorian period. The stores and the dresses that I describe existed. When I talk about a dress of gold tissue, caught up with stuffed hummingbirds with ruby eyes—well, you can imagine what the times were like. I was writing about 1870 in San Francisco; the people were new-rich, they spent money like water.

"I've always been interested in the Victorian period. My mother was a Victorian herself, and I was brought up on Victorian stories. She had books of manners and food and so forth, of that period, and it's fascinating to read the customs of mourning, for example—how many months you wore your veil down, how many months before you dared throw it back or add a little bit of white to the front of your bonnet. The whole thing went through three years, and by that time somebody else had died and you started all over again. My mother said she never remembered seeing her own mother out of mourning."

By this time, I'm beginning to realize that Andre Norton would be happy to tell me anecdotes about American ancestry for the next two hours. But I want to know more about her work; so I interrupt and ask about her first science-fiction novel.

"I used my home town of Cleveland and tried to visualize it deserted after a complete war, when people had returned to a barbaric state. That was *Starman's Son*. It has now sold well over a million copies." She smiles.

"Of course, for many years I sold well, but I had no critical standing whatsoever. I was a woman in a man's field. There were only about four of us women and we either wrote under men's names or under our initials. We had to! This didn't make me resentful; I accepted it as part of the customs of the times. There was no women's liberation movement then."

Does she feel that there's any general difference between male and female writing?

"Oh yes. Decidedly so. I think women are more interested in characterization than men are, and there are very few men writers who can draw a good woman." She mentions a well-known male name as an example, but asks to keep it off the record, perhaps not wanting to cause offense. "Most of their women are stereotypes, whereas women can write about a man and make him real. I know women who do."

She pauses, here, to cross-examine me on how many female writers will be in *Dream Makers II*. Will I be including Anne McCaffrey? C. L. Moore? Leigh Brackett? Marion Zimmer Bradley?

I explain that some of them write fantasy, which I don't enjoy.

"You class Anne McCaffrey as a fantasy writer? She is not. And she is one of the leading writers. If you leave her out, you are going to run into trouble." She tells me this very firmly.

"Jacqueline Lichtenberg is also of importance. Her books are difficult reading, but they are interesting."

Since most of the names that Andre Norton has mentioned have been active in the field for many decades, I ask if there are any modern women writers whom she admires.

"Of course right now I'm very upset, in the new attitude in fantasy toward homosexuality. I feel very deeply that this is wrong. At least half of the readers of fantasy are under twenty. Some of them, who are exceptional readers, are only ten or twelve.

"There've been some very bald books involving homosexuality. One of them fell into my hands, and I was so outraged that I simply threw the book in the garbage. And that book was up for a prize. Another was sent to me, and I opened it on a sex scene that was so absolutely nauseating that it made me physically ill!

"This trend is getting stronger and stronger. For a good many years, when I was in the library, they would not buy science fiction and fantasy books, because those were considered trash, as a result of those dreadful covers on the magazines. So I fought and fought to get them on library lists.

"I have friends who teach science fiction in high school, and they have to be so careful, now, in vetting the books that they use because of this new trend, for fear of using anything that any parent could object to.

"I feel that all the work that I tried to do, to establish science fiction as a perfectly good form of reading, is being undermined."

Is she objecting, for example, to the John Norman books about warriors and slave girls?

"Well, now, I've read exactly one of those, and I thought it was a very poor imitation of Edgar Rice Burroughs. No, those are sadistic, but another book, for example"—she asks me to omit its title—"not only described a homosexual relationship, but an incestuous one, between two brothers, in the greatest detail.

"You don't have to go in for sensational material in order to write a good book. Some people are now writing books that would strike an impressionable young person in a very questionable fashion. This is an evil and dangerous thing."

She feels just as strongly about other issues—the mistreatment of animals, in particular.

"I have not too much respect for the human race, for some of the things that they have done. For example, the clubbing of the baby seals, which is the most atrocious thing. The killing of the whales. In some states they kill animals in the humane societies by shutting off all their air in pressure chambers. It's horrible. We have fought it through the courts, in Florida, and they have outlawed it here. In fact, I wrote one book, *The Iron Cage*, because I was so angry at what was going on with animals."

And animals continue to play a large part in many of her fantasy novels. As if on cue, one of her cats wanders over, climbs up, and sniffs the microphone.

"This is Ty," Andre Norton introduces me to the cat. "She is an example of breeding for a red Abyssinian, so she's much more red than the majority of her breed. They tend to have a grayish tinge. Now, Ty, don't you get up there!"

She strokes the cat. "You know, I think the human race made a bad mistake at the beginning of the Industrial Revolution. We leaped for mechanics, and threw aside things that were just as important. We made the transition too fast. I do not like mechanical things very much. And I don't like a lot of the modern ways of living. I prefer to do things with my hands; and I think everybody misses that. People need the use of their hands to feel creative.

"In England, weaving had been done in separate cottages. Then they started these factories where the conditions were so dreadful. It seems to me the principal part of the Industrial Revolution was greed.

"But now, people are turning back more and more to the earlier ideas. I myself am not a scientist; so I'm not interested in hard-science writing. Recently I have been doing quite a bit of study into the occult and the various mental discoveries that we are making. That's what interests me now.

"Wicca is one of my interests. That is witchcraft—white witchcraft, not the black Satanism which is nothing but a sort of parasite that developed in the late seventeenth century as a reaction to the church. No, Wicca goes back to the old religion that deals with herbs and moon worship. It's a woman's religion, you see, because only a woman can control it. The horned priest is under the priestess.

"I don't try to do anything with it, but I study it. I use some of their spells in my books, and some of their ceremonies, but I always alter both the spells and the ceremonies. This is necessary. I have friends who are practitioners of Wicca and they tell me it must *never* be used straight, in any book.

"The friend of mine who practices it and lives close by belongs to the Irish Congregation of Isis, and their particular thing is helping animals in difficulty. The people who practice Wicca are strongly nature lovers. They are conservationists. They use herbs a lot. In fact, it was two members of Wicca, out West, who bred the unicorn. A real unicorn. It looks exactly like the ones in the tapestries. I even have a little sprig of the hair of the mane of one of them, that was sent to me.

"You see, the original unicorns were not horses. If you look at the ancient tapestries, they do not look like horses at all. They look like a variety of goat, and that's what has been bred, a huge white goat with the single horn, the chin-beard, the long mane, and the long tail.

"I'm also very interested in psychometry, which I have actually seen proven. In psychometry, a person holds an object and reads its history. I'm a skeptic unless I can see a thing work, but I saw this. I had three pieces of jewelry, all antique, and I gave them to a sensitive to read. The first piece I thought was Chinese, but she dated it and read it as not Chinese, because she described the man who wore it and he was distinctly Manchu rather than Chinese in his dress. Then she described the man who made it, and even the material from which it was made.

"I later showed it to a curator of Chinese jewelry, and he backed her up, in the date, the fact that it was a time when the Manchus were in power, and that there was a rebellion at that time. She had said that the man who'd owned it had been executed. So all her background was authentic, even her description of the material used in it.

"Another piece was a brooch made from mammoth ivory. To look at it, you would think it was agate. But she held that for a moment and laid it down, saying, 'I cannot stand this, there is a big animal, and it is dying, and screaming. I want nothing more to do with that.'"

We talk a bit more about magic and ESP, but it's not a subject I know much about. I'm more interested in her as a writer; so she takes me out of the living room and shows me her study.

In addition to being full of books, there are more ornaments and mementoes. Her readers send her models of the creatures and characters from her novels—finely sculpted soldiers and peasant people, dragons ingeniously fashioned from colored pipe cleaners, statuettes, drawings, clay models. There are her awards, too—a Balrog fantasy award, and other plaques and scrolls.

"I still type my own first drafts," she says, pointing to a Smith-Corona electric on a gray steel typing table, beside an old wooden desk piled high with papers. "I pay no attention to spelling or grammar; I just want to get the idea on the paper. I find nowadays that if I try to work from an outline, that kills it. So when I write, now, I do not know, from one page to another, what's going to happen or who's going to turn up.

"I used to type the second and third drafts myself, but I've had some back trouble lately, so I correct the first draft in ballpoint, then turn that over to my typist. She does a second draft, and I go over it again. Then she does the final draft."

She leads me through a door into what used to be the garage. She never travels, and dislikes even leaving the house more than necessary. So she owns no car, and the garage has been turned into a library. There are endless shelves of books on history, myth, and legend. There are large sections of Chinese and Japanese literature, in which she has a special interest. Everything is meticulously arranged by subject. But of course; for twenty years she was a librarian.

I suddenly realize how appropriate it is that she put her library in the disused garage. The books, after all, are her alternate means of travel. This polite, eloquent lady may seem isolated here in Florida, in a retreat from the world; but with the books, she can go anywhere. They are her tickets to adventure, to lands limited only by the imagination.

Note: Several paragraphs in this profile were deleted or modified at the request of Andre Norton.

BIBLIOGRAPHICAL NOTES

Many of Andre Norton's novels are interconnected with continuing characters and shared backgrounds, but the *Witch World* series stands apart and remains possibly her most popular work, consisting of ten books, from *Witch World* (1963) to *Trey of Swords* (1978). The scenario involves a number of elements, such as the use of magic, which earn the books a "fantasy" label, though they are sword-and-sorcery in the usual sense.

Andre Norton's first novel, *Starman's Son* (1952), is set in a post-holocaust Cleveland that has devolved into warring clans, subsequently united by a mutant hero to fight a common monstrous enemy. Over the many years and through the many novels that she has written since this early work, she has turned increasingly to female protagonists, often aided on an equal basis by telepathic animals, especially cats, in adventures on very far-off planets or worlds that exist only in the imagination.

Though she is regarded as a writer of children's stories, Andre Norton's various series are tailored for differing age groups, and frequently make satisfying adult reading.

PHOTO BY CHARLES PLATT

Piers Anthony

It's like Iowa with palm trees, this sleepy little town of Inverness, Florida, with stores selling fertilizer, feed, and farm equipment, and pickup trucks parked outside at the curb. Why would a science-fiction writer choose to move out here?

I run a quick mental inventory of all the fact and rumor that I know about Piers Anthony. Born 1934. He sold his first stories in the late 1960s. Acquired a reputation as a "difficult" author who has had some fights with publishers, some of whom he openly accused of blacklisting him and his work. Prolific; has produced ambitious science fiction (*Macroscope*, *Tarot*) with high stress on pure concepts, characters functioning symbolically in complex games and equations. More recently, has produced numerous fantasy novels (e.g., the *Xanth* series) that are beginning to make the non-science-fiction best seller lists.

He's a strict vegetarian—won't eat *or wear* anything derived from dead animals. And he seems reclusive: many people I know in the science-fiction field have never met Piers Anthony, and even Keith Laumer, who lives less than twenty miles away, hasn't seen him in fifteen years.

I drive along blacktop country roads, past fertile farmland and small patches of forest. Following complex route instructions, I take an unpaved road into a wooded area that's been remade as a residential development. But the developer's sign out front looks worn and faded, as if the scheme never took off quite as planned, and the area has a funky, low-rent look.

"If you're willing to brave the wilds," Piers Anthony wrote to me, replying to my request for an interview, "I'm free any time, except at horse-feeding time. . . ."

The dirt road turns into an even smaller dirt road. Simple wooden houses are scattered here and there among the trees. It looks to me as if human beings have hardly touched the land.

Piers Anthony's place is the only two-story building. A Volkswagen microbus and a Ford Fiesta are parked on the grass outside. There's a corral at the back with horses in it, and a pen full of dogs. Small outbuildings stand amid tall grass and succulent plants.

I stop the car. Here he is, running toward me from out of the woods, a wild-eyed bearded man in red T-shirt and old jeans, looking like some hippie-hobo of the forest. "How long are you going to be here?" are his first words after I've introduced myself and am closing the car door. "What I want to do is answer the questions, or whatever you have," he goes on, "and then there are some questions which I've written down, which *I* have to ask *you*." He talks quickly, nervously, as if he just got word of some impending disaster, and we don't have much time.

I meet his wife, who seems quiet, thoughtful, and slow-moving by comparison, and then Anthony leads me—quickly, quickly!—past the corral and the dogs and the chickens, out to his workshop, a small barn set well back from his home. Inside it's very rustic, like a summer house, but with lots of bookshelves. I barely have time to turn on the tape recorder before he starts talking, eager to maximize every moment.

"Just make sure any questions that you have get answered," he warns me. "I can talk—I overflow—I can write—I mean, I write more than almost anybody, last year it was 480,000 words of manuscripts turned in to the publisher, and I do three drafts, on a manual typewriter, I paid $450 for it at the time, I could have had a Selectric for the same price, but I don't want to be hung up by a power failure, and sometimes you can have them for four hours! This machine, office machine, has never let me down, and when I'm ready to go, I *go*, at my speed. That's why I use the special keyboard layout." (The keys are arranged by frequency of use, rather than in the standard Q-W-E-R-T-sequence.) "It's the world's fastest keyboard; I'm not the world's fastest typist, when I'm going well it may be thirty words a minute, partly because my brain is the limiting thing, and I do first drafts on this clipboard—see, it has a box behind it, where the sheets that I've written can be put inside, with spare paper. I have upon occasion done as much as a thousand words in an hour, in longhand. I used to type first drafts, but my little girl was born, she's fourteen years old now, but back when she was six months old, my wife went back to work, I wasn't earning enough as a writer, the number-one thing you need if you're a writer is a working wife to earn your living until you can make it, and so I took care of my little girl, I changed her diapers and so on, fed her, everything, I couldn't take my eyes off that little girl, she was precocious, she was hyperactive, she would get into trouble, so I had to find a way to do my work and watch her too, and I moved to the self-contained clipboard. So she affected my whole writing career, but in a positive way, as it turned out, because I always have the clipboard now, if I wake up in the night, or go anywhere, any time, I can write. If I'm standing in line waiting for something, like my driver's license, I'm writing several hundred words. I don't care if people think it's strange, some people think that maybe I'm an FBI man making notes, I don't care, I keep going, I'm working literally almost all the time that's available, if I'm not sleeping, or eating—actually, I write when I'm eating. And I have never been to a science-fiction convention, I don't travel, I stay home, and if I'm not writing I'm answering fan mail. I answered thirty-three fan letters last month, this is the consequence of popularity, this is recent, I mean, in earlier years I'd get about one fan letter a week—"

I manage to break in here to ask if his wife doesn't mind this non-stop work obsession.

"No, my wife understands, I mean, she had to quit her job because it got to the point where her total wages went to pay the tax on my income, and she got disgusted with that. You see, I used to earn $500 a year, $1,000, and then $5,000, but when I started earning $70,000, and $100,000, and I suspect it'll be about $150,000 this year, I have launched into the big time. I used to have arguments, I had one with Dean Koontz, he was saying he was earning almost $100,000, and he didn't need to pay attention to nitwits like me. Well, I don't know how Dean Koontz is doing now, he's writing cheap novels pseudonymously, so I suspect the positions are reversed. I am now earning it, but I don't make any claims to being suddenly a genius because I make a lot of money. The money, as you know, is likely to be inversely proportional to merit, and my most thoughtful pieces are likely to earn less than my least thoughtful. When I'm doing a Xanth novel, I go through it about double the rate of anything else. For Avon Books I write science fiction, for Del Rey Books I write fantasy, I wrote *A Spell for Chameleon* for them, it won the British Fantasy Award, and then the subsequent ones started selling better and better, and started paying. It's nice to write what you like, but you don't necessarily get rich on it. I may be one of the most commercial writers you'll interview, in the sense that I write the cheap stuff that sells big. By training—I have a degree in creative writing—by education—I was born in England, my parents each graduated from Oxford University, and I have the background, the literary background, and what am I doing? Light entertainment. But, I mean, the money—after struggling along all these years, at low-paying stuff, or trying to, I've made the shift. And I can't say I regret it. I regret it in the intellectual sense that I wish I could have done a piece of such quality that I would get an award from the Nobel committee, but the compensation for this is money, and I'll *take* the money! At the same time, I still make myself do some serious stuff, because I want to keep in touch, I want to be in good mental condition just as I want to be in good physical condition, which is the reason I exercise, I'm physically—one of my controversial statements!—I regard myself as one of the *healthiest* science-fiction writers of my age. You can see dirt-marks on the last beam over there, I do my chin-ups there, and in light clothing I can do twenty-five chins, which is twice as many as I could do in high school. Yesterday I did my run on schedule and I broke my record for my three-mile run, I'm very much into physical fitness, health, partly because I'm forty-seven years old, I'm middle-aged, and this is about the time when people become aware of this."

He pauses to take a breath. While he's been talking I've been taking in my surroundings. This large hut, or small barn, smells of sun-baked wood and dusty books. The peaked roof is of bare boards and beams. The working area is walled in with steel shelves of reference volumes on history, geography, science, and politics. We're sitting talking at the far end, on an old convertible couch. Behind me, the wood paneling is detectably warm from the sun outside.

I'm interested by Anthony's frank talk about his fantasy novels, but not entirely convinced. Surely, a serious novel like his *Macroscope* earns more in the long term than a lightweight fantasy that's soon forgotten?

"Okay. *Macroscope* was published in 1969, and it has brought me a total of about $28,000, I can look up the exact figure if you like, I'm very careful about such things. *Source of Magic*, which was published in 1979, ten years later than *Macroscope*, has already brought me $31,000. And I buzzed it out in a hurry, just because it went fast, and was fun.

"The kind of thing that you can spend five years working on, and end up with a hundred pages—there should be a place in the market for this, as well as for the stuff that you spend ten days writing and it sells 250,000 copies. I do both; the trouble is, I fail on the quality material, and so I am now known, probably, for the lightest material that I do. I'm sure that you assumed that I would defend the light material and say how great it is, but I don't defend it, I say it's great for money, it's great for fun, but I wouldn't call it great literature."

I ask him who he blames for this state of affairs. Himself? His readers? His publisher? The distributors?

"Everybody. Oh, there's blame to go *everywhere*. I struggle with this, I say 'Why-why-why?' and I beat my head against the wall. But I try to judge by my own reactions, when I'm watching television, and I don't eschew television, it may be a 'vast wasteland,' but when I hear that said I always think of the desert, which is a wasteland, but if you look you'll find it has its own ecology, there are things in the desert that don't exist elsewhere and should continue, so that 'wasteland' just means that human beings don't have much use for it, the animals and insects that are there do, it's not a wasteland to them.

"Anyway, what do I watch when I have complete freedom to watch anything on TV that I want to? That was the question I was trying to address by my circuitous route. Well, likely as not it will be some cheap, junk thing, Magnum, P.I., something like that, when I could be watching the New York Philharmonic. But when I've done hard work, I want to relax, I don't want something that's going to try my intellect, I want something where it doesn't matter whether I pay attention to it or whether I don't. I want it *because* it is junk. Same thing with my readers, I don't think they are determinedly negative or lowbrow, it's that they're tired when they come home, they don't want to read *War and Peace*, they just want to relax and be entertained, without any strain on body or mind, and TV is geared to do this, and so is some fiction."

But now that he's become successful, couldn't he write something more challenging and hope this time that it will sell purely on the basis of his name?

"Well, the series I'm about to sell to Avon, called *Bio of a Space Tyrant*, is space opera, deliberately, and yet I discover as I write it in first draft that I'm going to get into more direct social comment than ever before in my life. I'm not saying, 'Here's my name and reputation, pay attention to what I say.' I'm sneaking it in.

"I put it to the publisher: 'Supposing someone who *really can write* tried space opera?' You realize, a lot of what I say sounds conceited, and yet I believe it, I believe in myself, I *can* write, I don't claim I'm the finest writer, but I'm one of the good ones. I can do your kind of writing, I can do commercial writing, I can do it all, and not many people can do it all. I can do the lightest, funniest fantasy that's on the market—nobody's even competing with my fantasy, I've got that market to myself. And I can do the most deadly serious writing. *Bio of a Space Tyrant* is based on the Vietnamese boat people, really. They left Vietnam, they came up to Thailand, they weren't rescued. The men were killed, the women were raped, kids thrown overboard. The women would be raped ten times before they finally get to land, only two survivors, and nobody will believe them—they say 'Where are your witnesses?' All the witnesses were killed. I said to myself, 'Supposing that happened in space?' And my mind started working, and I've now got a five-novel series going. I've set it in the solar system, my people are Spanish-speaking, and they finally get to Jupiter, the land of plenty, 'Send me your homeless,' and so forth, but the people there say 'Sorry, there's a new administration, the policy has changed, we will tow you back out to space.' This is the Reagan policy, you understand. If he had his way he would tow them back out into the ocean and not worry about them."

I can't help wondering if everyone will take this series as seriously as he does—critics, in particular. Does Piers Anthony feel that he has been mistreated in the past by his critics?

"Yes and no. When I had trouble with Ballantine Books, which blacklisted me rather than be honest—and because I actually went to a lawyer, I can say this, if anybody was going to sue, I was going to sue. They sold a book in England, they sold a book in Holland, and in Germany. Not only didn't they pay me, they didn't even put it on their statements. I got angry, and I sent them a detailed letter. I understand that Betty Ballantine said it was the most offensive letter she had ever received in her life. All I did was demand a correct accounting. But I should add that reports at Ballantine Books are now made honestly.

"Anyway, this is where the trouble started, because I started getting blacklisted, and this went into criticism. There are still areas where I can't get reviewed, because people heard stories about what a bad person I was."

I get the impression from this that he feels publishers are liable to cheat anyone they can, simply for the money; and he tends to be careful of those he deals with in the outside world. Does this have anything to do with the childhood alienation that so many science-fiction writers talk about?

"When I was growing up I was small. When I graduated in ninth grade I weighed a hundred pounds and I was five feet tall. I was the smallest, shortest person, male or female, in my class, in Westown school, in Pennsylvania.

"In addition to being small, I came to this country when I was six years old, from England, and they were trying to correct my English accent, and I resisted it. So, outsider? Yes. And one who was small. I understand it.

"But, you see, I grew. From five feet to about five-eleven after that. I have some questionable pleasures, but one was at the twenty-fifth class reunion, and a man I stood next to there, he was about six feet and had gotten fat and paunchy and so on, and I was there with my little girl and picked her up, and he said 'Careful, she weighs a lot.' The pleasure in this was that he was the class bully. He was six feet back then, when I was five feet. He was beating me up. And twenty-five years later, he couldn't even *catch* me if he wanted to. If he did, he wouldn't be able to take me. I had a very sinister pleasure knowing that I knew it and that he knew it."

I also get a sense that he is a compulsive achiever, from his self-imposed work schedule to his physical-fitness program. When he talks, he stresses all the verbs—especially words like "can," "will," or "do."

"It's true that, even when I run, I try to break my own records, even though I know intellectually that I'm just doing it for exercise. If I run ten-minute miles, I know I'll get the exercise. Why, then, am I running seven-minute miles?

"I do get compulsive. When I get into something, I do drive, I like to do the best I can do in whatever I do. I do my work, I do my homework, you see all the reference books here.

"When I don't write, sometimes I find myself going into a depression, when I spend two days answering fan mail and not writing. It creeps up on me. I want to write. I feel a compulsion. And when I am writing I feel happy, I feel satisfied."

But where does this compulsion come from?

"I don't know. I look at animals and I see puppies raised together—we have two, and one is compulsive, always competing, and the other takes it easy. It's not anything we did, it's not the environment, it comes from the genes.

"My grandfather was called the Mushroom King of Pennsylvania. Half the mushrooms this country produces are still produced in that area. He sold out two weeks before the crash of 1929, but the people he trained went into business for themselves. He was dedicated to business and making money.

"But my *father* went into education. He taught Spanish, he became the intellectual and therefore was not rich. Now here I am; my father certainly wasn't going to shove me into business, he rejects the business ethic, the idea of driving hard to make money repelled him—understandably. I myself don't go for business that much, but I do have the drive, and I'm making the sort of money my grandfather used to. I am not foolish about money at all. I don't waste it, you don't see me going off and buying Cadillacs, no, you see me out there splitting wood, because we have a wood-burning stove, and solar-powered water heating, if the sun doesn't shine we don't bother with hot water, because I don't like to pay fuel bills. I'm a miser! I like to think that if my grandfather were alive today, and looked to see who has the attitude that most closely approximates his—it would be mine."

At this point, his wife buzzes us on an intercom from the house and says that lunch is ready. He's been talking for about an hour and a half (I have included, here, perhaps one-third of all that was actually said) and seems unhappy about stopping.

We walk out into the sun. I notice ants in the sandy soil, moving relentlessly to and fro, carrying enormous grains of sand in their mandibles. It seems appropriate, somehow, that Piers Anthony should work right next door to an ant hill. I imagine him figuring out some way to rate his work-day against theirs, so he can find out who's ahead.

The inside of his home is a cheerful but total shambles. He explains that they were cheated by a dishonest builder who gave them a galvanized iron roof instead of the everlasting stainless-steel one that they'd paid for. They sued the builder, he went bankrupt, and the house was never completed. That was four years ago. So the floor is of unfinished concrete, the ceiling of unfinished wood, and when I use the bathroom I notice that, although there's a shower fixture, the bath has never been installed. Instead, there's a huge mound of newspapers and magazines.

Piers Anthony explains more of his philosophy as we eat cheese omelettes together. He's used his royalties not on his own home (which looks, indeed, like a hippie commune displaced from Northern California). Instead, he's been buying up land all around the house; he says that he and his wife "don't care to gamble on the quality of neighbors who might move in. . . . So we buy all the land we can, to prevent it from being settled." They've accumulated thirty acres, so far.

After lunch, his wife, who used to work as a programmer, unearths their Atari home computer from beneath some plastic placemats that protect it from dust, and she demonstrates the word-processing program—which Piers Anthony doesn't use, because the Atari has a conventional typewriter keyboard, and he's adapted himself to the special layout on his manual typewriter. And anyway, computers are vulnerable to power cuts. He'd rather stick with his strictly non-electrical system.

He quizzes me for New York gossip, and tells me how hopelessly naive I am for believing that most publishers are honest and most editors can be trusted. "Most publishers are amoral. They don't believe what they do is wrong, but the writer had better beware."

And on this ominous note it's time for me to leave; because, this same afternoon, I must now go and interview Keith Laumer.

BIBLIOGRAPHICAL NOTES

Piers Anthony's first novel, *Chthon* (1967), describes the episodic adventures and gradual self-discovery of a resolutely capable man attempting to master and escape from the complex social system of an underground prison in an alien planet. It is claustrophobically powerful.

Anthony's next ambitious work after this was *Macroscope* (1969), which attempts a kind of unified cosmology of astrology and science, and micro- and macrocosms.

In the 1970s he began writing pure fantasy novels such as the highly popular *Xanth* series, full of puns and other light humor. His *Omnivore* sequence (1968–76) and *Tarot* (1979–80, conceived as one novel but published in three volumes) are his more serious work, in which great descriptive color is applied to highly inventive, exotic creatures and landscapes, with the human characters acting almost symbolic roles in the complex plots.

PHOTO BY JAY KAY KLEIN

Keith Laumer

The first time I met Keith Laumer he was tall and strong, a casually capable outdoorsman with an equally formidable intellect and not a shred of false modesty.

He had traveled widely while in the Air Force and while working for the State Department. He had taught himself something about almost everything, from history to language to gourmet cooking to engineering to art, and all that he knew was factually accurate, and most of it was fascinating. He showed a small amount of pity and a fair amount of scorn for anyone who was less demanding than he was—as though he believed that excellence was the only value that truly mattered. He was impatient with people who tolerated weakness or imperfection in themselves.

The second time I met Keith Laumer, one year later, his left side was paralyzed from what doctors had diagnosed as a stroke, and he seemed devastated by the frustration of what had been inflicted upon him. Fate was forcing him to accept the unacceptable: a disability that made a mockery of the code he had always lived by.

That was more than ten years ago. As I drive to Laumer's Florida home, now, I have no idea what has happened during the intervening decade.

He lives in wild, empty country. Down an unpaved back-road of fine, pale gray dust, between stunted trees and swamp grass; the telephone poles carry a single wire, and a single lonely bird is sitting on it.

I reach his driveway. And here is a strange, enigmatic sight: For some reason, the entrance is marked by two dented 1968 Mercury Cougars, abandoned here on flat tires, with numbers scrawled in black paint on their rusty roofs.

Approaching his house—a modern building on a spacious piece of land—I find more junked Cougars parked at the side of the driveway; and more are in the three-car garage; and still more are scattered across the lawn at the back of the house. There must be at least thirty cars altogether, all of the same year and model, all dilapidated, and all numbered in black spray-paint.

Keith Laumer greets me at his front door and we walk through his elegant home. He moves slowly, still encumbered with a leg brace, but he no longer has the air of despair that he showed ten years ago. He seems grim and determined, now, to overcome the catastrophe that almost ruined his life.

He tells me how he came to live out here. His father bought large tracts in Florida very cheaply after World War II, and became a real-estate millionaire. When Laumer decided he wanted to build a dream house, his father supplied an idyllic plot surrounded on three sides by a lake, in untouched countryside. Here, on what is virtually an island, Laumer supervised construction according to his own specifications—he was trained as an architect. Outside every window is water, and beyond that, wilderness.

Ever true to his code of self-sufficiency, he then started making his own furniture, to his own designs, in a woodworking shop in his garage.

"When I was out in Rangoon, Burma, in the Diplomatic Service, where the beautiful oriental timbers grow, I shipped home a bunch of slabs of three or four different beautiful woods. I was about halfway through furnishing the whole house when I was . . . temporarily interrupted.

"At first, you know, the medical profession told me, 'The likelihood of any significant recovery is minimal.' In other words, what they were really saying was"—he clenches his fist on the handle of his cane; he grimaces with rage, and raises his voice to a shout—"'Fuck you, stupid! Assholes like you spend your goddamn lives abusing your fucking bodies sucking on cigarettes and drinking booze and never getting any exercise, and when the goddamn thing finally rots you come crawling in here whining for a miracle. Well, you're not going to get one. Do you realize I'm late for the golf course?'

"And then zap, out the door."

The anger leaves him as abruptly as it came. I realize I'm flinching from him. While he was shouting, the intensity was frightening. But he continues, now, once again in a normal, conversational tone.

"Well, the fact is, I always took the best conceivable care of myself. I used to do a five-mile run every day, on trails through the woods. And it's almost as though I had a premonition that something was going to happen to me, because every day when I came in I'd turn around and say, 'All right, you sons of bitches, that's another five miles I took away from you. You can't get that back.'

"I never ate too much or too little, I ate good food, and I never did start smoking, so I never had to quit. I enjoy beer or wine, but there isn't any form of hard liquor that I like.

"One day shortly after I got into this horrible state I was reading an issue of *Time* on the subject of CVAs, which means Cerebro-Vascular Accidents, and it had a little checklist there. I scored zero all the way down; *nothing* applied to me. So I got through and I said, 'Okay, it'll never happen to me. So let me out of here!'

"And actually it *didn't* happen to me. What actually happened was a curious thing, to which everybody is subject, to some degree, starting before you are born, as soon as your intellect becomes aware of itself. Your mother bumps against something, and you didn't like that a bit, and you make a decision, 'I do not like to be knocked around, and I have got to be *tough*, so that it cannot happen to me anymore.' Your body responds to that absolute command by hardening itself, in the form of muscles tightening up.

"Everybody has a tight muscle representing some experience that you subconsciously shunted aside. Say a big black dog comes bounding out onto the lawn when you're three years old. That's too scary, so some part of your mind, way down deep, says 'This is too much!' and shunts that emotional energy into some place where it's safe, way down in a muscle next to the bone of your thigh perhaps. And little by little you get an accumulation of these things. And apparently in my case I got an accumulation of them that finally crossed a threshold—and something said 'Okay, execute Plan A.' And Plan A was to go—*crrrkkkkk*. And there I was, all fucked up."

I say that this sounds like the theory of Rolfing.

"The therapy that I'm getting is to Rolfing as champagne is to ditch water. The most visible part of what he does is the massage, using a knuckle or an elbow. He can feel that muscle down there that's harder than rock. When he squeezes out that muscle, it lets go. And I can feel it let go. And the funny thing is that I get the emotion that originally caused it. Either I'm scared shitless or I'm awful sorry for poor little me or I'm so goddamn mad I could kill somebody. The emotion comes flooding out, as fresh as the day it happened. And after that, the muscle can stay normal.

"And once he gets everything out, which is simply a matter of digging and digging at it, then everything will work freely." Keith Laumer says this with absolute, calm conviction. The therapy he is receiving, twice a week, has lasted four years now; but he knows it will work. Obviously, it has to.

"It hurts horribly, but it's just barely within what I can face. It's at least as bad as surgery without anesthetic. It's especially bad when he hits a fear pocket, because then you get terror along with the pain. Like when he starts working down in around the throat. You know goddamn well you're being choked to death, and you're panic stricken, and suffering agonies at the same moment.

"If somebody had tried to tell me about this before I got into this state I would have said 'Bullshit.' But when it happens to Number One, you can't deny it.

"When I first got into this state, for five years I didn't write anything. Then I slowly got started, doing a few short stories, and then I started writing one of the novels for which I had contracted before. And I have now completed four novels and half-a-dozen short stories, and am just starting a new novel which is due in a few months, and I have just signed a contract to do two more.

"I always used to type. Now, I have to do it in longhand. But I have a gal who comes in once a week to tidy up the place, and she also types up what I've written. So that works fairly well.

"I just turned in a new Retief novel, and before that was *The Star Colony*, and *The Ultimax Man*, which came out some months ago from St. Martin's Press."

Retief is Laumer's favorite hero, an interstellar diplomat whose lot in life is to grapple constantly, and comically, with a galaxy full of incompetents.

"I always enjoyed doing Retief and I still do. The world is so full of bullshit—there's always a fresh supply—and in the Retief stories I try to puncture some of it. And that's always worth doing."

He started writing the stories as a reaction to his time spent in the Diplomatic Service. I ask how long he was with the State Department.

"I was never *with* them," he corrects me grimly, "I was *employed* by them. I was, in fact, against them from the beginning. I was there for about three years; I was a Third Secretary of Embassy of the United States of America in the United States Diplomatic Service, and I was a Vice Consul of Career in the United States Consular Service, and I was a Foreign Service Officer of Class 7 in the United States Foreign Service. I ranked 'with and after a captain,' which didn't thrill me because I had already been a captain in the Air Force."

Mentioning these positions reminds him of all the publishers who have printed inaccurate biographical notes on his life. And this brings back his rage. One moment he's mild-mannered Keith, with a sly smile and a taste for gentle irony. And then, in a flash, he's Demon Laumer, screaming and swearing in vile fury. It's difficult for me to indicate, in print, how wildly he fluctuates to and fro.

"As a result of my going from the Air Force to the Diplomatic Service, and then back to the Air Force, the—*GOD DAMNED ASS HOLES*—who write blurbs on book jackets, instead of asking me, made up some—*CRAZY BULL SHIT*—about how I was some kind of a 'diplomatic aide' or some god damned thing. If the—*MOTHERFUCKING ASS HOLES*—had just asked me.... Anybody who knows anything about diplomatic practice would read that and say, 'This guy's a *phony*, because there is no such thing as a 'diplomatic aide.'

"When I go in there and see them and say a bad word, do you think that does any good? No, they put the same *GOD DAMNED SHIT* on the next book. They make me grind my teeth.

"And then the god damned editor of *If* magazine, when it was running all the Retief stories, constantly got out his *god damned editorial pencil* and changed the little technical niceties to something that seemed to his *god damned brainless mind* to be a little closer to Middle American blah, thereby completely destroying the verisimilitude. So anybody who was actually in the Diplomatic Service reading it would say, 'Well this asshole's never been near the Diplomatic Service.' The *god damned prick*!

"I said, 'Look, when I say the man was a counsellor, I do *NOT* repeat *NOT* mean that he was a member of a *council*. So will you kindly *FUCK OFF* changing the spelling to 'councillor'? It *AIN'T THAT*, see?"

Laumer relaxes back into his chair.

"But do you think he got it? He didn't understand. Perhaps—perhaps I didn't make it plain enough. Or—maybe he thought I didn't mean it, because I wasn't emphatic enough." He gives me a faint, ironic smile.

"Little things like that. For some reason unknown to anybody the word 'despatch' in the State Department is spelled with an E. So I spelled it with an E and he changed it to an I. I said, 'Will you *FUCKING LAY OFF*?' And he said, 'But I looked in the Web-ber Dick-on-ary. . . .' So I said, 'Look up your *FUCKING ASSHOLE*, jerk! *I* am the guy who was a full-time professional U.S. diplomat.'"

His anger subsides again, and he begins telling me an anecdote.

"One day I had a most interesting letter from somebody at the State Department Foreign Service Institute who asked me if, the next time I was in Washington, I would stop by and address the student body. And he said, 'Personally, I'm sort of a Magnan type myself.'" He chuckles.

"A what type?" I ask, not getting the joke.

"A Magnan type." He sees that my face is still blank. Suddenly, he grabs his cane and slams it against the floor. He lets out a terrifying, full-blooded scream. "You never heard of Magnan! *Gaaarrgh*! He is Retief's sidekick in *every* Retief story. *Aaarrgh*! *Nyaaarrgh*!"

It's a terrible, frightening sound, like a barbarian war cry. He lets go of his cane, grabs a saber in an ornamental sheath, and strikes it fiercely against the couch where he's sitting. He keeps screaming and scowling at me.

"I thought you said 'magnum,'" I try to tell him.

"*Aaarghh*! *Aaarghh*!"

"I'm sorry, Keith, but—"

"*Naaarghhh*! *Aaaargh*!" He pauses for breath. "Have I made myself clear?" he asks mildly, replacing the saber in its corner. "You see, I think people ought to know that Magnan is the sidekick of Retief," he goes on matter-of-factly, "and is a weak sister, highly ineffectual, and it's pretty funny when this guy put in his letter, 'I'm sort of a Magnan type myself.' I thought that was really charming.

"How are you going to transcribe my roars, off the tape?" he asks reflectively. "I suggest: 'A-R-G-G-G-H-H-H-H.'"

Feeling slightly dazed, at this point, I manage to agree that that sounds like a fine way to spell it. Hoping to put the conversation on safer ground, I ask why he seems so down on the State Department.

"The United States Department of State," he says carefully, "is as *filthy* an organization as ever existed on this planet, up to and including the Gestapo."

No, I object, it can't be that bad.

"*Worse*! It is rotten from the top to the bottom, and if anybody gets into it who isn't rotten, he's pounded on till he is rotten, or he gets out."

Really? *That* bad?

"*WORSE*! Think of something rotten, and they do it. Nothing as wholesome and decent as simply taking money for selling military secrets to the enemy. I mean, any red-blooded American boy might do that. But not these cocksucking bastards, they go way beyond that. If you've read my novel *Embassy*, which is not science fiction, you'll get some idea of my experiences. I poured my life blood into that book. A testament of two-and-a-half to three horrible fucking years out of my life. And editors said, 'Oh, yes, *The Ugly American* with sex.' Gaah! It's a horrible thing that that god damned book *The Ugly American* came out when it did. It was a piss-poor book, whereas *Embassy* was a marvellous book, and if *The Ugly American* hadn't come out right ahead of it, it would have sold twelve zillion copies. It should have been reissued when that thing was going on in Iran; because what went on in my book was the same kind of shit, and it showed exactly how it comes to pass, because of the venality and cowardice of the god damned bastards who've been running the American Embassies in the United States Department of State.

"If I were placed in charge, I would disband the department, fire anybody who had worked for it in any capacity, and no one who had worked for it would ever be eligible to work for the new Department of Foreign Affairs. Every building that had belonged to that organization would be gotten rid of, every vehicle. That's what it would take to clean it up. Nothing less."

I ask if he feels that bureaucracy is always inherently corrupt and inefficient.

"Of course. It's a concept that has flaws built into it, part of its nature. There are a lot of jokes that embody the truth, like the one: 'In the civil service they promote a man until he reaches a job that he can't do.' It's the fucking truth! Therefore you have an incompetent occupying every position.

"It is absolutely against the interests of any bureaucrat to cut down in any way on the scope of his duties or the number of people that work for him. Because his pay is based on these things. So you get one bureaucrat fighting to steal some section away from some other bureaucrat so he can have all those people added to his list, so he can get a raise.

"It's analogous to the U.S. legal system, which places a premium on extending litigation. It's not in the interest of lawyers to shorten litigation, but to prolong it as far as possible."

I ask if his dislike for bureaucracy is so strong as to make him a libertarian.

"No—that's anarchy, and under anarchy the biggest assholes gang up and beat the shit out of everybody else and take everything for themselves, and I'm not interested in that. It's Europe in the Dark Ages."

I mention that Poul Anderson is a libertarian of sorts.

"Well that simply establishes that Poul Anderson doesn't know shit from wild honey. People who express approval of that kind of thing aren't thinking in terms of, all of a sudden, no more TV, no gas in the gas station, no groceries in the grocery store. All of that is the product of a fantastic network of cooperation. If everybody just said 'Fuck it!' it would all stop. You could take off your clothes, go off into the woods, and start looking for nuts and berries."

Laumer's views on modern science fiction are almost as scathing as his views on the state of modern society.

"I find it very bad and uninteresting. A lot of it is very pretentious. Science fiction started off as a literature that was created for fun and read for pleasure. Now it's become a channel for social and socialistic ideas from writers who are avant-garde and new-wavy and liberal, and all those things make me puke, so there's just nothing there for me.

"Personally, I never said, 'I am going to write science fiction.' I just decided to write something that pleased me. I never even had the intention of becoming a writer; one day, in Rangoon, I told my wife, 'I'm going to stay home from that god damned office today and write a story.' And I did, and I sold it, and all the ones since.

"I went on doing jobs, like going back into the Air Force. It was a long time before it occurred to me that I should quit doing all the other stuff and write full-time. But I finally did, resigned from the Air Force in 1965, came to Florida, and built the house, and settled down to live happily ever after. And five years later they tried to kill me. So that has drastically changed the pattern of my life. I've had to devote every waking and sleeping moment to fighting this god damned plague, to recover my life, which I am doing, *and will complete*."

During the last part of our conversation, we've been eating steak which he insisted on preparing for me—a very fine cut of beef, cooked to perfection. He clings stubbornly to his ideas about excellence. He still has detailed plans for the completion of his house: "Everything properly made, and perfectly maintained," seems to be his motto.

And I learn that the dozens of junked Mercury Cougars that he's collected are a strange part of this obsession with perfection. He's vague about how the collection got started, but he's quite definite about what he's going to do. He'll repair every last one of them, as soon as he gets his strength back. He'll restore them "to new condition—or better." He tells me there are thirty-eight cars in all, and shows me some hood emblems and instrument-panel trim that he's already removed and had re-chromed. "It gives me something to occupy my mind, when I'm not thinking about 'Topic A,'" he says quietly.

To me, it seems as if the cars are an externalization of his own condition; they mar the beauty of his land as his illness has marred his life, and he wants to restore their steel bodies as he would heal his own.

He shrugs, and doesn't argue the point.

Before I leave, he shows me pictures of his three daughters, one of whom lives in London, the other two in Texas, which is also where his ex-wife is located. "After I have completed the total recovery of my health," he says, "I'm going to marry an absolutely first-class young beauty and have another family. And I'll know a lot more about what I'm doing, the next time."

Then he walks outside with me, into the warm Florida evening.

I remark that the cruelty of what he has experienced would make me doubt the existence of a god, if I were not already agnostic.

"But it has had exactly the opposite effect on me," he says. "Before this happened to me, I was always content, but never happy. Now, I have a whole new view of life. I appreciate life with a depth and scope I would never have imagined. And it cannot be an accident. I believe in God, now, and could not have come to this realization any other way. There is some principle, some force, which is active in controlling the universe, and I definitely believe that this applies to the individual."

For now, at least, he seems to have vented all his resentments. He speaks with a strange kind of equanimity.

"I sure wish some of my old friends would stop by," he goes on, as I get in my rented car. "Though I wouldn't ever tell 'em that," he adds gruffly.

I can see why they stay away, of course. No doubt they dread his spasms of rage, and the way he reminds us of the shadow under which we live. Keith Laumer was stricken at age forty-five, in excellent physical shape; obviously, then, it could happen to me, or you, or anyone. I suppose it's poor form to emphasize this. Most of us naturally prefer not to dwell on mortality, and so we feel uncomfortable visiting disabled friends, or even reading profiles of them. Pretending to be invulnerable is a common enough way of coping with life.

Keith Laumer, of course, now lacks that option.

BIBLIOGRAPHICAL NOTES

Keith Laumer's most popular books are probably those in his "Retief" series, featuring an interstellar diplomat of that name, mediating comically between nefarious and devious aliens and his incompetent superiors. The series began with *Envoy to New Worlds* (1963) and is still continuing. All of the books subsequent to the second one are identifiable by the name "Retief" in their titles.

Laumer has written with less humor and more drama of parallel worlds and the control of time paradoxes in his *Imperium* series, which commenced with *Worlds of the Imperium* (1962). A similar theme is given lighter treatment in the Lafayette O'Leary series, comprising *The Time Bender* (1966), *The World Shuffler* (1970), and *The Shape Changer* (1972).

His new novel, *The Star Colony*, was published in 1982, and *Rogue Bolo*, one of a series featuring robot fighting machines, is forthcoming.

PHOTO BY CHARLES PLATT

Joe Haldeman

"I got my draft notice. Being a naive young college graduate, I thought to myself, 'What the hell can I do about this?' So I went to the army and asked *them* what I could do, to get out of going to Vietnam. And the guy there rubs his hands together and says 'Well, if you're drafted, you're in for two years and you don't get shit. But if you sign this piece of paper, you're in for two years and you never have to go into combat.'

"What I did not realize was that he would get fifteen bucks for my signing that piece of paper; and no matter how you join the army, if there's a war on, you have to join a combat arm.

"He told me I would be a scientific assistant. I'd be cleaning out test-tubes and that sort of thing. Well, I was put in basic training. That was when I realized the depth of my error!

"So I applied for nuclear power-plant school. I was willing to extend my enlistment for two years, and spend a year in Antarctica running a power plant, which shows you how much I wanted to stay out of Vietnam. But they wrote back and said that, with a degree in physics, I was overqualified. That was when I knew I was doomed.

"I ended up in the army as a combat engineer. Basically, I carried a shovel and a chain saw and a bag of explosives, walked along with the infantry, and when we got into combat my main function was to drop back a ways and blow down enough trees with the explosives so that they could bring in a helicopter to evacuate the wounded. In a practical sense I was an ancillary to the medics, rather than a builder of bridges or anything else that 'engineer' might imply.

"In combat, I made my position clear. I had tried to be a conscientious objector before I was drafted, but because I have no formal religion, it was not allowed by law. (That law was later challenged by someone smarter than me, and annulled.)

"I told the guys in my outfit that I didn't see how I could actually kill anybody, unless I could see someone actually trying to kill me. But the way it worked out, even when I was in combat, I never had to shoot at anybody. I only had direct orders to do so once, when they sent us out to find this guy, and I found him, but didn't say anything about it. He had fired on a convoy and brought it to a halt. If he had had a weapon and brandished it at me, I probably would have killed him, because by that time I was fairly numbed to it. But he didn't. He had had the sense to stash his weapon and just hide behind the trees there, and evidently nobody else saw him. So I just left."

Out of these experiences in Vietnam, and his sense of the changes that had occurred in U.S. society while he'd been away, came Joe Haldeman's first science-fiction novel *The Forever War*. It pictured a "shockingly" sexually liberated interstellar army, and poked irreverent fun at some timeworn adventure-fiction cliches. It was orthodox science fiction wrenched into the real world, with the radicalism and self-knowledge of a young man fresh from the 1960s. It was as if *Star Wars*, say, had been rewritten by Jerzy Kosinski. It perfectly matched the mood of the times, and won both Hugo and Nebula Award as Best Novel.

Vietnam and the 1960s seem a long way away, now, as Haldeman sits talking quietly at his dining table, in his home on a back street not far from Daytona Beach. The small house is unpretentious and comfortable; there's some modern, expensive-looking living-room furniture, and a home computer/word-processing system in the other room, but these seem rare instances of splurging in an otherwise very simple life-style.

Some people assumed he wrote *The Forever War* as a left-wing reply to Robert Heinlein's strongly right-wing *Starship Troopers*. But Haldeman says it didn't happen that way at all.

"I didn't even think of *Starship Troopers* until I'd written sixty or seventy pages of *The Forever War* and somebody pointed out how similar it was in structure. That was the first time I'd thought consciously about it.

"I find the combat scenes in *Starship Troopers* pretty well done, but Heinlein's experience is that of an elite young officer who didn't stay in the service long enough to get shot at. I was a soldier, a fighting soldier, and much of my book came out of my emotional reactions to combat.

"Heinlein has told me that he's read *The Forever War* several times, and when it won an award he sent me a very warm letter pointing out that, although we didn't see eye to eye on much, we did agree on two particular things: the evil of the draft, and the senselessness of fighting a war that you know you can't win."

Puffing on his pipe, a can of Budweiser at his elbow, Haldeman himself projects a very unassuming image, as if he likes to keep life as calm and simple as possible.

Almost everything that he's written has strong social relevance or political implications, so I ask about his own political bias.

"I'm essentially apolitical. I try to keep an open mind, because any political solution seems to leave something out, including those for which I feel a knee-jerk sympathy because of my generation: pacifism, maximizing socialism at the expense of capitalism, anarchy, and so on.

"I suspect that no political institution or ideology is adequate to the problems we have now. This bothers me, as a science-fiction writer, because I can't come up with anything much smarter. Not only aren't there any easy answers, there aren't any hard answers.

"In my fiction, I think I'm overall optimistic about the future. In the world at large, I do see a gradual decrease in the inhumane things that go on. After all, the things we regarded as part of everyday life in the past are now seen as outrages."

I mention Jerry Pournelle's outlook, that history teaches us to expect war as an inevitable fact of life, and we shouldn't expect the future to be any more humane than the past.

"That sounds like the attitude of anyone in the Politburo right now, unfortunately. Jerry may well be right, but reasoning by historical analogy is a limp way of proving anything.

"If I have one fundamental tenet, it's rejection of *belief*. I realize that that in itself is a belief system, but I reject axioms, I try never to be dogmatic. This makes me a sort of wishy-washy person, on the one hand, but it does mean I can be flexible. For instance, Jerry Pournelle is no less my friend for holding what I consider to be very bizarre beliefs; and at the same time, I have equally good friends who are just this side of being bomb-throwing radicals."

In Haldeman's *Worlds* trilogy, he suggests that space colonies orbiting the earth could be testing grounds for very free political systems, near to anarchy, with no built-in resistance to change. Is this pure wish-fulfillment, or a serious prediction?

"I don't think it's too likely, though it is possible. I don't see us putting the enormous effort into building space colonies so long as their benefits seem so abstract, and I don't see Russia doing it either. We would need fundamental changes in our priorities, or in our technology—for instance, if we came up with something less brute-force than the Shuttle or the heavy-lift launch vehicle. The most economical methods they're talking about now, of putting up a colony, are still an order of magnitude larger than the Apollo program, and there was a good, sound political reason for doing that, whereas there's no sound reason for putting a bunch of yo-yos into orbit where they're liable to have a revolution and declare their own independence, just as we did in America."

Does he see any hope for private enterprise opening up space?

"There was every material reason to build a railroad from the East Coast of this country to the West Coast, and the technology existed, the material existed. But it took the government to push the big individual investors into doing it. In the same way, I think space industrialization can pay back, eventually, and a lot of industrial people know this. It could then go very much the same way as the railroads. We allow the government in as a basic driving force behind the private industries that are actually doing it, and wind up with a lot of featherbedding and regulations, and just an outgrowth of the government 22,500 miles up."

Does this imply the same anti-government, pro-business outlook that I've found in other writers of technological science fiction?

"Of the people I've met in government and private industry, I like the private industry people better. They seem more honest about their avarice, anyway. And in terms of their track record, at least until recently, private industry has done better than our government in terms of general success and growth. Our government has had to keep generating wars in order to keep making a profit."

That, again, sounds like a phrase from the 1960s.

"I do think about the 1960s a lot. At the time, I missed what was going on. I was just trying to get a handle on differential equations and keep a marriage going, that sort of thing. I had my nose stuck in a book, smelled tear gas now and then, saw people demonstrating on campus and just dismissed them as being too lazy to do the work for their degrees.

"But I was less than half right. When I got back from Vietnam, I realized that the year of 1968 had been very pivotal in American history. I'm going to write a book about that, titled *1968*, about the time I missed in American society. It will investigate the period from the point of view of a paranoid schizophrenic." He smiles. "A totally unreliable viewpoint character."

Joe Haldeman was born in 1943, the son of a public health official whose work entailed endless traveling.

"People ask me where I grew up, and I say 'Alaska,' but that's because I spent three years there. In fact, I had already lived in Puerto Rico, New Orleans, Oklahoma, and Washington D.C."

In college, he studied physics and astronomy. He wrote some stories in his spare time, but didn't sell any until he returned from Vietnam. For a while, he went back to graduate school in mathematics, because "at three or five cents a word, you don't think of writing as a career."

But he lost patience with college in 1970, and just happened to sell *War Year*, his non-science-fiction novel about Vietnam, one week later. He and his wife Gay picked up and moved to Florida, "because we could live cheaply here, and I could write full-time for a couple of years to see what would happen, while she taught high school."

Next came an interim period at the Iowa Writers Workshop, "where all the literary greats come through to dispense wisdom. It was pretty heady stuff, talking lit. with people like John Cheever, Vance Bourjaily, Steven Becker, John Irving. It was also wonderful discipline for writing, and a gold-plated ego trip, because I was selling what I wrote.

"I had a teaching assistantship, and Gay had a research assistantship, which moved us up from poverty to near-poverty. We stayed there for nearly five years. We'd still be there if we didn't love the ocean and hate winter."

So they returned to Florida, and have been in this slightly remote part of the world ever since. "I don't enjoy publicity," he says. "It's not in my nature. Down here we're away from the main stream of science-fiction life."

But the Haldemans keep close ties with some science-fiction people, and use the field almost as an extended family. The license plate on their van reads "SF FAN."

Ironically, Haldeman himself hardly reads the stuff any more.

"I stopped when I started writing for a living. Each year, around the time the awards come up, I sit down and read all the nominees, but let's face it, writers don't read much for pleasure. It's only when somebody does something that we haven't done, we stop in our tracks and try to see what's happening.

"In what I have read, there's been a strong tendency to recycle established ideas. Maybe we really have used up all the basic ones, or maybe it's just laziness, I don't know. I find myself writing stuff and then realizing it has strong roots in what I was reading when I was thirteen years old. Maybe this is something that affects all writers, but it's awkward when it happens in science fiction, because of the ideational component of the stuff."

He still remains loyal to science fiction, in a sense. But he has no time at all for heroic fantasy.

"God, I detest it. I think that fantasy books are published in lieu of science-fiction books, and if they sell better, they're going to start taking over the market. This endless stream of unicorns and dragons and people with swords—it's so dull.

"I think I understand the kind of person who reads this stuff. It's not quite as bad as sitting watching situation comedies day after day, but I think it's the same kind of mentality: someone who likes having the same buttons pushed over and over. And maybe I have some element of that when I watch TV, but not where literature is concerned.

"I wish it didn't have the obvious effect on publishing that it has. I don't believe it's done any harm to my career, but I do think it's kept other people out of science fiction and turned them onto fantasy."

Haldeman's own writing has been strong on science, written as factually and realistically as possible. He's one of the few newcomers of the 1970s to have truly established himself as a significant presence in the field. Following *The Forever War*, his novel *Mindbridge* was given best seller treatment in 1976; there was then a gap until the publication of *Worlds* in 1981. I ask him what happened during that time.

"I got very busy on a couple of books that turned out to be disasters. I guess everybody's career is cyclic. I had agreed to write two Star

Trek novels; I thought I could just gloss them, I figured they wouldn't take more than three or four months apiece. But I spent a whole year doing the two of them, and was not satisfied with either.

"I had *Worlds* started conceptually back when I was in Iowa, and had written a few pages here and there, but didn't feel like going for a whole trilogy. I wanted to get a financial base and free myself of all the other work. I finally wrote it in eleven months, which is the least time I've ever spent on a full-length novel. I think that was largely a reflection of relief at not doing any more purely commercial work.

"You have to understand, I don't really have career goals. I just want to make a living. I would like to be to science fiction, let's say, what Robert Heinlein was in the 1950s and 1960s. But there are strong negative aspects to being that well-known.

"It would be nice to have more financial security than I have, but I don't have any specific goals in that area, either.

"I've been lucky with my career, not having to go through a lot of poverty or a lot of real prostitution. Even the commercial work has always been some sort of a challenge or some sort of a lark.

"I always want simply to become better with each book. It seems to me that if I stated some ambition and actually held to it, then that would be limiting. I have projects planned five or ten years ahead, but I generally don't follow through, because by the time I've finished the current book, my ideas have changed.

"I'm not sure what I would have ended up doing, if I hadn't become a writer. I was getting disillusioned with the people in computer science. IBM gray suits and narrow ties—I didn't fit in there. I probably would have drifted into teaching." He grins, quietly, modestly. "I don't have a lot of ambition financially, so I probably would have wound up in some cow college."

In fact even now he does a little teaching on the side, at a weekly creative writing class. And since it happens that today is the day the class meets, he invites me along.

I sit in the back of a room full of serious college students, and I discover that Haldeman in public, talking to the class, is no different from Haldeman at home, talking to friends. No formalities; he sits there with his pipe, and his Budweiser, and tells them the qualities he feels are important in fiction. This is a topic, incidentally, that he has analyzed at greater length and depth than have most of his contemporaries.

Later, as his wife drives us home in their van after the class, I ask him how he manages always to take things so calmly.

"Drugs!" he jokes, gesturing with his pipe stem at another can of beer.

We laugh—but it turns out he's not entirely joking. As the van cruises on down the interstate highway, through the warm Florida night, Haldeman self-consciously explains that his tour of duty in Vietnam was not quite as uneventful as he had implied earlier. He was severely wounded by shrapnel and a .50 caliber machine-gun bullet. He spent six months in a hospital over there, and was awarded a Purple Heart. Today he seems fit, tanned, and healthy, but he's still classified as forty percent disabled, partly because of severed nerves. He's been on a succession of tranquilizers until quite recently. If he tries to take things easily and simply, this is his way of coping with, and allaying, his persistent anxieties.

I gather that he doesn't object to my mentioning this, because it's relevant to his whole writing career.

"I might never even have become a writer, without the intensity that the war gave me," he says quietly.

BIBLIOGRAPHICAL NOTES

Joe Haldeman's first science-fiction novel, *The Forever War* (1975), evolved from short stories of a space infantry whose time-dilated interstellar missions totally alienate them from their Earth origins. The book is notable for discreet satire of science-fictional cliches, and a post-1960s sexuality. It is rare as an example of high-tech military science fiction that has a left-wing bias.

Mindbridge (1976) tells basically a conventional space story, featuring aliens, telepathy, matter transmission, etc.; but uses a mosaic narrative incorporating multiple viewpoints and documentation in scrapbook form, in obvious homage to Dos Passos.

Worlds (1981) is the first volume of a trilogy featuring space colonists who have developed radically different sociopolitical systems partially facilitated by advanced biotechnology.

Joe Haldeman has in addition published several short story collections and two "Star Trek" novels.

PHOTO BY JAY KAY KLEIN

Fritz Leiber

People glance curiously at the elderly man sitting in the hotel lobby. It's not really his long, dense mane of white hair that attracts attention, or his determined frown, as if he's pondering some deep problem. It's more that he doesn't have a suntan and is wearing slightly shabby street clothes. What can someone like *that* be doing somewhere like *this*?

I'm still in Florida—Boca Raton, to be exact—at the annual Conference on the Fantastic in the Arts. Yes, science fiction and fantasy have become so academically respectable, these days, that there are honest-to-God deadly-serious scholarly *conferences* on the subject, at expensive hotels conveniently located in vacation resorts. English professors from all over America come here to read erudite papers to each other, on obscure topics like "Utopian and Dystopian elements in the Barsoom series of Edgar Rice Burroughs," or "Jungian Archetypes in Vargo Statten's Monthly Magazine." The professors' colleges pick up the tab for their travel expenses, of course, plus accommodation in this big hotel patronized mainly by middle-aged Florida vacationers.

Here come some of the vacationers now, moving aimlessly across the lobby, staring vaguely around them, the way vacationers do, in Florida. The men have white patent-leather shoes, beige jackets, and white shirts with collars opened outside their lapels. The women have white shoes, too, and white blouses, and beige skirts, and elaborate hair like mounds of Reddi-Whip. And they're all showing off wrinkled suntans and lots of gold: gold neck chains, jacket buttons, signet rings, bracelets, earrings, shoe buckles, purse fasteners. The vacationers promenade past the frowning elderly gentleman, and give him brief, puzzled looks—sensing he doesn't fit, somehow—as they head for the automatic doors out of the lobby (which, like them, is all beige and white). The doors slide aside like lock gates making way for an armada.

I notice, for the first time, that there is a full-size tree growing in the middle of the lobby. Florida is so full of the weird and the surreal, you stop seeing it after a while. For instance, in this hotel's "Gallery Cafe," the menus are pasted onto artists' palettes, and the waitresses all wear black berets, beatnik makeup, tiny black miniskirts, and black smocks; and no one gives them a second glance.

But the bushy-haired, elderly man, still sitting and frowning to himself, is another matter. Everyone notices him. Too pale to be a tourist, and he's over forty, so he can't be on the hotel staff, and he's not wearing horn-rimmed glasses or clean blue jeans or carrying a briefcase, so he can't be one of the academics. In fact, he must be the only person in this whole hotel who doesn't give a damn about his image.

But then, Fritz Leiber never has been one to worry about fitting in with everyday social customs and morality. As he tells me himself when I talk with him in his hotel room the next day, he's always been too naive to know the social and sexual rules.

Oddly enough, this is why Leiber's science fiction of the 1950s seemed so avant-garde and sophisticated for its period, tackling all kinds of sexual and political themes. He didn't know any better; he'd never learned to be repressed like the rest.

He receives me into his room, barefoot, dressed casually in a blue terry-cloth bathrobe. He's in his seventies now, and slightly stooped, and he moves more slowly than he used to; but he's writing as powerfully as he ever did. And he still talks in a beautiful window-rattling baritone that he inherited from his father, a Shakespearian actor who had his own touring company.

Leiber normally lives in San Francisco. He's here at this junket—I mean, this Conference on the Fantastic in the Arts—because they invited him as a guest of honor. All the more ironic, then, that he can sit in the lobby and attract puzzled glances from vacationers and academics alike, who fail to recognize him as one of the pioneers whose work created the field that made this whole conference possible.

Back when Fritz Leiber was earning half-a-cent a word writing for pulp magazines in the 1930s and 1940s, did he ever imagine such an exotic science-fiction social event?

"No, I didn't. And just last year, when the Science Fiction Writers of America had their Nebula Awards banquet at the Waldorf Astoria hotel in New York, I went there to get my award as Grand Master of Fantasy, and I was thinking, 'This is very high living *indeed*, for science-fiction writers!'" He chuckles.

Is he at all bitter over the long years in which it was hard to make a decent living writing science fiction and fantasy?

"Not really. Oh, in detail, I could complain or grieve over some of those early book contracts. For instance, the contract on *The Big Time* with Ace, which was written when Donald Wollheim was their science-fiction editor, entitled me to one cent per volume, in royalties, with no provision for an increase if the price of the book increased. Well, earning a penny a book was a reasonable amount when the book was being sold for thirty cents. But not when it's two dollars! Still, that contract has now been revised, twenty years later. And even when things were difficult at home, the money from translations helped out."

Personally, I suspect that Leiber has been overlooked in many places other than hotel lobbies; that his liberal attitudes placed him ahead of his time, and for years he was shunned, by some, as a result.

"As far as actions went, I was very inhibited. But my ideas about sexual morality very much derived from H. G. Wells and Bertrand Russell, so I early had just the simple attitude that sex was a good thing, and I didn't see why there should be all these taboos. It seemed that Puritan morality was just screwing people up. So I did take a very liberal attitude in my books and felt this was something to encourage. I wrote stories picturing communities in which there was free love, or complex marriage.

"The editor of *Galaxy* magazine, Horace Gold, used to say about one story of mine, 'Coming Attraction', that the readers complained it was un-American because it pictured America in a decadent state after an inconclusive atomic war with Russia. I think people were upset because I pictured a decadent America with motorcycle gangs—though this sort of thing existed, actually, and was in the public imagination at that time. The Marlon Brando movie, *The Wild One*, had already appeared. But combining that and the idea of male-female wrestling and so forth—it just had enough feeling of decadence to seem convincing as a sort of prediction of the way urban life was going in the United States."

Why were other writers so much more cautious about such themes? While Leiber was dealing with near-future decadence here on the earth, Asimov, Bradbury, and most other well-known names of the 1950s were keeping their robots and rockets as far away from serious issues as possible.

"Yes," Leiber says, agreeing but not really explaining. "I did stay closer to home most of the time. At least, the stories that annoyed people tended to be set closer to home. The story 'Poor Superman,' for instance, which pictured a sort of fucked-up America, described the government working with a fake computer, and pretending they'd sent spaceships to Mars, whereas they'd only been able to get as far as into orbit.

"You may remember, though, that by the time that period was ending, in the middle 1960s, the science-fiction community split up into two camps, of people who disapproved of American involvement in the Vietnam war—I don't think they went further than saying any more than that—and people who said we should fulfill our commitments to the government of South Vietnam. So some liberal spirit had developed in the field, by then.

"The only time I was ever politically active myself was in the 1960s, when it seemed very important to elect Lyndon B. Johnson, because it seemed important to stop Goldwater, who we felt was going to escalate the war in Vietnam. Of course, Lyndon Johnson did it just the same, so I became very disillusioned about that, and wrote my novel *A Specter Is Haunting Texas* to give expression to my feelings. That one time I got into politics, I was on the wrong side, or at least, that's the way it turned out. So I wasn't politically active again, after that."

Since Leiber has set some of his stories so close to everyday reality, does he feel frustrated never to have been published in the mainstream of literature?

"Not particularly. I've got more satisfaction, really, out of mixing categories. In *The Book of Fritz Leiber* and *The Second Book of Fritz Leiber*, which Ace have published, I was even able to mix nonfiction with the fiction."

So does he feel, now, that all his early ambitions have been fulfilled?

"At the very beginning of my working career, my father felt that I should become an actor. Until I was in my twenties the plan was that

I should act in his Shakespearian company.

"Then, during the Depression, he saw the writing on the wall and realized it wasn't going to be possible to do much on the stage, and so he shifted over into the movies just to have a way of earning a living for himself and his family, and I was left to my own devices.

"My first jobs were all in editorial work. I worked for an outfit called Consolidated Book Publishers, in Chicago, for about five years all told, and then I was an associate editor of *Science Digest* for about twelve years, before I became a full-time writer.

"When I got into writing, in the 1940s, there wasn't much prospect of book publication if you were writing science fiction—it was something you merely dreamed about. My first book, *Night's Black Agents*, was published by a small press, Arkham House, and the idea of making any sizable amount of money that way didn't seem very practical. The only income you could rely on was from selling stories to the magazines, until paperbacks came in at the end of World War II.

"My earliest stories were supernatural horror stories, to *Unknown Worlds*. The Fafhrd and Mouser stories. Heroic fantasy. You see, I liked science fiction, but I had trouble writing it, whereas supernatural horror provided a shock, a transgression against the laws of nature that could create a crisis important enough to write a story around. That was the way I approached it. It was a while before I found that similar shocks were possible with a science-fiction theme. My first science-fiction sale was the novel *Gather Darkness*, to *Astounding*, and that worked because it was about fake witchcraft that was powered by scientific miracles. I'd just read Heinlein's novel, *Sixth Column*, in which a whole new science of space, time, and energy was discovered by military scientists in America just after America had been conquered by an invasion from the Orient. That gave me the thought of basing the story on the same theme, but with the conflict between a science-powered religion and science-powered witchcraft. So I was able to get some of the effects of supernatural horror into a science-fiction plot.

"I kept on working for *Science Digest* magazine, while I was writing science fiction on the side, in Chicago, till 1956. That was when alcohol really climaxed as a problem for me. I was able to stop drinking afterward, but at the time, I had to quit my job, and since then I've made my living just as a writer.

"For almost the first ten years, it was a touch-and-go business. I mean, through the 1960s, I was just managing to scrape along. During that period I moved from Chicago to southern California, to be near my mother. My father had died back in 1949 but my mother survived him by about twenty-two years. My wife Jonquil and I lived with her or near her for that whole period.

"I was scraping along, you might say, on, oh, something around $5,000 or $6,000 a year income during that period. I sold the house that we lived in in Chicago, on the South Side, and that provided something in the neighborhood of $10,000, which we spent while I was eking out my new income.

"My writing has always gone by fits and starts. My wife Jonquil, to whom I'd been married for thirty-three years, died in the fall of 1969, and for the next three years I didn't do any writing, I went back to drinking, which had been a problem off and on throughout my life, and I pretty well held a three-year wake. We'd been living in Los Angeles, in Venice, on the beach, and I moved up to San Francisco and spent three years of almost medicinal drinking up there, just to tranquilize myself. I didn't get into any particular trouble, but I didn't attempt writing other than a few very short stories.

"Then I managed to pull out of that around October of 1972. Since then, some good things have happened—in the late 1960s the Fafhrd and Mouser stories finally got book publication, through Ace. Although they are now one of the commonly referred-to series, it wasn't easy to get them into paperback. But now all the stories have been rather carefully collected into chronological order for the series.

"I moved out of the small apartment I had had in San Francisco, and into a larger one, which I occupy still. I have a couple of friends close by, but I live pretty much alone now."

I ask what his next plans are.

"I've got to finish up enough material for another volume in the Fafhrd and Mouser series, and I do want to write another long Change Wars story, a sequel to *The Big Time* and *No Great Magic*. I have that story laid out, and it's sort of reassuring to me that I have, because I know I'll have something to do."

Does he line up a publisher before he writes a story or a novel?

"No, I'm very leery of selling anything in advance, getting money for a book before I've written it, because I don't feel certain of any particular project until the writing is actually finished. I've always tried to avoid working by that method.

"For instance, when I wrote *The Wanderer*, I didn't get any advances on that. I had had to put in about two years of work on the book. It was one of the first long science-fiction novels ever to be published. I remember Jim Blish had a lot of trouble with *A Case of Conscience* because Ballantine wouldn't let him make it any longer than 60,000 or 70,000 words, which was their standard length that every science-fiction book had to conform to, for economic reasons. *The Wanderer* was one of the first long science-fiction originals.

"Anyway, I'm just going to do stories for a while. I also have planned a supernatural horror story in the Lovecraftian tradition, called 'The Hurricane Horror.' It's a sequel to 'The Terror from the Depths,' that originally appeared in a collection called *The Disciples of Cthulu*, very much a Lovecraftian sort of endeavor.

"You know I actually had a correspondence with Lovecraft, for a few months before his death, and this was really my first contact with another writer. It gave me the feeling that writing was important work and worth careful effort. Lovecraft's enthusing over the samples of my writing that I showed him, a good two years before I managed to sell anything, was very encouraging. I wrote him that I was planning to do a novel set in Roman times, and he wrote me a couple of huge letters, giving me lists of books to use in getting background material, and taking it all so seriously.

"Meeting him through his letters that way gave the impression of a very well-balanced, extremely friendly, kindly person. I wrote him about how I very much enjoyed the books of Charles Fort, and he wrote back saying that they did contain interesting material for the writer of horror stories, but of course you had to completely reject them. He wrote from the point of view of the genuine scientist, explaining why this sort of anecdotal material, with observations that couldn't be repeated or verified, couldn't be made the basis of any refutation of science. He wrote as a defender of science and as a complete materialist.

"So you might say that the thing that made me accept Lovecraft at the intellectual level was that he was a scientist. He was definitely not a crackpot or an occultist in any way."

Leiber is one of the very few writers to have spanned all the imaginative categories, from genuine science fiction, through fantasy, to horror. I ask him why he likes horror stories.

"I'm not sure I *like* horror stories. I was able to write them at first, just because the structure was simpler. A supernatural horror story builds up to a frightening moment. You know that you're going to prepare a reader, and then try to scare him at one point in the story. So I knew what the writer's task was, whereas in science fiction the central point of the story was more elusive."

He was writing horror many years before its renaissance as a fashionable, big-selling category in the 1970s. Doesn't it seem a little unfair, somehow, that his work has never been as popular as books by newcomers such as Stephen King?

"Well, King worked terribly hard to establish a way of writing that would emotionally involve the reader. I associate him with John D. MacDonald, who wrote an introduction for King's collection of short stories, and said that things that go bump in the night were the least important part of Stephen King's work, and he expected King to end up writing stuff that would be considered mainstream. And it has sort of worked out that way."

Leiber says this without any rancor, as if he's perfectly happy with the way the world has treated him. He seems very philosophical—passive, even—as if he doesn't believe in fighting fate.

"Perhaps that's true," he agrees. "But you see I have the feeling that I can write exactly the sort of things I want to. I don't feel trammelled by the genres, really. Supernatural horror, and science fiction, and heroic fantasy, these are the things I want to write. And I can fit almost anything into these categories."

As I get ready to go, I ask him if he's been enjoying the academic conference.

"Oh yes. But what I've got to do is get back to San Francisco and concentrate on *writing fiction* again."

Which sounds, indeed, eminently sensible.

We too will transfer our attention to San Francisco now—to some of the other Dream Makers who make their homes in that part of the world.

BIBLIOGRAPHICAL NOTES

Fritz Leiber's large range and output make it hard to pick out highlights, but *The Wanderer* (1964) remains one of his most ambitious books, using multiple viewpoints in a fashion that anticipated subsequent disaster novels. It describes in detail the global chaos that results from a near miss between Earth and a wandering interstellar body.

In the science-fiction category, his *The Silver Eggheads* (1961) remains a classic of comedy and social satire, depicting a future in which writers have devolved to the role of "wordmill operators." Leiber is remembered more, however, for the "Change War" series, a maze of alternate worlds and time paradoxes; *The Big Time* (1961) is part of this sequence, which is otherwise composed of short stories, many of which are collected in *The Change War* (1978).

Leiber's fantasy writing has predominated since the late 1960s. His "Fafhrd and Mouser" stories have acquired a minor cult following, and continue to appear in paperback collections in the U.S. A good selection of his other short work, including pieces of nonfiction, appears in *The Book of Fritz Leiber* and *The Second Book of Fritz Leiber* (1974 and 1975).

PHOTO BY ROGER RESSMEYER

Robert Anton Wilson

It's 1968, and Robert Anton Wilson, self-described skeptic, is playing games with what he calls "absurdly ridiculous conspiracy theories." He links up with like-minded prankster-radicals and they plant all kinds of bogus scare stories in the American underground press, claiming that everyone from Richard Nixon to Lee Harvey Oswald belonged to the Bavarian Illuminati, an extinct secret society that Wilson and his friends "prove" is plotting to rule the world. Only the Discordians (another cult, invented by Wilson *et al.*) can save us.

Wilson and his friend Robert Shea use this and some even more paranoid possibilities when they write the crazed and self-satirical *Illuminatus!* trilogy, which quickly grows into a cult classic.

Years pass. Wilson digs deeper into conspiracy lore and the occult. He starts getting obsessed with all this weird stuff. He winds up reporting his researches in *Cosmic Trigger*, which some see as an extension of the *Illuminatus!* joke but others say is a serious testimonial.

Something is going on, Wilson claims in his introduction to that book. By "something" he's referring to psychic phenomena of all kinds, UFO sightings, von Danikenesque enigmas, visions, peculiar coincidences (which he prefers to call "synchronicity"), myths, magic, and mystery. Yes, he agrees, some reports may be faked, some reporters may be frauds, and some experiences may be delusions. *But not all.*

There is a hard core of data that cannot be explained away.

Well, many of us might go along with that. But there's more—such as Wilson's claim that in 1973 and 1974 he was quite probably "receiving telepathic messages from entities residing on a planet of the double star Sirius." Or his report that, after many hits of mescaline, he saw a little green man with pointy ears dancing in a corn field—one day *after* his last trip. Hallucination? Not necessarily, he claims. According to Carlos Castaneda, pointy-eared green men are well known to Mexican shamans as spirits of the peyote plant. Frequent peyote eaters may be attuning themselves to psychic signals from the vegetable kingdom. Or—the little fellow might have come out of a UFO. Or—he might be a manifestation of our collective unconscious, since by "a strange coincidence" (synchronicity!) pointy-eared persons appear in many myths of different cultures. Irish leprechauns, Peter Pan, Spock of Star Trek. . . .

Readers of Wilson's earlier work found all this hard to take seriously. After all, *Illuminatus!* had been one big belly-laugh.

But then Wilson went on to write *Masks of the Illuminati* and the *Schrodinger's Cat* trilogy, a mutant mix of quantum theory, UFOs, Crowleyesque magic, particle physics, hallucinogenic drugs, and cults of every description, downplaying the humorous content and inviting the reader to consider that some of these obsessions might be extremely meaningful.

Arriving at Robert Anton Wilson's home in San Francisco, I'm trying to keep all this in mind. I'm not sure what to expect; but I do know that this man must have a strong sense of the absurd.

He greets me at the door of his apartment, and I'm struck immediately by his lazy-lidded eyes. They look exactly like The-Eye-in-the-Pyramid—the symbol that crops up on Illuminati documents, dollar bills, and Wilson's own book covers. I feel as if I'm face to face with his own mythic lore, in his own corporeal self.

Then we sit down and start talking, and my second surprise is that I can find no sign—none at all!—of the humor in his books. On the contrary, he's deadly earnest about everything.

You're in San Francisco, now, Platt, I remind myself. The land of hot tubs, home-grown dope, and personal growth. People here believe all kinds of weird shit that folk back East would say is completely crazy.

Yes, but . . . telepathic messages from Sirius? "Are you sirius?" I ask him, trying to imitate the playful spirit of his earlier work.

He just stares at me.

A bad start, here. Minutes after unpacking my tape recorder, I seem to have alienated my interviewee by implying he's mentally unbalanced. I try to backtrack by mentioning the dedicated psychic researches that I have conducted myself over the years: The Hieronymus Machine that I built when I was fourteen, from plans published in *Astounding Science Fiction* magazine, in an (unproductive) attempt to tune in to the psychic continuum. The dowsing rods I constructed, to search (unsuccessfully) for drains in my best friend's back yard. The deck of Zener cards I made, to test (fruitlessly) for telepathy.

Wilson seems distinctly unimpressed. "People who reject the idea of telepathy remind me of creationists," he says flatly. "Creationists reject everything that orthodox science has discovered for the last 120 years. They claim it's all self-deception and juggling of the evidence. And skeptics use the same argument against parapsychology. I think the evidence for that, over the last hundred years or so, is good enough that the people who reject it must have simply made up their minds not to look at the data."

I object that the "data" he's talking about are seldom better than hearsay, that some scientists running supposedly tightly controlled experiments have subsequently discovered that they were fooled by frauds, and some famous psychics are known to have faked their results. Uri Geller, for example.

"I still regard the Geller case as a very open matter. I know people who worked with Geller who are convinced he's a fraud, and others who worked with him who are convinced that things happened which they couldn't account for.

"But where ESP is concerned, for me, it's not a matter of trying to judge which of the factions seems to have a better case. It's a matter of, either ESP exists, or I'm crazy. I'm not a professional psychic—I don't know when these things are going to happen to me. I just know they happen often enough that I've got to accept them."

Listening to this, I can't help wondering what Wilson thinks of a skeptic like Martin Gardner.

"People like Martin Gardner remind me of the holy inquisition in many respects. Take the case of Wilhelm Reich. When Gardner was busy attacking Reich, and then the government burned all of Reich's books in an incinerator, I was so young and naive then I was sure that Martin Gardner would come out with some kind of statement to the effect that 'I don't agree with Reich, but I didn't mean they should burn his books.'

"But he didn't. He was silent as a graveyard at midnight. Over the years I kept waiting for him to say something, and I finally came to the conclusion that having Reich's books burned was exactly what Gardner wanted. He certainly didn't object to it. That way of disposing of heresy seemed totally acceptable to him, as far as I can see.

"The well-documented conspiracy to intimidate publishers from printing Velikovsky's books is another example. I really think there is a holy inquisition mentality in that Martin Gardner, Carl Sagan faction. I don't believe we are living in a free scientific community."

But even if ESP exists, it seems so quixotic that, surely, there can't be any practical applications?

"I don't know what we're going to do with ESP; that remains to be seen. To me the chief interest in this whole area is that I've become convinced, over the years, that it is intimately connected with what Leary calls brain change and what is loosely called 'growth' in the consciousness movement. Oddly enough, Freud was the first to point that out in a book called *On the Uncanny*, in which he noted that experiences of this sort seemed to happen in therapy when a patient is on the verge of a major change in self-understanding.

"I think the best scientific model of the mind, so far, is the one given by the much-despised Dr. Leary. His eight circuits of the nervous system. You can take any moment of your life and examine it and decide which circuit you're on at that time. You can classify people by which circuit they prefer to be on most of the time."

I'm listening to him in his living room, in one of a cluster of modern, anonymous beige apartment buildings southwest of central San Francisco. The room is large, its wide windows overlooking a strip of dense dark-green woodland, beyond which lies the Pacific Ocean.

The decor is modern. There are framed pictures of Wilson's children; a giant poster of the integrated circuit chip from a KIM-1 microcomputer; a bronze Buddha; and a little collection of model pyramids ("People keep giving them to me," he explains, with a shrug).

I ask him if he always wanted to be a writer.

"When I was a child I wrote and drew comic books and distributed them to the kids in the neighborhood. I thought I would like to be a cartoonist when I grew up. Then—and this gives you an idea of how impoverished my background was—I discovered there were books without pictures in them! And I decided it would be easier to just write the stories without having to draw the pictures too!

"All through my teens I wanted to be a writer. I wrote several stories which all got rejected. Eventually I decided to become an engineer because I have a certain talent for mathematics. It took me a while to realize that I didn't really have the personality of an engineer. What I was looking for was something to support me so I could write at night.

"I went into advertising for two-and-a-half years. That was unrewarding. I worked on a couple of schlock tabloid newspapers, I worked on Ralph Ginsberg's *Fact* magazine, on *Home Furnishings Daily*, and a variety of other things. I was once an ambulance attendant; I once distributed samples door-to-door for Procter and Gamble.

"Ultimately I worked for *Playboy* magazine, editing their letters column. But I always had the idea that I would make it as a writer eventually. I got things published in weird places like *The Realist* or *The East Village Other*. But I couldn't hold it together to write a whole novel, because I was working eight hours a day and raising four kids. I didn't even have enough concentration to do short stories; all I did were articles, which were either scholarly or polemical or popularizations of science."

Then came *Illuminatus!*

"About a dozen of us started collaborating on this complicated prank. Someone found there were some right-wing cranks who believed that the Bavarian Illuminati still existed and were behind everything they disapproved of, from the anti-war movement to pornography to sex education to rock music.

"We started putting things in the underground press by various officers of the Illuminati, to give the right wing more to feed their paranoia. At one point after this joke had been going on a couple of years, Shea said, 'Why don't we write a novel about this?' And that's how it started.

"By and large the basic plot was Shea's and I did the digressions. But I also started adding things to the main line of the plot, as we went along.

"Shea and I submitted about seventy pages and got a contract. Then we wrote the whole book, which we finished in 1970. The editor was wildly enthusiastic, and shortly he got fired. It took a long time to establish communication with the new editor, who didn't know what the book was or where it was. He finally found the manuscript, and *he* got enthusiastic. Then he was either fired or quit, and they kept going that way—we went through five editors, and it took Dell five years to publish the books."

I ask if he was surprised at how successful the trilogy became.

"To be absolutely honest, I expected it to be more successful than it was. And I still do. I still think *Illuminatus!* hasn't reached its full potential yet. I feel that it could reach as big an audience as *Catch-22* did. It's that kind of book. It's a satirical comedy. I think promoting it as science fiction limited the audience; I never thought of it as science fiction until Dell promoted it that way.

"Personally, I feel that life doesn't fit any particular category of literature. Nobody lives in a gothic horror novel, and nobody lives in science fiction, or in a naturalistic Theodore Dreiser novel.

"So I try to mix different forms in my work. But of course, the publishers don't know how to deal with an approach like that, so they pin a label on it. *Masks of the Illuminati* they promoted as science fiction, though I don't see how you could possibly call it that. If you had to put a label on it, I should think it would be 'Detective Story.'

"As in my writing, I've always been ecumenical in my reading taste. I was reading science fiction as far back as I can remember, but I've also read a great deal of every other type of fiction, especially James Joyce and other experimental modern writers. Borges, Faulkner.

"I'm also a big fan of H. P. Lovecraft. And John Dickson Carr was one of my favorites for a long time. He frequently has several solutions to the crime; his books are playful intellectual riddles. That influenced me; I do the same thing in a lot of my books. There'll be an explanation, and then it falls apart and there's another explanation.

"What I'm *always* doing is trying to break down the one-model view of reality. Whatever the reader takes for granted is going to be knocked out fifty pages later, and, if they think they know what one book is saying, if they go on with the series they'll find it wasn't that simple after all."

This game-playing in his fiction reflects his belief that in real life there is no single reality, and no such thing as objectivity.

"One of the biggest influences on my way of looking at the world was Alfred Korzybski, the founder of General Semantics, who is regarded as a crank in many quarters. There were certainly defects in his system, but by and large I think it is something that everybody should grapple with. What he is saying is what modern physicists are dealing with all the time: You've got to recognize that every perception you have is a joint phenomenon of the world and your nervous system, and is therefore partially your creation. In physics, a more technical form of that is the Copenhagen Interpretation of Niels Bohr, which states that physics is not a model of the real world per se, but a model of how our mind makes models of the real world.

"You don't find physicists these days talking about 'the truth' at all. What they talk about is what model looks best right now. Models these days are changing so rapidly that any physicist I know—and I think this is also true outside California!—will say that there are several models that look good right now. They've always got at least three in their minds at once, and quite often five.

"I think General Semantics and ethno-methodology and comparative anthropology all indicate that we've got to think that way about everything, not just about the subatomic realm. Eskimos do not live in the same reality as New York cab drivers and Ohio farmers do not live in the same reality as Marin County cocaine-sniffing millionaires. Each person carries his own reality around with him wherever he goes.

"There are what I call reality streets, reality neighborhoods, nations, and so on. We can communicate with other people on our own reality street, but move a little further and the communication gets harder. If you sat down and had a conversation about basic philosophy with a Japanese businessman who does zen meditation every day, and a disciple of the Ayatollah Khomeini, and Jerry Falwell, you would find the problems of communication quite great. It's obvious they are not all living in the same reality."

Wilson expresses this relativism, in his books, by giving several different answers to any one problem, without saying which answer is the "right" one.

"Readers think I'm playing a joke on them and they write and ask which one is *really* true. I have to tell them, 'Look, I honestly don't know—do you think because I wrote a book I'm omniscient?' An awful lot of people think everything has a 'yes' or 'no' answer, and if you wrote a book you must know everything, and if I'm not telling them it must be because I'm deliberately being perverse."

He is quite firm, however, in one belief: that libertarianism is an answer to global problems.

"I believe that the greater the liberty of a society, the greater its wealth will be. As I see it, wealth is the alteration of the physical environment by intelligence, and the freer a society is, the less restrictions on inquiry and voluntary association there are, so the faster wealth increases.

"In the novel I'm working on right now, the Italian hero is in London in 1766, and he realizes that England is so much richer than Italy not because the English are smarter but because they don't have a holy inquisition. And if you look at the chemical elements, you'll find that twenty-two were discovered in the British Isles, and not one was ever discovered in Italy, which is just one way of measuring the influence of the inquisition.

"The last thirteen elements, incidentally, have all been discovered in California, and I don't think that's a coincidence, either. It shows that this is the freest part of the world right now, where the most creative energy is. The freer a community is, the richer we'll all be. The whole human race collectively."

I object that cooperation can be just as powerful a system as total independence, and there are some rigid or regimented societies where innovation in science and technology still flourishes. Japan is an obvious example.

"I admire what Japan is doing, yes. But you've got to look at it historically. Japan is a fantastically free society now compared to what it was before 1945. I think a great deal of energy has been unleashed by the comparative move forward toward freedom there. Just like England in the eighteenth century: you could hardly call it a free country by modern standards. People couldn't vote, illiterate peasants and children were dragged into the factories, the African slave trade was going on; and yet it had made such a *comparative* advance in freedom that inventiveness flourished. It became the center of the industrial revolution and the richest country in the world.

"I think anything that interferes with human freedom prevents the maximum success that we're capable of. We're capable of a world in which everybody is not only affluent but super-affluent. They can still make themselves miserable if they try hard enough, but it will require more effort than when most of them are starving, as is the situation at present.

"I'm a great advocate of space, and I'm assuming that we're going off the earth to get additional physical resources, but even without the expansion into space we could make enormous discoveries right on this planet. To take a wild example, in Heisenberg's uncertainty principle there's zero point energy, which some physicists regard as a mathematical convenience which happens to be in the equations, and others say is probably real. If it does exist, and we can tap it, it's been calculated we could get enough out of one cubic centimeter of vacuum to run all the factories on earth for the next fifteen million years."

Wilson himself is from Chicago, and spent a lot of his life working there or in New York City. However, he has become a confirmed Californian.

"I don't feel at all like a heretic here. Everybody I know has opinions no more remarkable than mine. Most of my friends are interested in longevity research and presume that there's going to be a major breakthrough in the near future; they're into space and computers; and a tremendous amount of conversation goes on about psychic experiences people have had, and their theories to explain it. People accept that these things are happening all the time, to them and everybody they know. The ones that I find congenial have a mocking satirical attitude toward professional occultists, cultists, and so on, and are all looking for scientific theories to account for these phenomena."

My own view is that the only people who believe in ESP are the ones who feel that they have experienced it personally. Their talk of tests and experiments is just a way to support the intuitive belief they have already reached. By contrast, people who have never experienced ESP will look at the very same tests and experiments and find them totally unconvincing. And I fall into that latter group.

But this either-or, true-or-false thinking is obviously out of place in Robert Anton Wilson's world. Not only does he think that we each live in a separate reality, but, as I understand it, he holds that different beliefs, from the different realities, can be equally valid. So there's not much point in arguing; as far as he's concerned, we're maybe *both* correct. Or, perhaps, it's a matter of "which model looks best right now."

As I get ready to leave, I apologize if my skeptical attitude has offended his mystical sensibilities.

"But you don't seem to realize," he says. "The last thing I am is a mystic. I started out as a skeptic, and compared with most of the people I know in San Francisco, I still *am* a skeptic."

Note: After I sent him this profile, Robert Anton Wilson sent me the following reply, which he asked me to publish:

"Nobody sounds more shifty than he who loudly asserts his honesty; and nobody appears more loony than the chap insisting that he is quite sane. Although I understand this semantic trap, and earned my Ph.D. in psychology for a dissertation on such communication jams, Mr. Platt has taught me that understanding these processes does not make one immune to them. When he arrived in my living room with his heavy cargo of prejudices—which the intelligent reader can perceive in his vocabulary ('cult,' 'cults,' 'obsessions,' 'weird shit,' 'cult' again, 'obsession' again)—I became trapped in the pointless game of defending my own rationality. Naturally, all the symptoms of irrationality appeared out of that defensiveness. Since that is a no-win game, I hereby surrender formally. I am indeed stark staring bonkers, the 'apartment building' where he interviewed me was actually a hospital for the agnostic, *Cosmic Trigger* says what he asserts that it says, anybody who thought parts of that book were playful or joking is as crazy as I am, my books are only funny when satirizing other people's dogmas and become unfunny when satirizing Mr. Platt's dogmas, there is no such place as California, and colorless green ideas sleep furiously. Furthermore, in the immortal words of Baron Frankenstein, 'Mad, am I? I'll show them all—'

"Robert Anton Wilson, State Home for the Hopelessly Perplexed."

BIBLIOGRAPHICAL NOTES

The *Illuminatus!* trilogy, written in collaboration with Robert Shea, was Wilson's first work that could be considered science fiction; and the label was probably placed by default, other categories being even less appropriate.

The conspiracy theory that is played with in *Illuminatus!* is documented, along with speculations on aspects of the paranormal, in Wilson's *Cosmic Trigger* (1977), a nonfiction account.

Masks of the Illuminati (1981) describes the long-drawn-out induction of a naive Edwardian gentleman into a psychic cult run by Aleister Crowley; James Joyce and Albert Einstein appear in cameos.

The *Schrodinger's Cat* trilogy takes the same mystical obsessions, plus sex, drugs, and rock 'n' roll, and links them with speculations about particle physics and quantum theory. These books can better be considered science fiction than Wilson's earlier work.

Poul Anderson

Interviewer: "Mr. Anderson, I'm beginning to get the impression that you try to see both sides of *every* question."

Anderson: "Well, yes and no. . . ."

Poul Anderson didn't say exactly that, but he came close. It's hard to exaggerate how careful and diplomatic he can be in an interview. Hesitating to commit himself to any strong viewpoint, sidestepping and backtracking, he reminds me, in a way, of Gerald Ford.

This isn't intended as a derogatory comparison, and I doubt if Anderson himself would take it that way. So far as I can see, Anderson in science fiction really does have some similarities to Ford in politics.

He's well-known not for spontaneous flashes of brilliance, not for impassioned statements, but for his solid, consistent hard work. He's a central figure, but not one of the names that everyone thinks of first, perhaps because he has an anonymous image and prefers a low profile. He's conservative, both politically and personally.

He was president for one year, of the Science Fiction Writers of America; he did the job in a characteristically methodical style, without fanfare or favoritism. He spoke hesitantly at meetings, as if he preferred private contemplation to public pronouncements.

"Give Poul a few drinks and he becomes a great raconteur," I've been told, but, alas, I haven't seen it happen. At gatherings of writers or science-fiction fans I've noticed him one step removed from the action, smiling politely but with a distant look in his eye, as if he has tuned out the chit-chat and is mentally computing orbital velocities or planetary mass in some story he's currently working on.

He certainly seems more comfortable with science than with strangers. Born in Pennsylvania in 1926, he originally planned, in fact, to be a scientist.

"My ambition was to be an astrophysicist, and any writing I would do would be on the side. I went to school in Minnesota, and majored in physics there.

"I'd been writing as a hobby, sold a few stories while in college, and then graduated with a bachelor's degree, at a time of recession. There were no positions available, and there was no more money left for me to continue school; so, being a bachelor who had not yet had a chance to develop expensive tastes, I thought I would support myself by writing while I looked around for a job. And somehow the 'while' got longer and longer.

"Later, when I thought the matter over, I realized that I would never have made a first-rate scientist in any case. For one thing, I don't have mathematical creativity. I can follow most mathematics well enough, but I don't do well at employing it myself. And just being a second-rate scientist did not seem very attractive."

We're talking in the home of Jim Benford, a physicist himself and brother of science-fiction writer and physicist Gregory Benford. Anderson has a rule against ever conducting interviews in his own home, so Jim, who lives nearby in the hills east of San Francisco, volunteered to host this event. He, myself, Poul Anderson, and his wife Karen sit in a circle in the Benford living room, looking vaguely self-conscious about the affair—Anderson most of all. I feel as if we all want to help him through the ordeal—but no one quite knows how.

Solid science has often been central to Anderson's work, so I stick with this topic and ask him if he's disappointed by weak science in modern science fiction.

"But I don't know if there ever *was* very much of what you could call true, hard science fiction," he says, very slowly, carefully, with long pauses between one word and the next. "There was always a lot of pseudoscience, gobbledygook. The sort of genuine science fiction that Greg Benford writes, for instance, never has been too common."

Still, I persist, many writers say it's harder to write scientifically accurate stories now, because the science itself is more complex.

"I wouldn't say it's more difficult," he objects, as if he's happier arguing a point than giving a straight opinion. "I don't think the present pace of scientific development creates a problem, per se, and anyway, scientific obsolescence seldom seems to prevent good stories from getting reprinted. For example, Heinlein's are still in print, in the wake of Viking and everything.

"I do wish there were more real hardcore science fiction on the Hal Clement or Greg Benford level, simply because I enjoy it. But there are, after all, a good many things other than science fiction to read. Good heavens, I've yet to read all the works of Aristotle."

In his own work, Anderson has often been described as "versatile," having written pure fantasy, highly technical science fiction, and historical sagas, in styles ranging from traditional action-packed adventure, to belly-laugh humor, to medieval-lyrical.

And yet where style is concerned he is more a master of imitation than innovation. He seems to have a long-standing love for pastiche, as if he's happier paying his respects to other stylists than striking out in a direction all his own. He's cautious and conservative, also, in his methods of storytelling.

As author of more than thirty novels and fifteen short-story collections, he's obviously a prolific writer. But when I mention this, once again he prefers to shrug the question off.

"People always call me prolific, but I never have been. I've simply been at it a long time, over a period of about thirty years. Spreading the work over that period, it's just not in the same league as, say, Robert Silverberg and Barry Malzberg, in their productive days." (These are, of course, the two most prolific writers in all of science fiction—not a very reasonable yardstick to use.)

Anderson keeps winning awards for his short stories, but remains most famous for some of his early novels, such as *Brain Wave*, in which the earth emerges from an interstellar force-field that has been keeping all living creatures much stupider than they otherwise would be. The intellectually elitist overtones have always had great appeal to a lot of science-fiction readers. I ask Anderson if they complain that his old stuff was better than his new stuff.

"They're more polite about it than that. The *implication* is that nothing since then has been as good. But they were younger then. If they read something like *Brain Wave* when it first came out, good heavens, that's nearly thirty years ago.

"I hope I've developed since then. In fact I no longer consider the production of my first several years readable. Fortunately the public of that time was a bit more tolerant.

"It's been said, and I think is true, that every writer worth his or her salt always hopes the best work is going to be the one currently under construction."

Which is . . . ?

"I've been interested off and on in the fact that if this industrial civilization of ours suffers a hiatus, we may never be able to rebuild it, not because the knowledge will be lacking but because we won't have the rich natural resources on which the first civilization was founded. For example, these days, when hematite is getting into short supply, we can mine taconite, but that takes a rather large industrial plant.

"My book is set in the far future when civilization has been partially rebuilt. The actual scientific knowledge is somewhat greater than we have now. In advanced parts of the world the technology is quite sophisticated. But for the most part people are making do with low energy and human resources. For example, there are very few aircraft, not because they can't build them but because the metals and the fuels are too expensive. On the other hand, there are extremely sophisticated sailing ships.

"A very few stories of mine have already been published, set in this future, but so far they have only concentrated on the Pacific basin."

What about some of his earlier series, such as the novels featuring interstellar trader Nicholas van Rijn? Has he stopped writing within that particular format?

"I have a feeling that the Nicholas van Rijn future history is mined out—or, to change the metaphor, tied up in knots of its own making. If you try to stay consistent, the more material you accumulate, the more restricted you get in what you can do later on."

Some readers have complained that the books in Anderson's various series have been published so erratically that it's extremely hard to tell which ones are part of what. Does he feel he was badly published?

"Well, I never set out to write some sort of Tolstoian epic from beginning to end with the Flandry and van Rijn books. I would write one whenever I had a good idea for it, and they would appear almost randomly. It's not like, say, Frank Herbert's *Dune* series, which was obviously conceived of as something to read straight through from beginning to end.

"As regards bad publishing practices, in those days there was a great deal of physically sleazy publication, copy editing that could most kindly be called random, and god-awful titles thrust onto books. Fortunately, that is fairly well behind us.

"However, the publishing industry is having other problems right now, and some of them are self-created. There's idiotic distribution, and increasingly idiotic management as the publishing houses become absorbed by these large conglomerates. You're familiar of course with the alarm over the current emphasis on the so-called blockbuster novels, and so on. I don't think that that will destroy the business, because there's always going to be a sufficient number of people who want something else, and I trust there will always be either some executives of large corporations or some entrepreneurs who will have the wit to provide it. It may not make a fortune, but it should be viable.

"As an example of bad distribution, science fiction is and for a long time has been very popular in college and university areas, but distributors never make any particular effort to make it available there. They distribute it randomly. It's only bookstores whose managers know what the situation is and put in special orders, that take advantage of this market. And thereby of course do a service to the reading public."

He pauses, perhaps wondering if he has Said Too Much or Gone Too Far.

"I'm not one to give you great thoughts about the publishing industry," he adds, backtracking carefully. "I'm really rather naive about it. I've told you practically everything I know," he adds, as if to make it clear that there's no point in my asking him any more questions about *that*.

However, he must be well aware of one recent development in science-fiction publishing: the growth of fantasy in the last ten years.

"I remember many years ago, when he was editing *Fantasy and Science Fiction*, Anthony Boucher remarked that, to judge by his mail, more of his readers preferred fantasy to science fiction, but they didn't know it. It's a question of definition."

Still, I persist, there are a lot of books actually labeled "fantasy" now. And, surely, they're becoming a bit repetitive.

"Of course, when any field becomes popular, you're going to get a great deal of routine work appearing. Personally, I'm delighted to see more fantasy being published. I like to read it. I like to write it, insofar as I like to write anything. In fact I might mention, when my current piece of work is finished, Karen and I have a fairly ambitious collaborative fantasy novel in mind.

"It is true that fantasy has to ignore the scientific and technological revolution going on around us. You *can* write a pure fantasy about, let's say, a computer. But if you really want to try to deal seriously in fictional terms with how it's going to affect people's everyday lives, you probably have to use the science-fiction form."

I ask him why in many of his fantasies and fringe science fiction he seems to have a fascination for feudal societies.

"I think it's a very interesting relationship on a number of counts. For one thing, it occurs again and again in history. In fact, in one story I went so far as to suggest that perhaps some kind of feudalism is what you might call the ground state of agricultural man, to which he always reverts, and any other form of civilization is unstable." He hesitates. "I'm not saying that's *necessarily* true," he adds carefully. "I just threw it out as a thought.

"Then also, of course, it gets you into some areas that I think are very basic and important, such as the relationship between master and man, if you will—leader and follower. What are the obligations on both sides? One thing that history makes pretty clear, for example, is that an aristocracy which ceases essentially to serve, and begins essentially just to exploit, signs its own death warrant. For example, I would say that the British aristocracy signed its own death warrant with the Enclosure Acts.

"There's also the interest of a highly structured society, which feudal ones tend to be. It's not a simple hierarchy; they're actually quite elaborate, frequently with a lot of picturesque details, which add color to the story. If nothing else, you can perhaps in a way bring in the feeling of tradition there, which tends to be lacking otherwise in science fiction. The societies depicted in science fiction stories usually seem to have no tradition."

Politically, Anderson has a reputation as being fairly far to the right, and has been called a reactionary.

"I've seen a lot of such remarks. My usual answer, if I'm challenged on it, is—just look at what I'm reacting against. But I don't think we want to get into political polemics, do we?" He looks hopefully at the rest of us in the room.

"I'd like to," I say quickly.

He looks glum. "Well—how should I put it without sounding too snobbish?—for at least a certain part of what's usually called Western civilization, the concept of individual liberty and of strictly limited government was one of the greatest advances ever made. I don't say it would necessarily work for all cultures, but for, let's say, at least most of Western Europe and a few other countries it's definitely proved itself, with all its drawbacks, to be materially the most productive and, what's really more important, it has given the individual more opportunity to realize his own potential or simply to enjoy his own life.

"So, in view of this, it distresses me to see the walls closing in." (I assume he is referring to the increasing regulatory role played by government in American society.) "I say this not so much on my own account," he adds. "Because I've had an extraordinarily good life. But I feel sorry for young people.

"I haven't given up all hope—I intend to go down fighting, or at least kicking and screaming. But the odds are certainly against us. The real danger is probably runaway inflation followed by a complete breakdown of the economy, which of course will lead people to scream for all sorts of emergency measures. It's happened again and again in other countries, you know, and I see no reason why we should be immune."

Does he see more individual liberty, with less government interference, as a real antidote?

"Oh, it would be, but of course even if you have an ideal solution, you can't get to it overnight. For instance, Social Security, in this country at least, is probably the largest fraud ever perpetrated; but too many people are dependent on it. We can't abolish it just overnight, even if it were politically possible. It would be a monstrous thing to do. We'd have to phase it out over a twenty-year period.

"I try not to preach in my fiction. I often say that if readers want sermons, they can go to church; all I really do is tell stories. But we all inevitably stand on one or another philosophical platform and speak from it, and this is bound to show to some extent.

"If I had to call myself something, it would be either a conservative libertarian or a libertarian conservative. But I prefer to avoid labels.

Basically, I feel that the concepts of liberty that were expressed in the eighteenth century by people like the Founding Fathers were actually the radically bold concepts from which people have been retreating ever since. And I don't believe that it's necessarily reactionary to say so."

BIBLIOGRAPHICAL NOTES

Poul Anderson has written a large number of books and stories that share various elements of a common future history. The van Rijn series describes the sometimes comic adventures of a colorful interstellar merchant prince; the Dominic Flandry sequence chronicles the exploits of a tough interstellar Terran agent in a decadent empire that is descended from the laissez-faire system of free trade that prevails in the van Rijn books. A complete listing of all the novels and stories is not possible here, but will be found in Nicholls and Clute's *The Encyclopedia of Science Fiction* (see the Bibliography at the end of *Dream Makers II*).

Of Anderson's non-series work, his early *Brain Wave* (1954) remains a classic, postulating the removal of a cosmic field that has repressed synapse speed and thus human and animal intelligence.

Three Hearts and Three Lions (1961), in which a 1940s earthman is translated into a fantasy universe, is noteworthy; *A Midsummer Tempest* (1974) is its lyrical sequel.

Other important works are *The High Crusade* (1960), in which medieval Britons seize an alien spaceship, and subsequently an alien empire; and *Tau Zero* (1970), one of the purest examples of technological science fiction relying heavily on relativity theory and astrophysics.

A new novel, *Orion Shall Rise*, is expected early in 1983.

Jack Vance

"Hello? This is Charles Platt, Mr. Vance. You remember, I wrote to you—"

"Charles who?"

"—about doing an interview, for *Dream Makers*."

"Dream what?" There's a trace of humor in his telephone voice, as if he knows perfectly well what I'm talking about but he feels like being playful—or awkward.

"You did write back to me and say it would be okay," I remind him.

"I did, did I?"

"Yes, and I'm in San Francisco now, and I'd like to drive out and interview you some time this week."

There's a pause. "Well, I tell you what. I'll give you ten minutes. From 11:42 to 11:52 tomorrow. How's that suit you? Eh?"

"I might need a *little* longer than ten minutes," I reply, playing it straight. "About an hour."

"An hour! Do you realize how much I value my time? Are you going to pay me for it?"

"Ha ha! No, actually, I'm not, Mr. Vance."

"Well, then, you'd better be a *really* interesting fellow. Otherwise I'll do what I do with other people who come up here and waste my time."

"Ha ha. What do you do with them, Mr. Vance?"
"Throw 'em out."

Driving up into the steep, wooded hills north of Oakland the next day, I replay this telephone conversation in my mind, feeling apprehensive about confronting this ogre—and irked, too, by the indignities that are sometimes heaped upon the heads of innocent interviewers.

The narrow road gets narrower, and steeper, and winds back and forth, and finally I find Jack Vance's house half hidden amid the tall trees. I park the car, and I get out, and an intimidating voice bellows down: "*Who's there*?"

But when I finally meet Vance, he shrugs off his irascible act and is very friendly. He dismisses the matter of the phone call. "I just like to tease people," he says, with a sly grin. "And you seemed like a pretty amiable fellow."

He's a brawny man in old jeans and a short-sleeved shirt, with an anchor tattooed on his forearm. He once worked as a sailor, and still looks the part. His wife brings out some pomegranate wine, and we sit together on a porch swing on his stone-paved patio, beside the house that he designed and built with the help of his son.

Jack Vance values his privacy. He won't have his picture taken, doesn't like being interviewed, and doesn't even socialize much with other writers. "Some of these are quite decent chaps," he admits, as he flicks through the pages of the first volume of *Dream Makers*, which I've brought along for him to inspect. "But others in here, who I won't name, are horses' asses. My God—is this the company in which I'm going to be placed?"

I ask him if his reclusiveness is a deliberate, conscious decision.

"Yes, deliberate. Naturally I have friends—Poul Anderson lives near here, and we are good friends—but professionally, I don't care to make my living through my personality."

And he avoids visiting publishers in New York.

"I bypass it. Detest the place. Don't even think about it. My part is to sit home and write, send out manuscripts, and then run down to the mailbox to see when the check arrives."

Despite this tendency to hide himself, he has become a much-admired science-fiction storyteller, known for "voluptuous prose and soaring imagination," as Robert Silverberg has put it; or, in the words of Norman Spinrad, "perhaps the premiere stylist . . . in terms of fusing prose, tone, viewpoint, content and mood into a seamless synergetic whole."

He shrugs. "It hasn't come easy. It's been a matter of plugging away, finding what I can do, and then trying to do it properly. I'm not one of these chaps who was an instant success. There was a long period in which I wrote a lot of junk, as an apprentice, learning my trade. I found out I was no good at gadget stories, or at least they were very boring to me, and I found out that I didn't enjoy writing whimsy, and I finally blundered into this thing which I keep on doing, which is essentially a history of the human future.

"I didn't start selling until kind of late in life. I was doing other things. Working, gadding about—I was a merchant seaman, a deck-hand. The only way I could get on a ship, with my bad eyesight, was to memorize the eye chart. See, every time you go on a ship, they'd parade you in front of doctors and have you read an eye chart. Luckily, they always used the same chart.

"I wrote while I was at sea. I did this so-called *Dying Earth* thing."

"Why 'so-called'?" I interrupt.

"It wasn't my title."

"What was your title?"

"Damned if I know." He chuckles. "Anyhow, I wrote that, sitting looking out over the water, and then I got tired of that particular life for various reasons. I met a friend of mine who'd become an apprentice carpenter; he said I should try it. Have to go to school for four years, but after that you'd usually get a job. I said, 'all right,' 'cause you gotta do something. I went down to the union hall, they asked me what size a saw-horse is, I held out my hands like so. They said, 'Why do you place studs sixteen inches apart?' and I said it was probably because plywood sheets are four feet wide. They asked me which end of a nail goes in the wood first, so I said, the sharp end is usual, in this case. Fine, they sent me out as a journeyman—full-time carpenter, forget the apprenticeship. I hardly knew which hand to hold the hammer in, lasted on the first job one hour, the second job two hours, finally learned the hard way.

"But I was still writing, and one of the worst stories I ever wrote I sold to Julian Blaustein in Hollywood; he saw a sentence in it that inspired him. Bought the story for what was then a lot of money, and so for a while I worked in Twentieth Century-Fox's West Coast studios. Then my producer got another job and I was fired, politely.

"So we went to Europe, stayed there nine, ten months. We toured England by bicycle. Came back penniless, to New York, where Scott Meredith, the literary agent, got me the job of writing Captain Video scripts. Worked on that for a while, then came back to California, to the mountains, and that's where I met Frank Herbert. He was working as a reporter on the Santa Rosa *Press Democrat*, and he came out to interview me.

"Three months later we drove down to Mexico with the Herberts and set up a writers' household in Chapala. We had a wonderful time, but the period was financially arid. We came back to California and the Herberts stayed on for a while longer. We found this place, and have lived here ever since, except for when we travel. On our last long trip, the three of us—Norma, our son John, and myself—took thirteen months to go around the world. We set up housekeeping at Madeira; at Fishoek, Durban, and Graff Reinet, in South Africa; a houseboat on Lake Nagin in Kashmir; and Hikkadua in Ceylon. And many other places for shorter periods. I wrote, Norma typed, and John studied his lessons.

"I write in longhand, Norma types it out, I go over that draft, she retypes—does all the real dirty work. She probably edits a little bit too, I guess. It's a very essential part of the process."

He talks in an offhand, earthy style, pausing now and then for a quiet chuckle. He seems to like telling anecdotes about his life and the manual labor he's done, but he avoids talking seriously about his books.

"It never occurs to me to even try to analyze my writing," he says. "I just write more or less what I think I would like to have read myself, at the age of sixteen or seventeen."

As a teenager, he studied to be a mining engineer, then decided it was "too damned dull" and majored in physics at the University of California, then decided physicists tended to be "single-minded, one-dimensional people" and became a journalism major, since he enjoyed working on the college newspaper. It's evident from this that he's an educated man; but he comes across more as a craftsman than an intellectual, so I ask if this means he has no time for academia or literary criticism.

"I don't have much respect for so-called intellectuals. I think to call somebody an intellectual is the same thing as calling him a fool or a blackguard." He pauses thoughtfully. "Critics are intellectuals. It's their role. They work with ideas, words, thoughts. Their tool is a pencil or a typewriter. I won't go into a long discursion on esthetics, but a critic—I won't say he's necessarily a deviant, or a criminal, or a disgusting person; he can be very nice, pet his cat, treat his wife nicely. Who knows? But still, to admit *that's* what you do for a living! It's like saying, 'I give sex shows down at the Burlesque for a living.' Something you'd have to blush to admit."

Does he feel this way because he receives negative criticism?

"No. I try to avoid it, certainly. But criticism simply doesn't interest me."

I mention that Don Herron, a critic who contributed to a symposium on Vance, deduced that Vance had been heavily influenced by the work of Clark Ashton Smith.

"That's true. Can't help it; Smith is one of the people I read when I was a kid. But it only influenced *The Dying Earth*.

"I was one of those precocious, highly intelligent kids, old beyond my years. I had lots of brothers and sisters, but I was isolated from them in a certain kind of way. I just read and read and read. One of the things I read was the old *Weird Tales* magazine, which published Clark Ashton Smith. He was one of the generative geniuses of fantasy. The others, Lovecraft for instance, were ridiculous. Lovecraft couldn't write his way out of a wet paper sack. Smith is a little clumsy at times, but at least his prose is always readable.

"When I wrote my first fantasies, I was no longer aware of Smith—it had sunk so far into my subconscious. But when it was pointed out to me, I could very readily see the influence."

I ask why he has never drawn directly on his global traveling experiences, to color his fiction.

"I do, more or less, on a subconscious level. And I wrote one murder mystery called *The Deadly Isles*, set in Tahiti, with a deep-sea sailboat, navigation, things like that. Also, a suspense-thriller, *The Man in the Iron Cage*, had a Moroccan locale.

"I particularly don't like these movies that call themselves science fiction, with a Star Trek type of spaceship and everybody in uniform—essentially all they are are navy ships, floating around in space, very boring and dull. When the time comes—if it ever does come—that we're traveling in space, the experience will be so different from the everyday. We've had just a little taste of it; what's going to happen eventually will obviously be much richer and more complex."

He takes another sip of pomegranate wine. "I'm talking a lot more *theoretically* than I enjoy talking," he complains. "Theoretically, or, what's the word? Didactically." As if he doesn't like being quizzed on his outlook and ideas.

I ask him if, similarly, he dislikes putting messages in his fiction.

"Well, I have done it a couple of times. There was one book that used a very simple fact, which everybody knows but doesn't want to admit. I have heard American Indians complaining about the wrongs done to them by the white man, who stole their land and so on. Which is true. But something which everybody knows is that the forebears of these Indians had stolen the land from some other Indians, and those had stolen the land from some earlier tribe, and the white man was just the latest tribe to come along and kick somebody off the land. No doubt some time in the future, *we'll* be kicked off.

"Same thing in England. Should we check out the Domesday Book, see who owned the land in A.D. 1000, and give it back to 'em on the theory that the Normans shouldn't have come there in 1066? In that case, you can think, well, the Saxons were kind of marauders themselves, so you can give the land back to the Britons. And so on.

"So the central idea of this thing was that there's no state in the world whose title does not derive from violence, which seems to be a harmless thing to point out, except that the word 'violence' is kind of like a red flag to many people. It made the peaceniks get very, very furious.

"In the other book I did, the theme was even less inflammatory, in fact it was so trivial as to be trite. Essentially, I said that socialism, the welfare state, is debilitating. That is such a trite thing to write a book about, that I'm ashamed of it, in a certain sense. But the idea of this very, very large welfare system carried to extremes had such grand possibilities for picturesque episodes that I decided to go ahead with it. And some British fellow, evidently left-wing in his political opinions, sent me this long analysis. He seized upon these two books to prove his theory that I'm from the extreme right wing. Which, of course, in my opinion, is *absurd*. I'm *nowhere*, not left or right or center of anything. I'm an *ad-hoc individual*."

This angry, emphatic refusal to be typecast as a member of a political group reminds me of his refusal to join in with the science-fiction crowd—or, for that matter, his large family, when he was a child. Preservation of his individuality seems very important to him; his fictional heroes likewise tend to rebel against becoming loyal members of any particular social unit.

I ask what he's working on now.

"A very long medieval fantasy. It's not sword-and-sorcery, although there are wizards and swords. This is quite different. It's romance. Trying to do something to sell to the general public, a broader audience. These particular situations and characters, I think, will have a wider appeal than some of the other stuff I've written.

"If it goes over well, I've got plans for another two or three more, for Berkley-Putnam.

"Also, one of my favorite books that I've written is *Eyes of the Overworld*—not my title, incidentally. I want to do a few more stories dealing with that same protagonist, to make up a second volume there."

I ask how many books he writes each year.

"I don't keep track. I don't like to think about it. I don't do enough; I waste too much time."

This sounds like a self-imposed work ethic.

"Uh... yeah, in a way. Life is too short not to get as much into your life as you possibly can. That doesn't just include work; that includes exerting yourself to have various experiences. For instance, Johnny and I are getting our boat ready to sail down to the South Pacific. We've got a forty-five-foot ketch, a sea boat, in fact we should be at sea right now, except for, oh, money problems. But we probably will sail to the Hawaiian islands, or down to Mexico, next year."

At this point, Vance's wife comes out and tells us lunch is ready. "All right," he says, pulling out of his relaxed mood and remembering to be grouchy again. He turns to me. "Have I disemboweled myself sufficiently for you? You see, I'm not a recluse. I just keep myself reclusive in a certain sense here, because I don't want to be associated with the goddamn science-fiction field. Myself; that's all I want to be. Just me. I don't want to be lumped in with this person and that person.

In fact, I don't like even being in your wretched book! For all I know, you'll put me in face-to-face with some fellow I don't approve of at all." He chuckles, a little bit playfully—but only a little.

Note: Portions of this profile were rewritten by Mr. Vance.

BIBLIOGRAPHICAL NOTES

Jack Vance is still known for his first book, *The Dying Earth* (1950), a collection of six highly colorful stories set in our planet's most distant future.

Subsequently he has written more about exotic cultures on worlds very remote in space and time, with a flavor of the fantastic, if not of fantasy. Science is loosely invoked to justify strange life forms, as in his popular *The Dragon Masters* (1963). Three other popular titles have been *To Live Forever* (1956), *The Blue World* (1966), and *Emphyrio* (1969).

He is now under contract with Timescape Books to write two more novels sharing the Dying Earth scenario: one, a sequel to *The Eyes of the Overworld* (1966), will detail further adventures of Cugel the Clever, who Vance says is his favorite character.

His connected novels include the "Demon Prince" series, comprised of *The Star King* (1964), *The Killing Machine* (1964), *The Palace of Love* (1967), *The Face* (1979), and *The Book of Dreams* (1981).

His short fiction has been collected in *The Best of Jack Vance* (1976), including commentary by the author.

PHOTO BY MARC ZICREE

Theodore Sturgeon

The glass towers of downtown Los Angeles stand less than a mile away, hazy in the smog, but this little back street of Spanish-style houses is a backwater untouched by time. I climb some steps, pass through an archway, penetrate a tunnel of unkempt semi-tropical foliage, and emerge in a small courtyard. Old-fashioned, three-story apartment buildings stand on either side, their sandy-brown walls half hidden behind cacti, shrubs, and palms. Insects buzz and hum in the hot morning sun.

I locate a tiny door into the basement of one of the buildings. The door is no more than four feet high—as if built for children, or gnomes. There's no name, and no bell. I knock.

The door opens and a gaunt, pale, gray-bearded figure squints up into the harsh light of day. He reaches for my hand and draws me down the steps into his subterranean refuge. I have to bend double to squeeze through the doorway; and then I find myself in a tiny cluttered place barely bigger than an elevator. "Sit down," says Theodore Sturgeon, watching me steadily with his pale blue eyes, "and make yourself at home." He smiles a secret smile as he closes the door, cutting off the daylight.

A water bed takes up more than half the space in this cubicle. A ventilation fan hums steadily. The one tiny window is heavily curtained; a metal-shaded desk lamp sheds dim yellow light; boxes of books are piled in the corner, in the shadows. A doorway leads through to a tiny toilet and metal shower stall to the left, and a miniature kitchen to the right.

There's hardly room to turn around; I feel like Alice in Wonderland, a giant in a shrinking house. Sturgeon describes it as his "crash pad"—one of three dwellings he maintains on the West Coast. Some would probably classify it as fit for monks or prisoners in solitary confinement, but he seems to enjoy it—perhaps because it embodies some of the virtues he values most. It makes do with less, it's home-renovated, and it's quite eccentric.

While I set up my tape recorder, he tells me how little he had to pay to make this dwelling habitable. The water bed was a mere fifty dollars. His work-table was improvised from salvaged wood and packing crates. The carpet was found on the street. The paint for walls and ceiling was ninety-nine cents for one gallon, because the color had been discontinued. Halfway through the paint job, he realized he hadn't bought enough, so he had to dilute what was left with white. It still wasn't enough, so he had to dilute it again, and so the ceiling fades from beige at one side to off-white at the other—"Do you realize how much you'd have to pay an interior decorator, to get that kind of effect?" he asks me, surveying his handiwork with obvious pride.

He lights his pipe, explaining that he only smokes because it induces vasoconstriction—shrinking of the blood vessels, which, he says, alleviates his low blood pressure and enables him to think better. He goes on into some of his other theories about health, involving herbal remedies, spices, vegetarianism, and vitamins. And then, on another tangent, he mentions a gadget he made recently, to hold a book with its pages open, so he can read without suffering from tired arms. The gadget consists of a piece of coat hanger and a couple of paper clips. He shows it to me. "Do you realize how little that cost to make?" he says, amazed by his own ingenuity.

I realize that I am not, after all, in Wonderland. This must be Looking Glass Land, because the man sitting opposite me, watching me with those strangely steady, pale blue eyes, can be none other than the White Knight. At any moment, he will demonstrate an upside-down cookie box that keeps the rain out.

I don't mean to make fun. It simply seems that Theodore Sturgeon loves being an eccentric, and delights in his nonconformist ideas, any one of which he can justify with impeccable logic. It's all part of the rich (albeit recycled) tapestry of a life full of fantasy.

Since he seems to avoid the obvious and orthodox, I ask him if he could be described as an unreformed radical.

"Radical? Perhaps, in a way—in my refusal to accept certain things. Most people are constantly in the habit of accepting things which are totally nonsensical. For instance, until recently, when an airplane was flying across the state of Kansas, they couldn't serve drinks. Did you know this was the last touch of the Ptolemaic universe in the law? Because it had to do with a static earth with a sun that traveled around it. You could logically own land from the center of the earth to the zenith.

"We're surrounded by this kind of thing. People obey laws which have no real rationale behind them; or customs, or so-called morality. But morality is just the leftovers from ethical thinkers. There's a very important distinction between morals and ethics. Ethics are really species-survival oriented. But morality is a static thing. When an ethical thinker comes up with something new, they usually crucify him or cut his head off or crush him under a stone or evict him. But ultimately the idea survives and it trickles down into the morality, which gradually absorbs it. And most of our moral structure has come to be that way.

"We're constantly faced with things that simply don't make any sense. And we don't sharpen our tools and our lenses and what-not to observe these things. And I *do*. And it's gotten me into some very interesting trouble—and I wouldn't have missed a minute of it."

He speaks softly, gently, persistently, in a lulling rhythm. He pauses and smiles, still watching me intently, as if trying to discern whether I'm with him—whether he's dealing with a kindred spirit.

I say that he seems to be describing a world in which a few enlightened individuals perceive things more clearly than large conformist groups. Does he see life in terms of us-versus-them?

"No! I do my best never to think in those terms. I don't think I'm special, by blood or by. . . . I do have a talent. A huge talent. But that's like a guy I knew one time who was six-feet-four and weighed 230 pounds. If it was convenient for him, he'd crook his elbow and rip his shirt up the back. But he had nothing to brag about, he didn't do a *thing* to get that way. Talent is just the same, like eye color, or anything else that's given to you.

"My feeling about 'us and them' is: When you come right down to human nature, if you get an ardent Russian communist and a real right-wing American, and they're both in agriculture, and you dump them together, I doubt they're going to get into a political dialogue. They're going to talk about seed corn.

"I'll never forget what one of the astronauts said, when they looked down from 163 miles: 'I don't see any lines.' I love that. 'I don't see any lines.' People are people.

"I'm not a joiner. I belong to very few organizations. Politically, I usually vote for what seems to be more or less liberal; I voted Libertarian last time, and before that I voted Peace-and-Freedom. Libertarian, at the moment, feels more like home to me than anything else.

"I have a certain amount of scorn for people who don't vote and then complain about what the government does to them. You realize Ronald Reagan was elected by twenty-two percent of the registered voters in the United States? And then you get the screaming and hollering that's going on now.

"My favorite all-purpose bumper sticker is, 'Keep the Faith and Reelect Nobody.' You like that? Hm? I think that is an operating political principle. It's right in line with my feeling that the entire universe is in flux, and we ought to be, too. Build nothing that we can consider permanent. Long-lasting? Sure. Solid? I agree. Forever? No."

I interrupt his flow of axioms and epigrams to suggest that, even if he's unsure about the term "radical," he could still be called rebellious.

"Yes. That's true. I have a right to my own life-style, and I don't like yahoos coming along to correct me. I happen to be of a nudist persuasion, and I don't wear clothes unless I have to. The one thing that really bugs me the most is if somebody knocks on the door, and it's a stranger, then I have to go put some pants on before I open the door. The essence of that is that I am being forced to obey somebody else's rules on my own turf.

"I do insist on my own life-style, and I like to protect my own way of thinking. At the same time, I constantly attack the stasis that overcomes people. You know, when someone says, 'Uh-uh, I don't want to hear that, I don't want to know that.' Well, that person just died. You've noticed the symbol that I use on all my correspondence?" (It looks like a Q with its tail elongated into an arrow.) "It means *ask the next question*. I counsel people to do that, because the moment they stop doing that, they die, and then they walk around with all the millions of other zombies you see walking down the street, who just don't care anymore."

I manage to interrupt to inquire whether I may, in fact, ask the next question.

He smiles self-deprecatingly. "Of course, go ahead. I tend to ramble on, I know."

I mention another personality trait that I sense in his work: an almost paradoxical mix of grim visions and lyrical sentimentality.

"I am a highly tactile person. And I'm a lover, I believe in that. You mention the word 'sentimental'; this is a pejorative in England, among English critics particularly."

I try to object that, although originally British myself, I didn't mean "sentimental" as a put-down. But he continues:

"Expressions of sex and love embarrass the British very much. They take refuge in words like 'mawkish'—I've had that used against me, and I can't even define it. I think it essentially means feelings of love, which embarrass them. But love does not embarrass *me*, and it never has. James Blish once wrote an appreciation of my work in which he said that many writers are afraid to say certain things 'in case momma might see,' but Sturgeon apparently doesn't give a damn. And that's true. That is why I don't, for example, hide my association with *Hustler* magazine." (At the time of this interview, he is writing a regular review column for *Hustler*.) "I admire Larry Flynt. He is honest and he is devoted and he has absolutely no tolerance for sticky-fingered politicians and blue-nosed moralists—like the right-to-life people, for example who want the state to move in and protect any conceivable speck of life, even though the state then puts a number on this speck of life when it is 18 years old and sends it out to get its head blown off. This is the kind of inconsistency which I insist on fighting, and Larry Flynt feels much the same way. His magazine is vulgar and gross, but he does not like people who beat on women, or people who beat on children, and as far as kiddie-porn is concerned, he has no patience with it. Well, he'll hint at it, maybe, and it will sell magazines, but his own convictions are totally, strongly against that kind of thing."

Interesting. But I would like to talk more about Theodore Sturgeon's fiction—and science fiction in general.

Of course, he's happy to do so; happy to talk on any topic. I begin to feel as if he has anecdotes at hand for every possible occasion.

"As far as science fiction is concerned," he tells me, "I want to proclaim my everlasting love and devotion to it, because outside of poetry it is the only form of literature which has no parameters whatsoever. There's no ceiling, there's no fence, there's no horizon, you can go anywhere. I refuse to let any definitions of science fiction limit me, because I have my own definition of science, which derives from *scientia*, which is the Latin word that means knowledge. To me, science fiction is *knowledge fiction*, and it's knowledge not only of physical and chemical laws but also the quasi- and soft sciences, and also matters of the human heart and mind. This is all knowledge, and so to me it's all legitimate science fiction.

"You know, one of the most exciting things I've ever thought of in my life is that someday there'll be a generation ship [a starship that takes several generations to reach its destination] and on that ship, by statistical necessity, there will be a science-fiction writer. What will he be writing about? What *will* he be writing about! I think science fiction is the cutting edge of the human psyche. Isaac Asimov once said that there are only three basic science fiction stories: *What if?* and *If only!* and *If this goes on*. . .I truly believe that.

"It is also what I call the 'pigs with wings' form of fiction. We know perfectly well that pigs don't have wings, and probably can't, but we can *conceive* of them, and the fact that we can conceive of absolute impossibilities, and even construct whole narratives around them, is a very special thing that I think our species has."

But to turn from the general to the specific for a moment: Are there any trends in modern science fiction that Sturgeon dislikes or disapproves of?

"The proliferation of series, right now, saddens me a lot. It's a nice comfy thing for a writer to fall into a contract which will guarantee for sure he's going to be able to sell four books. But I think that in itself is pretty sad. After all, where is the real importance in science fiction? It's always in people who *break* the trends. Ray Bradbury wrote Ray Bradbury right from the beginning, when nobody was about to buy things like that. He would not—and could not, I think—write what other people wrote. He wrote Bradbury until ultimately the markets opened up for this snowstorm of manuscripts, and let him in.

"I was just sent a huge book from one of the universities, for my comments. And I'm sending it back, refusing to comment. Article after article, essay after essay, each striving to be the one which comes up with the ideal cubbyhole in which to put a particular kind of thinking. I find it insupportable. There are too many people in the world—and most of them seem to be in academia—who feel that an application of the handles is an understanding of what you are handling. And it isn't. It is not. Nobody alive now seems capable of reading a novel by simply sidling up to it, and saying, 'Hey, tell me a story.' No, they have to put a label on it. They want to know if it's a mystery, science fiction, romance, or what. *What's it about*? And to find out, they read the book jackets, which are generally written by people who haven't read the books properly anyhow, and give away part of the plot. The author who structures his book very carefully and takes trouble to place all his surprises, has his surprises taken away from him. What use is fiction without surprises?

"For years I have avoided any book that has the word 'sword' in its title. What gets me about sword-and-sorcery fiction is that there is a very basic lack of surprise in these stories. I don't care how exciting and bloody they get; the hero always wins. He may get limbs lopped off, but he will always win in the end, and I prefer the kind of suspense where you cannot be sure whether he is going to survive."

As regards Sturgeon's own work, we've seen little from him in the last decade, although he continues to publish short stories and reviews, from *Omni* to *The Los Angeles Times*. I ask if readers and critics still typecast him as the man who once wrote *More Than Human*.

"You get that all the time. My first story was sold forty-three years ago; but some of my recent work has been very much appreciated. 'Slow Sculpture' won both the Hugo and the Nebula awards," he reminds me.

"Of course, *More Than Human* still goes on. It's now under film option from Robert Gordon, a film editor, who edited *Blue Lagoon*, which might have been a stupid picture, but was a beautiful one. So we may also end up with a stupid picture, but I guarantee it's going to be a beautiful one.

"At the moment, Jayne [his wife] and I have been asked to write a sequel to *Alien*. We have a marvelous plot for it. I am at the moment doing a narrative for the most expensive and elaborate Laserium show ever. Laserium is an unforgettable experience. Have you ever seen it? Almost beyond description! This will be syndicated all over the United States and probably Europe as well."

And he says he is still working on his epic novel, *Godbody*, which has been in progress for ten years but which he cares about too much to finish by a specific deadline. In addition, he has contracted to write an entirely separate new science-fiction novel, *Star Anguish*.

Of course, life wasn't always quite like this.

"In order to stay alive, I have done all kinds of different things. I'm a very skilled short-order cook, for example. I'm a class A heavy equipment operator—I can run anything with tracks or a boom on it. I have five ratings in the Merchant Marine. I play enough guitar to do three-chord work in a bluegrass band. And I trained as a circus performer. When I was twelve, in high school, I was the original ninety-seven-pound weakling, the brunt of all kinds of bullies. Within one year I gained about sixty pounds and grew about four inches, became fascinated by gymnastics, and ended up with an A.A.U. title on the horizontal bar and a free scholarship to the most advanced gymnastic organization in the city, and I was going to be a flyer at Barnum and Bailey. Writing was the last thing in my mind.

"Then one fine day I woke up with a 105-degree fever. My stepfather would not permit me to be sick, so I dragged myself to school. Same thing on the second day. On the third day I couldn't get out of bed at all. I had acute rheumatic fever, and a sixteen percent enlargement of the heart, every joint in my body hurt, and my brains were fried by holding that high a fever for so long. This was 1934, so there were no miracle drugs, just aspirin and bed rest.

"After four months in bed I was able to walk, but that was the end of gymnastics for me. However, within six months I passed a physical examination for nautical school.

"I learned something there that I will never forget: that people in authority will purposely amuse themselves by hurting others. I mean, standing at attention with a piece of rock salt in your mouth until you collapse; stuff like that. I took absolutely all that was coming to me as a fourth-classman, moved into third class, and then ran away—I was not going to quit under fire.

"On the basis of having been a cadet, I had no problem getting seaman's papers, and that's when I took off on merchant ships.

"In 1939, I was in the merchant marine, and by then slogging away at trying to become a writer. We docked in New York and there was mail waiting for me—a letter of acceptance for a story I had sent to a newspaper syndicate. Not a science-fiction story. I was so excited, I quit my job and went ashore.

"They paid me five dollars for this story. For the next four-and-a-half months I wrote for that news syndicate, and they would buy no more than one or two stories a week, so I made five and sometimes ten dollars a week. Now, my room cost me seven, and any money that I could save, I could use to eat. Have you ever noticed that pound cake has no crusts? Well, what do you think happens to the crusts? At that time, Cushman's Bakery used to sell a shopping bag full for a nickel. That's one of the things I survived on.

"My room was on Sixty-third Street, where Lincoln Center is now. My brother lived in Brooklyn, and I used to go and see him—walk all the way, downtown and across the Brooklyn Bridge. Subways then were a nickel, so I'm telling you what I learned about saving money in those days.

"But then somebody showed me the first issue of *Unknown*, and I was just thrilled. I ended up selling so much to John W. Campbell that at one time I had four of my stories in his two magazines. This is why I used pseudonyms at that time: one was E. Waldo Hunter, and the other was E. Hunter Waldo, because Campbell remembered it wrongly from the time he'd used it before.

"He was the strongest influence on my writing, my best friend and my worst enemy, in that he kept me in science fiction when this category was indeed a ghetto, and it was very hard for me to get decent attention from any serious critic.

"Then later I suffered writer's blocks; I wrote nothing between 1940 and 1946 except "Killdozer." I had a wife and two kids at the time, and things got very tough, very hard indeed. Later, when I married Marion, and we had four children, things got terribly hard, and I finally had a major breakdown in 1965. I almost didn't make it that time.

"But things have been much better since then. Recently I feel I've paid my dues and it's all coming back to me now. One of the most important things that has happened to me, as far as my head is concerned, is est training. I went through est in October of 1979. It's a hugely effective course, it is not what people think it is, it is not fascistic. I'm seriously considering going back and taking it again, now that I have a little more consciousness of what it's all about."

He pauses, finally. It's almost mid-day, which was our agreed cut-off time for the interview. Throughout the past ninety minutes, Theodore Sturgeon has maintained his intense focus on me, while talking in his gentle, persistent rhythm. At first, I thought he was watching to discern whether I was sympatico. But I think it meant more than that. His epigrams and axioms seem like phrases from a manifesto, outlining a whole belief system—a system that Sturgeon seems to be offering as an invitation, for those willing to shed the conformist preconceptions of the straight world, and join him.

If this is the case, I suppose I haven't been a very cooperative subject. I've maintained an interviewer's detachment, neither agreeing nor disagreeing with him. And so as I leave his little hideaway, I have the odd feeling that I've just rejected a gentle but persuasive invitation to some sort of philosophical communion.

BIBLIOGRAPHICAL NOTES

Theodore Sturgeon has always been primarily a short story writer, the bulk of his well-known work appearing in the 1950s. *More Than Human* (1953), an assemblage of stories and connecting material, continues to remain his most famous book. It chronicles the coming together of six physical and mental freaks, each with a different paranormal faculty; together, they form a super-powered group mind.

Sturgeon's stories are frequently lyrical, dwelling on love as a motivating force, and he was to some extent a pioneer of sexual themes in the 1950s, as in "The World Well Lost" (1953), a story of homosexual aliens whose deviance has resulted in their being exiled from their culture.

Venus Plus X (1960), one of his few novels, postulates a utopia resulting from transcendance of stereotypical sex roles and the divisiveness that they induce.

There have been many collections of Sturgeon's stories, including *The Worlds of Theodore Sturgeon* (1972) and *The Stars Are the Styx* (1979). Forthcoming is a new collection, *Slow Sculpture*.

L. Ron Hubbard

Some of my more paranoid friends warned me not to try to interview L. Ron Hubbard. They said I'd get my name on "the Scientology hit list," and I'd be the target of mind-games and covert investigations.

They told me that an interview was impossible, anyway, because L. Ron Hubbard lives in perpetual retreat on a huge yacht cruising the Mediterranean, protected by an entourage of fanatical disciples in Scientology—the global religion of which he is the founder.

Of course, I said I was far too sensible to pay attention to wild rumors and hearsay. But as I subsequently became tangled in a tantalizing correspondence with Mr. Hubbard's various officers and agents, I couldn't help wondering if I was acting like some "Skeptical Investigator" in a ghost story—the kind of character who laughs at doomsayers warning him to stop before he rouses the Wrath of Hbbrdu with his reckless investigations. "Heck, I don't believe any of that foolishness," he scoffs. "Why, that's just a lot of—Aaaarrrgghhh!"

And the wise ones shake their heads and say, "We tried to tell him, but he *just wouldn't listen*."

Forgive me for running off into fantasy. It's hard not to; because the life of L. Ron Hubbard is the stuff of which myths are made.

As a teenager, he traveled through the Far East. A member of the Explorers Club, he was awarded three Explorers Flags. He became a pilot, proficient in both powered flight and gliders, in which he set records for time aloft. His real career, of course, was as a writer: He wrote screenplays for Hollywood, and he wrote prodigiously for American short story magazines of the 1930s and 1940s. Much of his work appeared under pseudonyms, much of it was adventure fiction, and some of it was science fiction. His writing was fluent and dramatic, sometimes laconically humorous, and always highly imaginative.

But he stopped publishing fiction in the 1950s. On the basis of some private research he founded Dianetics, the "modern science of mental health," and opened training centers across the U.S. Many of the centers failed when the organization expanded faster than its capital would allow, but Mr. Hubbard regrouped, returned, and became the central figure in the Church of Scientology, which he built into an international organization. It now claims more than a million members, who regard him as a great spiritual leader.

This is all I can tell you about Scientology, because it's all I know. And Scientology is not what concerns us here, anyway.

What interests me is that, thirty years after he left science fiction, Mr. Hubbard has now returned to it. His 430,000-word novel *Battlefield Earth* was published in the fall of 1982, and is just as vigorous and dramatic as the writing of his youth.

In his introduction to this epic he says that he found himself with time on his hands, so he decided to write a novel. Clearly, he didn't do it for the money; I'm told he was a millionaire even before he started Scientology. Perhaps he was lured by the challenge of writing a science-fiction best seller, on a scale equal to that of his old contemporary Robert Heinlein. Or perhaps he simply couldn't resist marking the fiftieth anniversary of the start of his career as a writer.

My quest for an interview, to answer questions like these, was long and full of mystery—though I was never quite sure how much of the mystery was in my own head. I began by writing to one of L. Ron Hubbard's literary agents, Forrest J. Ackerman. Ackerman seemed miffed that I didn't want to interview *him*, but he said my request to interview Hubbard had been forwarded—though he didn't specify where. I began to get the impression that people associated with Mr. Hubbard were careful never to state in writing that they had sent something to him or received something from him. Maybe it was just an accident of phrasing; but it fascinated me.

Within a few days I received a letter from Wally Burgess, the International Director at Hubbard's Office of Public Affairs in Florida. I liked the letterhead—L. Ron Hubbard's name was embossed in gold foil at the top, just like the cover of a best-selling novel. Not exactly subtle . . . but impressive!

Burgess said he could put me in touch with a Hubbard bibliophile; not with Mr. Hubbard. I wrote back again and repeated my original request.

Next I got a letter from Vaughn Young, another Director of Public Affairs, this time of Author Services, Inc., "Representing the Literary Works of L. Ron Hubbard" in Hollywood, California. Young's letter discreetly implied that *something* might be arranged—though he didn't say what. He told me to send him my interview questions, and wait for developments.

The Author Services letterhead included a Los Angeles phone number. I tried dialing it, and got through to an answering service that claimed never to have heard of Author Services. When I persisted, they went and checked their records and found they did take messages for that company—but they had never heard of Vaughn Young.

This really fed my fantasies. I imagined endless protective layers around L. Ron Hubbard: an infinite series of dummy corporations, false names, and forwarding addresses. I began to feel I was pursuing a science-fictional Howard Hughes.

Anyway, I sent my list of questions to Mr. Young, and he wrote back enigmatically: "I believe I will be able to help you out." He added: "I look forward to the response as much as you."

Note: "the" response, rather than "Mr. Hubbard's" response. Again the phrasing seemed odd—but by this time I was beginning to realize how easy it is to read hidden meaning into any sentence, and how myths can multiply around a myth-figure merely by the fact of his existence.

One week later, Vaughn Young sent me a letter saying—enigmatically, again—"I am pleasantly amazed at what your questions evoked." Well, I was pleasantly amazed, too; because enclosed with his letter were eleven typewritten pages of answers to the questions that I had asked. These pages constituted, in fact, the first interview of any kind that L. Ron Hubbard had given since 1966. Witty, fluent, and full of character, the complete text appears below. I have included, also, most of the text of my questions, because I like the contrast between my somewhat earnest approach and Mr. Hubbard's laconic attitude to the whole affair.

Well, this almost seemed too easy; it was certainly the last thing I had expected. And maybe it *was* too easy. I started wondering if, in fact, the typed responses were genuine. After all, I didn't know who I was writing to, and I didn't know where the responses had come from. Vaughn Young—assuming there *was* a Vaughn Young—had never specifically stated that he had written to Hubbard, or that he had received anything from him. And so, a trifle nervously, now, and trying to be as tactful as possible, I wrote and asked for proof.

While I was waiting for that, a friend pointed out something to escalate the paranoid fantasies still further. The typewriter used in Vaughn Young's letters to me had a slightly damaged capital "A"; and this was identical to a damaged letter "A" in the typed responses that were supposedly from L. Ron Hubbard. Moreover, the paper had the same distinctive watermark.

Did this mean that "Vaughn Young" had made up all the answers *himself*? Or (a more exciting idea!) was Vaughn Young *really L. Ron Hubbard*, writing to me under a pseudonym? Or (and this, surely, was the classic piece of conspiracy thinking) had "they" deliberately used the same paper and the same typewriter, hoping I'd notice, and it would make me paranoid?

Well, I hate to spoil a good story, but within a few days I received a handwritten authentication from Mr. Hubbard, by express mail, from a P.O. box in California. It is reproduced at the end of the interview, and I must admit, it does look rather genuine. I also received another letter from Vaughn Young, patiently explaining that he had used his typewriter merely to transcribe responses that Mr. Hubbard had dictated. Young subsequently telephoned me, and told me that the Author Services letterhead was out of date, and they now have a new phone number listed on a new letterhead. Moreover, Los Angeles telephone information verified it when I called them a few days later.

Well, I'm particularly grateful to Mr. Hubbard for taking the trouble to answer my intrusive questions, and I'm also indebted to Vaughn Young for acting as go-between and tolerating my skepticism. And yet, it might have been more satisfying, in a way, never to have received a conclusive response at all, and to have gone around in circles forever, from one mail drop or answering service to the next, building more and more crazy, complex fantasies in the process. Mystery and myth must always be more enticing than dull old reality; paranoid theories are more fun than any rational explanation. At the end of a ghost story, we feel cheated if the Skeptical Investigator emerges unscathed, and proves that there was no ghost at all—merely the night breeze blowing through an open window.

1. Since Mr. Hubbard was last active in science fiction, it has changed greatly. The magazines have declined while paperback novels have proliferated. Technically accurate, predictive stories have given way to novels of the "soft" sciences. In the last fifteen years, some people complain of a trend toward reworking the old formulas endlessly as if there are no new ideas left. Finally, some science fiction has grown to best seller status and some authors now receive million-dollar royalty advances while the rest still earn only $5,000 to $10,000 for a book. What are Mr. Hubbard's opinions on these various trends?

You reminded me how I came to enter this field.

It was the day I met John W. Campbell, Jr.

I had been called down to that dirty old building on 7th Avenue in New York City by F. Orlin Tremaine and some other top executives of Street and Smith. I didn't know what they wanted but S&S was The Giant of the industry and so such "invitations" were heeded. It was like an audience with the king.

I wasn't the only one. J. Arthur Burks, another top writer, was also there—equally mystified.

Well, Tremaine tells us he wants us to write science fiction.

Burks and I look at each other.

Science fiction? We write about *people*, not monsters and machines.

Exactly the point, Tremaine said. S&S had just bought *Astounding Science Fiction* and sales were unacceptable. What the magazine needed was stories about people written by some headline writers like Burks and myself but it had to be science fiction.

A special company, A. B. Dick—sort of the Nielsen or Gallup of that day—had found that a few writers sold magazines and Burks and I were among that select group. All we had to do was write science fiction and write it about people, not monsters.

Burks and I may have been successful writers but that was hardly reason to say no to the biggest publisher of the day so we wisely agreed.

Astounding editor Campbell was called in and introduced to two of his newest writers and told that he would print whatever Burks and I wrote—no questions asked.

Campbell didn't like it one bit. He snarled but S&S was calling the shots. He was told to buy our stories and publish them. At our rates, it would ruin his budget. Besides, he had his own idea how science fiction should be done.

But Campbell gave in.

And that is how it began.

John and I became the best of friends and, frankly, I don't know how many of us were foisted off on him or how many he found but he ended up with a stable of writers second to none. He became the Czar of science fiction and he earned it.

"Dangerous Dimension" was the first fruit of my SF effort, followed by "The Tramp."

Rather than BEMs, "Dangerous Dimension" used a philosophic theory that predates Western culture—that an individual's location depends on that person's ideas and not the location.

The story centered on a meek little professor (henpecked by a domineering housekeeper) who stumbles on the secret and finds he is instantly transported anywhere by merely thinking of the location—sometimes to his embarrassment.

The story was unusual for its philosophy, humor, and its emphasis on people and not monsters.

"The Tramp" was a guy who acquires immense mental powers after a brain operation to save his life.

The fans loved it.

The "new trend" began.

Circulation soared and Campbell sighed and put his monsters and robot societies away.

That is history. But Campbell got even.

Although we became good friends, he got the fantasy I wrote out of *Astounding* by starting a brand new magazine to accommodate it—*Unknown*.

That handled that.

2. In the last ten years, fantasy of the sword-and-sorcery school has emerged as a separate category rivaling science fiction. Is this a healthy trend, or does it imply that readers have come to fear science and prefer to read about medieval societies run by magic?

I am very pleased that you make this distinction for too often fantasy and SF are blurred.

The two genres are quite distinct.

If you mix one with the other, you dilute both.

Fantasy deals with magic, mythology, the supernatural. There are no boundaries in fantasy.

When Einstein came out with his Theory of Relativity and the fixed speed of light, a tremendous barrier had been imposed on SF. No longer could a space ship just whip out to Xnenophean 5 for lunch and zip back for tea.

So SF writers had to come up with new ideas and "Doc" Smith was one of the best. He had to come up with new drive systems to circumnavigate around Einstein more than anything else.

But in fantasy, you don't have that problem.

It's all "magic" in this genre.

You see, "Dangerous Dimension" was actually fantasy because it was based upon a spiritualistic idea. "The Tramp" was science fiction.

So when you ask if readers prefer to read about medieval societies, I think it is more the case that they prefer the freedom of that genre.

Fantasy predates SF.

It is as old as storytelling itself.

One is not necessarily better than the other.

They are just different.

3. Does Mr. Hubbard have any social or psychological theory to explain why so many people are willing to take ideas seriously which used to be laughed at? Many adults now read about dragons, monsters, or far-off galaxies, whereas twenty years ago that kind of thing was ridiculed as "kids' stuff." Does this reflect a turning away from the problems of real life?

Your question about what was "kids' stuff" twenty years ago brings back memories!

I think if you will look at the trends of the last forty or so years, there was a development towards being very "serious" and "scientific."

This happens every now and then as some new theory takes hold—and then passes.

But I think it would be a bit inaccurate to say that just because people today are enjoying SF and fantasy they are "reverting." What they are doing is getting rid of the ideas that were imposed upon this society by the man-is-mud-and-trapped-in-mud practitioners.

Fantasy is as old as Man. It is only in the last century that someone has come along and said that we are made of little wiggly-wogglies. They promise that they'll have it all explained for us any moment as soon as we pour another billion dollars into their lab. But all we've gotten so far is a nuclear nightmare.

SF and fantasy hold out the prospect of possibility and in possibility you have choice and in choice you have freedom and *there* you have touched on the basic nature of every person.

This society offers just the opposite—and I am not singling out any one society.

People walk about knowing that something is wrong but they just can't seem to put their finger on it.

If you really want to be blunt about it, this world we live in with its insanities and madmen ready to blow it up is more unbelievable than any SF or fantasy.

So when one grows up in that kind of world, anything else is easily believable.

4. My second and third questions, above, relate to levels of faith and belief in the general public. As the founder of Scientology, Mr. Hubbard must have a particularly good perspective on what people believe today and whether mental health, overall, is improving or declining. Does the popularity of science fiction imply that people's minds are more open now than before, or are people less prepared to deal with the real world? Does this mean, in turn, that there is more need today for Scientology as a system to enhance our mental abilities?

I've always found the phrase "deal with the real world" to be amusing.

Pick up a daily newspaper and read the headlines and then look about you and see how the two compare. Which is "real"? To believe the news, every other person is being shot, airplanes are falling like rain, every house is burning down, and tornadoes are as common as clouds.

Are newspapers reporting the "real world"?

I think not.

But you can sure begin to think the world is that way if you read enough papers and watch enough TV and don't LOOK. (And one of the results of too much "news" is that people think it is even dangerous to look!)

So to judge the "mental health" of society, where do we turn?

Do we use the information given by others or should we look around us and judge for ourselves?

A society composed of individuals who can look about and see what is there and see what is NOT there (an equally valuable skill) is healthier than one consisting of people who need Dr. Knowitall or Johnny Journalist to tell them what to believe.

To the degree a Scientologist learns to look for himself, he or she is sane and to that degree the society benefits.

As long as there is a need for sanity, there will be a need for Scientology.

It has made a difference to the degree that it helps the individual to help himself.

5. Elite secret societies of especially gifted people have been a common theme in science fiction. Often the elite are a jump ahead up the evolutionary ladder. Is this a valid parallel with Dianetics or Scientology? Were any science-fiction books influential on Mr. Hubbard when he conceived of a cohesive organization of gifted individuals using a new mental discipline?

People always enjoy the idea of an "advanced" society but this is always taken in a "vertical" sense—sort of "up"—as compared to an Eastern view that would probably be better described as "horizontal"—expanding out. It is also the difference between one and three dimensions.

Professor Mudge in "Dangerous Dimension" wasn't really all that "advanced" when he discovered how to teleport himself around the galaxy. In fact, he made his discovery by looking not for a "fourth dimension" but a "negative dimension."

Thus Mudge did not move "forward" but "backward."

Mudge's problem was not so much what he found or discovered but his inability to control it.

This is the problem that befalls every "advanced" society—it simply cannot control its creations but is controlled by them.

I found this to be a challenge for the individual for it is there that the battle or struggle is most real.

That is why Mudge and The Tramp are so similar. The two are from totally different backgrounds and both are fairly mundane individuals. But suddenly they "advance" (whatever that means) but they cannot control their newfound abilities. The "gift" was almost Mudge's undoing. It destroyed the hobo.

It was this problem that intrigued me and was what I researched. I knew that there was a mechanism in man that acted like a self-destruct button.

The results appeared in *Dianetics: The Modern Science of Mental Health* in 1950.

6. Why did Mr. Hubbard return to writing science fiction? Does he write only to entertain, or to communicate a message or even enlightenment?

Battlefield Earth was written to celebrate my fiftieth anniversary as a professional writer.

Possibly, by definition, every story has a message. It is a communication. A story that doesn't communicate isn't much of a story. It is just a question of how much *does* it communicate?

Writers who take their "message" first and then try to weave a story around it make better advertising executives than writers.

7. What were his original ambitions as a writer? Did he achieve those goals? Why did he stop writing science fiction? Did the obscurity of the field, its low literary status, and its meager rates of pay influence his decision? Where did he write his early work? Was he part of a regional group of writers? Did he feel at home among other science-fiction people?

At first, I wrote on anything I could find—if it took pen or pencil I wrote on it. When I traveled through the Far East (twice) as a teenager, I used old ledgers as well as stationery pads.

The only time I really stopped writing was for the first two years of the Second World War when security prohibited the keeping of diaries.

But I finally found a worn Smith-Corona or a Royal (I forget which) in 1943 and began to write.

My first story in two years was forgettable. It was barely over 1,200 words but it was a story! I was as proud as a neophyte who had just sold his first story.

I limbered up soon enough.

Like remembering how to ride a bicycle, it just takes some refreshing.

But writing for me has always been something more than a profession—and I think you will find this to be true with any true writer. It is a way of life.

So I never really stopped writing, except for those two years.

Looking back on it, it is amazing that all of us from that great period did what we did—given the publishers and the agents. It was a challenge.

But we hung out together and even today I consider them my friends. We traded stories and ideas while jealously wondering if what we described would appear under someone else's by-line.

We yammered and argued and celebrated and watched others come and go while we wrote.

My first professional story was in the *Sportsmans Pilot*, although I had been writing in college before that and while traveling.

So when the old golden anniversary came rolling around, I figured I would celebrate it in the only way I really knew how—I wrote *Battlefield Earth*.

8. Did he have any inkling that Scientology would become so successful? Has he now achieved all of his ambitions? Is, perhaps, writing a contemporary best seller the last big challenge?

We were all quite surprised at the immediate success of *Dianetics: The Modern Science of Mental Health* in 1950. The publisher was caught flat-footed when the book shot onto the best seller lists and just stayed there. (By the way, the first Dianetics article was NOT in *Astounding* as some contend. The first article was "Terra Incognita: The Mind" and it appeared earlier that year in the Winter-Spring edition of the *Explorers Journal*.)

As the book was the result of years of hard work supported by writing, I never suspected that I had only scratched the surface of what could be learned about the human condition.

I am very happy with the life I have lived and really regret no part of it. I have had one vocation—to understand life and do something to help my fellow man help himself.

My philosophy has been that wisdom is not something that should be locked away. It belongs to any who seek it and who can use it to benefit their fellows.

My greatest treasure is my many friends.

9. As a somewhat mysterious and powerful figure, Mr. Hubbard has become a focus for all kinds of rumors—much like the late Howard Hughes. For instance, I have heard that he lives in exclusive luxury on a yacht in the Mediterranean. It's said that he is a multi-millionaire. There is a cynical anecdote that at the last meeting of science-fiction writers which he ever attended, he told them they were crazy to write for a penny a word when they could apply their ideas to the real world. Are any of the stories true?

It is one of those curious phenomena of our times that people are asked to "set the record straight."

Over the years I've learned that it is like the plight of the Sorcerer's Apprentice. With each denial or correction, the rumor splinters into more rumors, and. . . .

I've just learned to laugh them off.

It's more fun that way anyway.

10. Will there be more novels by L. Ron Hubbard? Does he have plans for the next five or ten years?

Yes, I am just finishing another science-fiction saga—bigger than *Battlefield Earth*. Plus I just did two screenplays.

I'm planning on doing some cinematography, for the camera has always been one of my loves.

11. On the personal side: Is Mr. Hubbard married? Does he have children? Does he have hobbies?

Yes, and I am even a grandfather!

As far as recreation—I write!

14 May 82

Dear Mr Platt—

I was very glad to hear that the answers to your questions fulfilled the requirements of your book, Dream-makers II. Glad to help.

Wishing you every success with the book—

Best

[illegible]

The original copy of the above authentication has been examined by a handwriting analyst who, as I understand it, was employed by attorneys representing the Church of Scientology. These attorneys are contesting an action being brought by L. Ron Hubbard's son, who is trying to prove that his father is either dead or mentally incompetent.

I have been told that the handwriting analyst believes the sample reproduced above was written by L. Ron Hubbard and is genuine. The existence of my interview is further evidence that, as of mid-1982, Mr. Hubbard was indeed alive. Although the interview was conducted by mail, and at first I was skeptical myself, I have reached the conclusion that the style and humor are totally consistent with other work by Mr. Hubbard and could not have been faked. I have stated this literary opinion in an affidavit which may yet be used in contesting the case being brought by Mr. Hubbard's son.

Obviously some people have a great deal at stake, when it comes to establishing whether or not L. Ron Hubbard is alive, and where he may be hiding. We are witnessing a larger-than-life treasure hunt. It should be an interesting one.

ADDITIONAL:

I would like to comment simply on the title of your book—*Dream Makers*.

It was Descartes who used the dream to establish his certainty of himself and the world and, finally, God. He sought something that could not be doubted—and found himself.

There is a basic truth in that for all of us.

Those who dream give us future.

But in doing so, each man or woman should find themselves.

For dreams are too often pitted against "reality"—as Descartes did—when they might well be more real than this very page.

It was only in this century that dreams lost their value (except to analysts who made a fast buck) and it is a delight to see their value restored.

Dreams are the visions of man's future and it is only the future that will tell us if the vision was true.

Thus I wish you every best success with your second volume of *Dream Makers*.

BIBLIOGRAPHICAL NOTES

Almost all of L. Ron Hubbard's science fiction and fantasy was originally published in magazines between 1938 and 1950. Some of this material subsequently appeared in book form, notably *Final Blackout* (1948), in which Britain, debilitated by successive wars, is restored by a military dictator, to resist colonization by a politically decadent U.S.

Fear, a grimly paranoid fantasy, was collected in one volume with *Typewriter in the Sky* (1950), the latter being one of Hubbard's most well-known and playful pieces, in which a man who shares an apartment with an action-adventure writer becomes trapped in the imaginary world being described by that writer in the new novel that he's working on.

Battlefield Earth (1982), marking Hubbard's fiftieth anniversary as a writer and his return to science fiction, is the epic saga of devolved, post-holocaust humans struggling back from primitivism to repossess the earth from aliens who have established an outpost upon it. Like much of Hubbard's work, it entails an implicit theme of mental transcendence.

PHOTO BY ILEEN WEBER

Joanna Russ

Aggressively independent female heroines. A nonviolent, all-female utopia. Explicit sex scenes—between women and women, as well as women and men.

These are some of the "controversial" things that Joanna Russ has written about. Personally, I think other aspects of her work are more important; I'm more interested in her graphic but eloquent style, her social messages, and her talent for showing real, everyday characters reacting convincingly to alien situations.

But her "shocking stuff" is worth mentioning as a reminder that what can be published today was once taboo.

Before the 1960s, science fiction was strictly for kids. Aiming their books and magazines entirely at teenagers, publishers avoided any "heavy" or "offensive" material. They knew it would be vetoed by suspicious parents and librarians who would ban a book or cancel a magazine subscription if there was so much as a hint of sex. And by "sex" I do not mean pornography; through the 1950s, you could barely get away with using a word such as "thigh," let alone "breasts."

Looking back, it seems obvious that, sooner or later, science fiction had to grow up. But to say that change was inevitable is to ignore the courage and obstinacy of the writers who brought that change about.

Farmer, Sturgeon, Leiber, Ellison, Delany, Spinrad, and others were met with anger and outrage when they started putting sex into science fiction. And this backlash came not just from readers but from editors and even some fellow writers, who didn't like such a disturbance of their status quo.

Today, the radicals have mostly beaten back the censorship. But for one group the struggle was harder and the victory has been less complete. These writers were faced with an additional obstacle: they were female.

Apart from a few pioneers such as Andre Norton, Judith Merril, C. L. Moore, and Leigh Brackett, science-fiction writers were almost always men. To write it, you had to be an avid reader of it; and since almost all of it was action-adventure starring male heroes, it didn't attract many female readers. For decades science fiction stayed mainly male because it was written by men for boys. A classic closed circle.

When women writers first invaded the field in large numbers during the 1960s, they received a warm welcome—but not always for respectable reasons. Look at it from the male point of view: after long, lonely decades, women were actually turning up at writing workshops and science-fiction conferences, inspiring at the back of many a male mind the thought—*At last, it's going to be easier to get laid!*

In addition to this undercurrent of simple lust, there was some subtle literary prejudice—even among men who claimed to be open-minded. They didn't doubt that the women could write; but could they really write the hard stuff? Could they handle drive tubes and tractor beams and hyperspace? Shouldn't they leave high-tech to the men, and concentrate instead on more, er, appropriate material? Telepathic love stories, for instance, or whimsical fantasy, or cuddly little aliens. In effect, women were being welcomed warmly to the mansion of science fiction—but were naturally expected to spend most of their time in its nursery or its kitchen, rather than the study or the workshop in the basement.

This prejudice was largely unconscious, and not universal, but it did persist. Women who wanted to explore adult themes therefore had to overcome not only the usual resistance against publishing those themes, but also the slight but perceptible barrier to the idea of women writing proper science fiction at all.

Joanna Russ has assaulted both of these barriers more directly, more uncompromisingly, and more successfully than any other female writer I can think of. Ursula Le Guin is often mentioned as the one who has fought for feminism by describing courageous women in societies free from stereotypical sex roles. But Le Guin is well-mannered. She persuades people against sexism by being relentlessly *nice* about it. Russ is more radical, and full of rage. *No more bullshit!* her books seem to say, as she comes straight out with strident demands for female freedom.

And so some readers complain that she uses science fiction merely as a soapbox from which to spout feminist propaganda.

Joanna Russ says that this isn't true at all. She's not a literary missionary.

"The only times I've done things like that have been in a few book reviews or articles for feminist publications. I don't really like doing it; it gets to be an awful obligation. And I don't write fiction that way at all, with a didactic intention. I've never sat down thinking, 'In this novel I will try to promulgate *X* and clarify *Y*.' I start writing like, I suppose, anybody else, because I have some vague ideas about a plot, or something that just attracts me. I'm not really sure what I'm going to do until I've done it, most of the time. I structure the book beforehand only to the extent that I know I have to have a confrontation between these two characters, and then one of them has to go out and walk alone in a forest, and think, but I don't know what he's going to think . . . and I don't know how it's going to end."

But even if she's not deliberately trying to convince or convert a reader, wouldn't she agree that the kind of books she writes are liable to trigger changes in people's lives?

"No. I remember reading, once, an article by an editor of a large-circulation magazine who said that there was nothing he'd ever printed that had not brought in letters from somebody claiming 'You changed my life.' You can practically print a recipe for meat loaf, and somebody will write you and say, 'This thing has had such a tremendous effect on me, it's saved my life.'

"The messages go out, and I am not responsible for the receivers out there, and what condition they're in. If they twist the messages, there's nothing we can do about that. People are adults; they have to take their chances. That, presumably, is the reason we restrict what children can see and read, and we don't restrict what adults can see and read.

"In any case, after having had contact with students for so many years, I think it's a lot harder to change somebody's life than people think. People will *say* they've been changed, but what they really mean is they read something which crystallized an awful lot of things they were already feeling. I don't think books really change people's minds very often; I think that's awfully rare."

But isn't feminism based on the hope that people's old, bad habits of thought *can* be changed?

"I think, like other political movements, it's based on the idea that you can make people conscious of feelings that they already have but have never articulated. One really cannot do more than that; I don't think it's possible."

Nevertheless, a stable and apparently happy marriage could surely be disrupted by a book that caused a woman to question her situation in a way she never had before.

"If that happened, I would answer that she was suffering injustices which are so obvious that only by an enormous social effort can a woman be *kept from* questioning them. You see what I mean?"

I reply that I do, but I don't necessarily agree it's that simple.

"That makes me kind of angry, I'm afraid. It's the kind of attitude I've encountered when talking to people, say, about socialism, and they say things like, 'Yes, but what is a socialist world going to be like? What is art and literature going to be like?' And these are questions which they have never asked of the *present* world.

"In any case, what frightens me is not that I will do something horribly harmful to somebody and will ruin their lives. What upsets me is that it's really the other way around. For every one person who writes in and says 'You changed my life' there are 999 who turn a deaf ear. I have much more the sensation of shouting into the wind than anything else.

"In any case, if you want to change people's ideas, science-fiction books must be the least efficient way to do it. You're reaching so many fewer people than you would, say, in movies or television. And many of the people you're reaching are such techni-freaks, they have very decided ideas about things already."

Speaking of techni-freaks: Does she feel there are any overall differences between science fiction written by men and by women? Is it true that most women write fantasy instead?

"This is one of those generalizations that an awful lot of people would assent to, but I started actually remembering who has done what, and writers like Heinlein and Larry Niven, whom we think of as being hard science writers, have written quite a lot of fantasy.

"Then I made a list of the women who write science fiction, who include of course Vonda McIntyre, Ursula Le Guin, Octavia Butler, Suzy Charnas—she's never written a fantasy in her life; I don't think of *The Vampire Tapestry* as a fantasy, I think it's science fiction, pretty clearly—and, oh, Kate Wilhelm. I think the real difference is in tone. The tone of a typical Larry Niven story is, you know, 'If you get down to such-and-such atmospheric pressure in Venus, the temperature is such-and-such, and the rocket will malfunction.' Women don't use this kind of jargon."

Then is it true that men write engineering fiction and women don't?

"There I think you may have a point. But that's not the same thing as science fiction."

Are women innately better at dealing with the social sciences?

"That may be true, and if we *are*, we will go and enroll in those courses and get those degrees; it will take care of itself. But at the same time it's also true that an awful lot of this culture devotes itself to insisting that certain areas are not for me—that it's unladylike, unreasonable, dangerous, etc., etc.

"If there really are systemic mental differences between men and women, they are *not* the conventional ones, the stereotype ones. Those are just too convenient, too neat, too simple. I don't believe them. I really don't.

"I agree that where there are physical, organic differences you should get some psychological or temperamental differences accordingly, but so much of what people do and state is not a direct expression of anything physical.

"Samuel Delany once wrote a story in which some people, schizophrenics, can go through a space-warp and enter the fourth dimension, without being harmed, and nobody else can. In that world, that becomes an important difference. In the same way, if we find that, for example, payload is so critical in space travel that only very short women can run space ships, that's going to become a critical difference. But these kinds of differences are only important if we *make* them important.

"I would be very, very wary of anybody who says that the differences between the sexes just happen to follow the line that men have been laying down for the last 2,000 years."

This seems to mean that she does not accept sociobiology, which interprets almost all human behavior as being the result of genetically inherited survival traits, with man the hunter, woman the nurturer, and so on.

"No, I don't buy that. I think that kind of outlook has a lot to do with the economic depression that's going on, and with the kind of political backlash going on. There's an awful lot of mythology hidden in science. The pathology that was hidden behind nineteenth-century science is beginning to be fairly obvious. I think that the same thing goes on today in sociology and psychology, even in biology.

"From what I've heard of sociobiology it's very suspiciously harking back to—forgive the cliches, but I don't know any other way to say it—gender role stereotypes, capitalist stereotypes. I am very wary of anything so close to what I have always been told to believe, now coming at me from another quarter.

"The kind of research which I do think is fascinating is, for example—there was an article in the *New England Journal of Medicine* last month that links depressive illness with a particular chromosome. That's a very concrete, very one-to-one correlation in the human realm. That's solid stuff.

"What we have to watch out for, to keep from being suckered in, is when someone purports to explain not one particular concrete thing, but the way in which a whole species works.

"This reminds me of what happens to some women who become active feminists. The issues they want to talk about are limited and concrete, but the response they often get from their opponents will be something like, 'Yes, but what are the real differences between men and women?' The feminists are saying things like, 'The incidence of wife-beating is *X-Y-Z*,' and the response is, 'But are men naturally aggressive?'

"The abortion question is illustrative of this. Women say, 'We want the right to own our own bodies.' And the opposition, the Moral Majority, say things like, 'When does life begin?' That's not the point. I don't give a damn when it begins. I don't give a damn what the real differences between men and women are. I just don't want to be stepped on when I walk out into the street. I don't want to have to go out at night in terror. I don't want you to tell me that you won't give me a decent job. I don't want to have a low salary. I don't want to be maltreated."

Joanna Russ was born in 1937 and raised in New York City. She graduated from Cornell University with distinction and high honors in English, and received an M.F.A. in playwrighting and dramatic literature from the Yale School of Drama. Since 1977 she has been an associate professor of English at the University of Washington, in Seattle. (I was unable to visit Seattle, so this interview was conducted by phone.)

Russ's desire to write goes back a long way.

"I wrote my first story when I was five years old—dictated it to my mother. I did my first novel when I was sixteen, and I think finished another when I was about twenty.

"My father was very much into popular science and he did a lot of things like carpentry, and roofing—he was a shopkeeper, and there were a lot of crafts that he knew something about. My mother used to read poetry to us; she'd get out the *Oxford Book of Verse* after dinner and we would pick out first lines and she would name the poems.

"I got much more encouragement than most writers get, and I got most of it from my mother. But when I went out into the world I found out just how atypical my childhood had been. I had experienced an early utopian situation; then came the bump of coming down to reality.

"For example, when I was in college, I got a very good education in English literature—technically quite excellent. But I got it from completely male professors; there was not a single woman working in the Department of English at that time. They encouraged me to go on to graduate school, without ever pausing to consider where I would ultimately get a job.

"The same professors who talked about literature as an absolute value never talked about the sexist messages we were getting from it. The rules of conduct of that time, in the 1950s, were completely different for women, on campus, from what boys were permitted to do. There was a peculiar kind of tacit agreement to pretend that the absolute values were classless and sexless, even though they aren't.

"You become a kind of schizophrenic if you try to believe that, if you are a woman, or if you're black, or Asian, or working class; you go a little bit bananas.

"I didn't go to graduate school, and I didn't become a professor, which was the usual thing that writers did. I wanted to live outside of academia. Academic criticism in the 1950s was horrible; it was the New Criticism, which was really poisonous to anybody who wanted to write.

"So I thought I would teach theater. That seemed far enough away from writing to be a nice sort of cross-pollination. But it was impossible for me to get a job."

So she ended up teaching literature, speech, and English, and started selling short science-fiction stories on the side.

"For a long time I wrote two kinds of stories: action stories with men, and love stories with women. And in the love stories the women generally lost, and in the action stories the men generally won.

"Then I started writing the Alyx stories, and that was really where it happened."

Alyx was a character who continued from one story to the next: a small but rebellious female thief, transported accidentally through space and time. It was a breakthrough for Russ to write about such a pushy female protagonist, but the stories were still told in the form of conventional adventure fiction.

By the beginning of the 1970s, she was moving further and further away from the standard format. Ultimately, in *The Female Man* (1975), she published a truly experimental novel, full of pointed commentary on modern society, narrated in the first person by four different women, one of them from a future in which men have all been wiped out by an epidemic and women have constructed a utopia.

It wasn't easy for her to find a publisher for this book.

"It went around for about two years, to hardcover publishers, who would not touch it. Finally, my agent decided to try for a paperback sale, and Frederik Pohl, at Bantam, took it.

"These days I seem to be having more and more trouble getting stuff published—even though it's selling better and better, and the books are obviously making money. I understand that, of the series of books Pohl edited for Bantam, only two really made money, and they were *Dhalgren* and *The Female Man*. And they just happened to be the most 'controversial' of the lot.

"Most of my books have sold 100,000 copies in paperback over the years, and yet every time I do something new there is this complaint: 'Oh, we really wanted something like the *last* one you did.'

"I don't think New York publishers really know what they're doing. Book publishing, except for the most standardized stuff like Harlequin romances, is not a market-researched field. It's not a mass audience, compared with movies. I don't think they have the money to really find out what's going on out there, or to distribute properly. I think distribution is probably the worst part of it.

"What they all want is 'something like the last one.' Because they know that that one sold."

I ask if she feels that dividing books into categories is part of the problem.

"Yes, I think it is, and I think it's getting to be more and more of a problem for all fiction, because of the distribution system. They think that if you put a recognizable label on it, it'll sell.

"The covers of paperback books are, by and large, the only advertising that the books get, so each cover serves as a capsule summary of what kind of book it is. The cover tells you what to expect inside: a Western, a detective story, a romance."

But Joanna Russ's novels do not fit the categories, and as I've already mentioned in D. M. Thomas's profile, such books are not popular with publishers. Has Joanna Russ found that female editors are more willing to take a chance publishing her work than male editors?

"No, because almost all the women are low on the totem pole and have very little power in the organization they work in. They are often terrified of doing anything out of line; they don't really have the clout in the organization to do something controversial. I don't think it's any accident that a man—David Hartwell—has been one of the most adventurous editors in buying feminist science fiction. It's true that this isn't always the case, but it very, very often is. I suspect that the judgments editors make reflect what they think they can get away with—what they think will make money."

What about from the readers' point of view? Joanna Russ's work has such a personal tone; do her readers ever write and ask her, for instance, if she's a lesbian?

"Up to now, nobody has. But readers do tend to believe that what they read in novels is autobiographical. They say, 'You mention in one of your books that such-and-such happened—has it really happened to you?' And I have to tell them, very uncomfortably, well, yes and no. I steal things from everybody's life, including my own. But the novels are *not* autobiography."

Her current work has been beset not only by the usual publishing uncertainties, but by health problems.

"Several years ago, I began having trouble with my back—really bad trouble. Finally I managed to get a decent doctor, and an operation, and now I'm up again, but it's only been within the last five or six weeks that I've been relatively free from pain. It's been really, really tough, really difficult.

"I've managed to continue writing a little bit, but for a long time I had to do all my writing and reading standing up. It took me about a year to re-learn how to write by hand, which I hadn't done since I was about sixteen. I wrote an awful lot of book reviews, and letters, figuring this was one way to do it. And then I had trouble with my feet, because I do so much standing.

"I decided, finally, this year, that I would write a series of short stories. I'm always terrified that something is going to go wrong with my body, and I will be down in bed again, and I won't be able to do it. So I figured if I wrote a series of stories, I would at least have the individual stories, even if I didn't finish the series. I have one more to go now, and David Hartwell has expressed an interest in them. I think they may see publication."

This would have been the end of the profile; but when I sent it to Joanna Russ for her approval, she wrote back with the following additional answer to a question that I hadn't quite dared to ask, because I felt it wasn't really any of my business.

"I take it that your question, 'Do readers ask if you're a lesbian?' really covers the question, 'Are you a lesbian?' I think I have equivocated. I did want to explain (and still do) that fiction is pasted together from all sorts of things: one's own experience, other people's, friends, enemies . . . and so on. But it's perfectly true that the recurring themes in the work are the author's own choice and do indicate the author's temperament.

"In World War II (so I've heard), when the Nazis occupied Denmark, one of their first orders was for Jews to wear the dreaded yellow armband with the Jewish star on it. That is, in order to eliminate a group, you first have to make it visible. The day after the order was issued, the King of Denmark, King Christian (!) appeared in public wearing the yellow armband. Within a week, every adult in the country had them. And Nazi efforts to deport and kill Danish Jews were frustrated.

"I've heard that story used to indicate the importance of feminist support for lesbians. Now it's certainly a fact that I am very interested in gay women and their lesbianism, as a theme, appears in much of my work. On the other hand, it's taken me almost a quarter of a century to perfect that 'personal' tone. It is *not* spontaneous or easy, damn it. Writing is *work*. On the other hand, I do use a lot of my experience (real or imagined) in my work.

"Sure I'm a lesbian."

BIBLIOGRAPHICAL NOTES

Joanna Russ's liberated adventure-fiction heroine Alyx appears in her first novel, *Picnic on Paradise* (1968), in which time travel serves as a device to snatch the primitive young protagonist from ancient Greece and put her on a vividly described alien world, where it is her mission to save the lives of complacent future citizens stranded in a survival situation. This novel was collected with short stories featuring the same protagonist, in *Alyx* (1976).

And Chaos Died (1970), her second novel, describes graphically a man's acquisition of psychic powers on an alien world, and his ensuing suffering when he returns to earth society.

The Female Man (1975) is Joanna Russ's most direct feminist statement, depicting sexist hypocrisies in contemporary America through the eyes of a feisty, self-sufficient woman from an all-female future utopia.

We Who Are About To... (1977) reverts to an extraterrestrial setting, and unifies themes from some of the earlier books.

In addition, Joanna Russ has pointed out that this bibliography should mention *Kittatinny: A Tale of Magic* (1978) and *On Strike Against God* (1980), both published by small presses, conveying a strong feminist message.

Janet Morris

I'm sitting with Janet Morris in the Author Pit. They don't call it that, of course, but that's what it *is*, this sunken area with a rail around it, in the basement of the huge B. Dalton bookstore on Fifth Avenue in New York City. They put authors in the Pit, and customers come wandering over with idle curiosity, and stand at the rail like kids watching animals at a zoo.

It's Science Fiction Week at B. Dalton, so I'm in the Pit trying to promote *Dream Makers*, and Janet's offering to autograph copies of her novel *Dream Dancer*, and we're being heckled by a literary snob in a dirty raincoat. "I've given up buying science fiction," he complains. "There aren't any writers who use solid, up-to-date science, *and* have good writing style, *and* strong characterization."

I don't have the stomach to start arguing with him, myself. I can't take the situation seriously; it's too embarrassing.

But not many things in life embarrass Janet Morris, and she takes everything seriously that relates to her work. So she tackles the heckler. "There *is* one writer in the field today, who combines all those qualities you're looking for," she tells him.

"Yeah? Who?"

"Me," says Janet Morris, as if it ought to have been obvious.

Now, this kind of salespersonship may sell a few extra books, but, at the same time, it does rub some people the wrong way. Some men, in particular, don't quite know how to take it when Janet Morris comes on like a graduate from assertiveness training and lectures them on anything from particle physics to handguns. They don't like it when she beats them at pinball, either. And there are some women who resent Janet Morris, too—for not toeing the feminist line, for instance. Her first four novels (the "Silistra" series) starred some sort of science-fictional *prostitute*, for heaven's sake, who felt it was not only her function but her pleasure to be used by men. It seems that Janet Morris doesn't believe in sexual equality, and doesn't reject all the old roles. She even refers to herself as a "girl" once in a while—and she's only half kidding.

"There is a degree of satire in everything I do. But to some extent the Silistra books were meant as a kind of cultural antidote to the overkill of women's lib, which was just cresting then, and which I felt was and is wrong. You can't stand out there in the middle of the street and scream for your rights, throwing a tantrum, which is often a woman's idea of her way of getting what she wants. It doesn't work in the real world.

"Also, in Silistra, I was influenced by Ed Wilson and the whole sociobiology thing. I was taking societal conditioning away and showing what was left—the genetic reality, as I inferred it from sociobiology."

I ask her to give some idea of what sociobiology is about, since not all of us know.

"Well, Wilson says things like, 'The urge to creativity may be inextricably linked to the desire to own and dominate.' That's a bottom-line quote. Silistran females are female in their thinking, they're never guys in girl-suits. And the males are fight-or-flight, they're always going after their edge in a particular way, which makes them almost walking genes. I was trying to crystallize human sexuality and show the degree to which it could influence decisions. They're not meant to be realistic characters that you could put into this world, or characters whose world-views would work in this world, but all of our world-views are influenced by the subconscious awareness of the kinds of thoughts that Silistran characters will voice, which no male or female can deny. Any woman who is honest will tell you that rape fantasies were her thirteen-year-old nightly exercise. It's not fun in the real world, but it sure makes a nice way to get to sleep when you're that age."

Doesn't she feel that, if rape fantasies are common, they are a result of social conditioning?

"No. On a genetic level, women want a dominant male, the one that is strongest and best capable of producing the child that will be most successful. That's somebody who's at least your equal. We still have the old hunter-gatherer instinct of, you run as fast as you can and the guy that can catch you and hold you down is the one. And if he's not at least strong enough and clever enough to do that, then you don't want his child."

But shouldn't we attempt to civilize our behavior above this primitive level?

"In order to deal with the promptings of genetics, one has to admit that they're there. To overcome something, you have to be able to pinpoint it without guilt or societal tsk-tsks or any kind of negativity that is brought in from your conditioning. We have to take as a given that males are males and females are females, and the drives and the kind of thought-preconditioning that come from those drives are different. I'm a humanist, not a feminist. I know I'm a female, I have no doubt about it, I'm very comfortable with it, and I'm perfectly willing to accept that females and males are complementary but different. I certainly would neither like nor encourage a society in which across-the-board equality is legislated or demanded against the indications of nature. *Physical* equality is an impossibility."

This doesn't mean, however, that Janet Morris herself is the stereotypical female, docilely submitting to men as a slave of genetic programming.

"A lot of times, if I don't hold back I'm there before the guy is, I've solved the problem. I'm more than capable of solving almost any problem that comes up in daily life, and I'm a high-androgen female: I've had show horses and done a lot of traditionally male things, and now of course we're into competitive shooting. I'm getting reasonably proficient with my handgun. Intellectually, I do a lot of homework and research, and things interest me that don't tend to interest other women. Phil Klass said to me the other day that woman's proper study was man, and man's proper study was whatever caught his interest. By that definition, I'm a man. I like intellectual stimulation.

"My bedtime stories, when I was four and five, were Spenser's *Faerie Queene* and such—that's what they used to read to me. My father was at Harvard, and his field was English literature. My mom had a master's in education. So by the time I was seven I'd been through all the myths of every society, Greek through Norse, Mesopotamian to Roman—I was very interested in ancient legends and all the magical stuff.

"In my family, instead of an allowance I got a hardcover book a week. I started reading science fiction when I was about seven; I always liked it because in science fiction, it isn't easy to tell from the third page what's going to happen at the end of the book. There're so many more alternatives in science fiction—when it's good. It isn't as good as it used to be, partially because people don't do their homework, and you don't have the Hugo Gernsbacks who are interested in promoting ideas, you just have derivatives—people who've never read anything but science fiction, and therefore they get their science from science fiction, and they merely rewrite cliches."

She's critical of modern science fiction by female authors.

"I remember throwing *The Female Man* by Joanna Russ in the waste basket. That was polemic, a treatise, not a story. The only living female writer who interests me—let's not limit this to science fiction—is Marguerite Yourcenar. I think female writers generally tend to lack discipline and structure, and both discipline and structure are what I like in a story.

"I have a theory that there are authors, and writers. People who want to be *known* for doing something, and people who like to *do* it. And too many women in this field seem to fall into the first group. But then, there are plenty of dreadful male writers, too.

"Of the women writing science fiction, I think C. J. Cherryh is certainly the best. I concur with her main theme of romanticizing science, trying to put science back into science fiction. I think that the public's fear of science and technology is totally overblown and unwarranted. It tends to be worst in older people who are shell-shocked. Those of us who are comfortable with going into the future ought to open our mouths.

"Everyone's terrified of nuclear bombs, now, and some people have found they can make a living lobbying for causes with which no one can disagree. Who can disagree with *peace*? So all these folks are out there making a living getting everyone to march for peace. The Soviets poured all the initial seed money into the European peace movement, to try to freeze the 'balance' of theater weapons in their favor. But people don't go after information themselves, they believe what they hear. This is, historically, the failing of democracy. You have mass rule and you have ascendancy of the mediocre. It's happening in science fiction too. You get a readership which is wider, editors who are only doing science fiction on the way to something 'more exciting,' such as women's romances, and therefore you get mediocre science fiction.

"When I wrote the Silistra novels I felt I was very brave and talked about issues that meant a lot to me, and I assumed that everybody was smart enough to know when I was teasing them and when I was serious. But a lot of readers don't see any more than you write on the surface. They don't read into it, to get at the subtlety.

"For instance, one of the things that was important to me, which I was developing there, was my intuition about what physics is and how it works, and the ability of mind to influence probability. In this last year, long after those books were done, John Wheeler codified all of those intuitions in his anthropic principle—the participatory universe—and has pushed physics almost to the boundary of metaphysics, with pretty much the same ideas: that you create your future as you go along, that you are co-creator of the universe. These ideas are so complex mathematically, you couldn't put them in a story of hard science fiction, it would take too long to define the terms. But I dramatized them as Silistran mind control.

"I've had letters from fifteen-year-olds who knew exactly what I was talking about, and forty-year-olds who couldn't handle it. Each time I write a book I find out which things are difficult for people, and I try, the next time, to make them simpler, to get my points across. But because I read more and more, the points get more and more complex. With twistor theory and space-time manifolds, it got to where I couldn't even find anybody to talk to about it. And then I knew I was in too deep. There were too few people reading in this area of science in the country."

I ask Janet Morris why, if her feeling for science is so strong, she writes books which seem to have a fantasy flavor, and have even been published as fantasy.

"I'm sneaking up on people. People don't want to work; you have to spoon-feed them to some extent. This is true even in publishing itself. There are some powerful women in publishing who have said some frightening things—like, 'Fuck the science, what matters is if the boy kisses the girl,' or 'I never took physics in high school, so I just skip the technical parts.' It almost seems as if ladies generally don't, can't, or won't maintain the level of specialized concentration that I think is necessary to become premiere in your field. And yet they want to be there—without doing the work."

Further to my question about the fantasy flavor of her books, I ask Janet Morris why, if clarity and communication are so important to her, she uses a stylized kind of writing instead of straight storytelling.

"Sometimes I want to write 'art,' and when I'm feeling Homeric my stuff tends to come out with that 'ancient' feel to the prose. If I need to relax, I like to read the *Iliad*, so I have a soft spot in my heart for prose lines that are beautiful. To me, some of those lines were very beautiful.

"The other thing is, when you're dealing with higher math, and difficult concepts, and you don't think people are going to get them if you put them in such a way that you need 5,000 words to define your terms, you can convey it experimentally, almost as poetry. Then people are going to have it whether they know they've got it or not, and they don't have to be afraid that they're not going to understand it.

"There's so much fear—people are afraid to try to learn, because they don't want to fail. So if you start giving them information in such a way that it scares them, they're just going to quit on you. What I've given them, in a lot of cases, is experiential physics, without using the word 'physics' at all."

In addition to science, her novels also deal with political concepts.

"In *Dream Dancer* I described a computerized referendum democracy. Everyone had to do ten to fifteen study hours to qualify to vote, so you had people who were voting on issues with which they were familiar. They'd seen all the pros and cons. At the same time, anyone could lose degrees of their citizenship in the Athenian style. And if indeed they lost enough of their citizenship, from apathy and lack of participation, then at some point they would become non-citizens. Each person had a degree of government funding, which they would lose if they opted out. I think that if we would allow everybody this kind of conditional government kickback, then maybe they'd have some incentive to participate.

"Our problem right now is that we have a system where the people who make our decisions for us have become a parasitic class who do nothing but have lunch and pass judgment on a basis of little or no information. My half-sister was Carter's speech writer on economic policy, so I know just how uninformed those people are about what's going on. If he was going to make a speech somewhere, he didn't even see it until the day before he went. He had no idea even of the subject he was going to talk on, let alone a chance to generate some point of view that he wanted to discuss. They really don't know.

"The ideal would be a democratic society in which everyone did their homework and was qualified to participate and vote on issues."

And she brings this kind of thinking right back home to the book business.

"Every time publishers find they can sell a bad romance or a Ken Follett novel to multitudes of people, the standards of publishing go down. But this is where democracy would really work, if the readers would just send back to the publishers every piece of trash that they bought and read. You wouldn't even have to demand a refund. If you just sent the bad ones back, eventually they'd get the idea."

Janet Morris was born in 1946 and lives with her husband Christopher, a rock musician, in a modern home hidden in the woodlands of Cape Cod. They're such a tight, cohesive couple, it's hard to consider them separately: He goes with her to the science-fiction events, she goes with him to the recording sessions, he reads and comments on her first drafts, she critiques his demo tapes. They seem to share most things, including a fetish for technology—they even have his-and-hers remote-control TV channel changers. Outside the house is parked a custom-painted Ford van, for the music equipment; in the garage is a shiny black Jeep. Soon, instead of the Jeep, there'll be a Porsche.

Life wasn't always so laid-back or so lucrative.

"I sold the first draft of the first thing I ever did, which was the first Silistra novel, in 1976. I don't talk about what I was doing before then. There are a lot of things that I really can't discuss. Let's say I did a lot of on-site street research, getting into all sorts of trouble and then getting myself out of it, because you have to know what life is like to write about life. I went out and got on the wrong sides of guns and knives and got into plenty of trouble, and boy, does that help you. I don't think you can lead a sheltered life and be a writer.

"We still try to keep a balance, but I'm exercising my hard-earned right, now, to privacy. I do go to science-fiction events once in a while, and my meetings with the science-fiction public have become less difficult than they were in the beginning. I was really offended by the reception that the Silistra books got among science-fiction fans originally; I was shocked that those readers weren't bright enough to realize what I was saying, and it never occurred to me that a young crowd like that would be so prudish, when the books were very well received outside the science-fiction community, including *The New York Times*. I held that against them for a while. These days, I'm better in control of it."

She now plans to write a fantasy trilogy based on a character she invented for the *Thieves' World* series of story collections. But her real obsession, just lately, has been a novel outside of fantasy and science fiction altogether.

"When I wrote the Silistra books, I couldn't say the things I wanted to say about sexuality in a contemporary format. I would never have gotten a publisher.

"With the *Dream Dancer* series, the things that I wanted to talk about were very scientific, really, and the politics were very experimental, which entailed a science-fiction format.

"But what I'm doing now is writing a high-tech contemporary novel, dealing with contemporary politics. I feel it's time for me to stop hiding. In a sense, I've been hiding behind the fantasy and science-fiction screen, talking about my real-life society indirectly, in a critical way."

One last thing I have to ask—and this goes right back to my experience with Janet Morris in the Author Pit, and some of the things she's said about the science-fiction audience. Has she ever been called an elitist?

"Yes, I've been accused of that. But historically, a society becomes known by the best and the worst; the mediocre is forgotten. And one thing I don't intend to be is forgotten. One doesn't want to have to apologize for one's intelligence in a free society."

BIBLIOGRAPHICAL NOTES

Janet Morris's four "Silistra" novels (1977–78) were her first published work in the field, depicting a courtesan of high rank in an alien, or fantasy, culture, whose intricate social customs and rites derive from the writer's convictions about fundamental sex roles and genetic preconditioning. The complex scenario, revealed progressively throughout the series, includes a glossary of alien terminology and argot.

Since then Janet Morris has written *Dream Dancer* (1981), *Cruiser Dreams* (1982), and *Earth Dreams* (1982), in which a young woman from a devolved earth enters a higher alien culture and pursues regal ambitions. Although superficially reminiscent of fantasy, with a lyrical tone, the books incorporate a serious scientific rationale.

Janet Morris has also written stories for the *Thieves' World* series of collaborative collections edited by Robert Aspirin.

PHOTO BY JAY KAY KLEIN

Joan D. Vinge

Joan D. Vinge is a nice person. Don't just take it from me; ask anyone. Even the hard hearts and sour spirits who claim that they don't like her books will still add, quickly, that in person Joan Vinge herself is—well, really nice.

How do you get a reputation like this? Perhaps by being shy, gentle, and continually careful not to trample on anyone else's feelings. In fact, her motto might be "live and let live." I ask her if she feels this is a fair way to phrase it.

"I guess you could say that," she agrees cautiously. "As a writer, you need drama and conflict in order to have interesting literature. But in your own life, you wouldn't necessarily care to have a great deal of drama and conflict. I do a lot of thinking about why people treat each other like shit, generally. I watch the evening news and say, 'How can people possibly do that to each other?' This is not to say that I'm some pure goody-two-shoes who's never angry or jealous, because God knows I am. It's just that I tend to internalize it a lot. I get depressed instead.

"I don't see why people can't see other people as potentially friendly. I suppose you never know how to react to someone else, because you never know how they're going to react to you, and it sort of feeds on itself. But I have the feeling that if people could take independent thought in each situation they encounter, rather than falling back on stereotypes and simplistic black-and-white definitions of how they should relate to other people, the world would be a better place. And I think it's extremely important that our world should be a better place, because if it doesn't improve soon, there may not be one. I'm going to have a baby, and I don't want it to be for nothing. I thought about this considerably even before I got pregnant."

She sits on the edge of an old plaid couch and speaks softly, shyly, her hands clasped in her lap. We're talking in the living room of her rather charming, cottage-like house in Chappaqua, thirty miles north of New York. It's a sleepy little town, a refuge for many urbanites who've traded grime and crime for trees, grass, front yards, back yards, and kitchens large enough for two people to eat in at the same time.

Joan D. Vinge (her name rhymes with "stingy") was born in 1948 and grew up in San Diego. The "D." stands for Dennison, her family name.

"When I was young I swallowed the line that girls don't really need to know about math, and in any case, I'd wanted to be an artist since I was about eight years old—I drew and painted compulsively.

"My best friend and I used to play with dolls like good little girls, but we never wanted to read 'Marcie Goes to the Prom.' We preferred the kind of books where the back flap listed 'Other books boys will enjoy.' Our dolls would get into *strange* adventures sometimes, and we'd play Roger's Rangers and adopt male pseudonyms and live out elaborate fantasies. I was lucky, I'm very grateful that my parents never interfered in my fantasy life.

"I started reading science fiction in junior high school. I went to the corner grocery store and saw *Storm Over Warlock* by Andre Norton on the book rack. I didn't know what it was—I didn't know what 'Terrans' were and I was afraid it would be too weird for me to cope with. But I bought it anyway, and reading it turned out to be one of those moments of epiphany—'Where has this been all my life?'—and after that I mostly wanted to read science fiction.

"Though I never got a strong background in technology, I still find new scientific discoveries very exciting, and I've always been particularly fond of astronomy. When I was little my father had a telescope out in the back yard and we used to look at the stars and planets. Today, I like to think of myself as a science-fiction writer, and essentially I think science-fictionally, because science, progress, and technology excite me a great deal and impress me a lot, and I always want to know more about them. When I have an idea for a story, frequently it will begin as a normal everyday idea, and then I'll find myself asking, How can I make it into a science-fiction story? How can I set this out in space somewhere?"

Is she equally interested in modern fantasy?

"I like both science fiction and fantasy, and have always read both. I'm very interested in mythology because of my educational background—I have a degree in anthropology. But I classify myself as a writer of science fiction. When I think of fantasy I tend to think of classic fantasy, high fantasy—*The Lord of the Rings*, for instance. And I enjoy that a great deal, but when I try to write it I feel inhibited by the sense that everybody has already done this, and probably better. In science fiction there are so many new ideas floating around. I probably will continue to write some fantasy, though—and to use the mythic elements in my science fiction, which gives it a fantasy aspect.

"To my mind science fiction has tremendous potential for being great literature, simply because you can do anything. You can set up parameters which are totally unfamiliar. You can put characters into alien situations and run them through strange changes which still relate to universal problems that people face today. This is also how I feel about anthropology. When I see something that's done in another society—entirely different from the way we do it, and yet it works for them—there's this sudden moment of expansion of perception. With science fiction, you can expand people's perceptions in that same way. You can have people read something and say 'My God, I never thought of it that way before.' I think that's good for the mind. And that's why some people can't read science fiction at all, because it's far too threatening to them.

"I get infuriated by *The New York Times*, which every few months seems to feel it has to do the old 'if it's science fiction, it can't be good' thing. I don't necessarily think that the great American science-fiction novel has yet been written, but I think the potential is really there, whereas contemporary fiction is in rather a static state, and I find much of it extremely boring. I like science fiction because it deals with change and new things."

I ask her to name a few books which excite her in this way, since, from my perspective, a lot of science fiction seems to have become a bit dull and repetitive.

"I find John Varley's works very exciting." There's a long silence while she tries to think of other writers. "This is terrible; it's like asking someone if they've heard any good jokes lately! Let's see—*Windhaven*, I liked that." Another long silence. "I'm sorry, my mind has gone blank. I'll send you a letter about it."

(Subsequently, she sends me the following list of "Books that I've really enjoyed, for reasons as different as the books themselves: *The Sardonyx Net* by Elizabeth Lynn, *Camp Concentration* by Thomas M. Disch, *The Left Hand of Darkness* and *The Dispossessed* by Ursula Le Guin, and Samuel R. Delany's early work." I can't help noticing that, with one exception, all of these were published eight or more years ago.)

Getting back to her own work, I mention her novel *The Snow Queen*. For those of you who don't already know, this is *not* the saga of a homosexual cocaine dealer. It is in fact a lyrical, mythic tale of the ruler of a far-off world trying to transcend the laws of her culture. Though it is only Joan Vinge's second novel, the writing carries great conviction and the book was immensely successful, winning a Hugo Award.

I comment that it seems less rooted in science—less science-fictional—than her previous writing.

"In one sense, maybe it is. Some of my earlier work, such as the stories in the Heaven Belt future history, were written partly under the aegis of my ex-husband, Vernor Vinge, who has a hard-science background and was my technical advisor. Heaven Belt was in fact a concept of his which he gave to me to write about, because I was writing and he wasn't, at that time. Even now, I still call him for technical advice, because I don't have the background and I like to get my facts as straight as I can.

"*The Snow Queen* is more romantic because it does have a heavier fantasy element, and I tie fantasy and romance together. I still think of it as a science-fiction novel, and I wrote it thinking that I was writing science fiction, but at the same time I did see that people who liked fantasy could be drawn to elements in it."

Does this mean that she specifically intended it to appeal to a wider audience?

"No, I didn't do it intentionally. What really gave me the idea for the novel was a fairy tale by Hans Christian Andersen which is, as far as I can tell, a retelling of an old folk tale, as most fairy tales are. I have an interest in fairy and folk tales simply because they are a part of mythology, and I'm very interested in that.

"I was intrigued by this particular fairy tale because it did not have a prince as an overlay—none of the paternalistic religious fixtures that were added into so many tales. Stories like *Snow White* are riddled with allusions which, if you've read very much mythology, you recognize instantly. The prince gets to do all the good stuff, and the female characters are either boring little wimps or wicked old witches. What I liked about this fairy tale was that all the main characters were female. I thought I would like to do something with that—create as many different female characters as I could and let them do as many different things as possible.

"Then, just as I was beginning to really settle down and think about working on this, I read Robert Graves's book *The White Goddess*, which is fascinating if you're interested in mythology at all. It was so detailed that reading it was like wading through molasses, but to me, it was as exciting as a good novel. I steeped myself in all the various mythological elements which could be applied to my novel. I feel there are certain universalities that people recognize almost instinctively, that seem to occur world-wide in different myth structures. I thought that if in some way I could tap into that, I might be able to get hold of some 'elemental force' that the readers would really respond to."

And indeed, readers and reviewers alike did respond, very favorably—with a very few exceptions.

"It doesn't matter what you've written, there's always someone who doesn't like it. There were those people who criticized it as 'mere entertainment' and nothing more. There were some cases where it was simply a man who didn't like reading a book which was all about women. Then there were people who felt there were spots in it that were overwritten. I think that's probably true. I love lots of colorful images, and I hope I still have things to learn about writing—subtlety, control. And my editors could have been a lot stricter. I loathe criticism after the fact, but I do like editorial feedback. I get so close to my work sometimes that it's impossible for me to see what it is.

"There were some people who criticized me for selling the book to Jim. [Jim Frenkel, her editor, whom she married and now lives with in Chappaqua.] One person, who shall remain nameless, said, 'It must be nice to pay your girlfriend $60,000 for a book.' This to Jim, while I was standing right beside him. But a year later, when the book was selling wonderfully well, Jim was then able to say, 'Yes, it certainly is nice.' Science fiction is a small town, and naturally people are going to talk. But the whole thing's absurd; Jim was not my only editor on the book, and he had to have the approval of a considerable number of people at Dell before he could spend that much of the publisher's money."

Was *The Snow Queen* written as pure entertainment? Or does she feel there are messages in it, and in her other work?

"I like to be entertained a lot; I make no bones about that. So I write stories that I hope are entertaining. But in addition, they do have messages. A lot of reviewers miss the messages entirely, which I find amusing or annoying, depending on my mood; but I do have basically important things to say about the human condition. I suppose my favorite themes are the difficulty of communication between beings—human, alien, and otherwise—and the importance of that communication, of overcoming the misunderstandings that cause most of the problems in our lives. I also feel that it is very important to write about strong female characters, and male characters who have human emotions and are allowed to feel human and make mistakes and see through to the other side of them. I have known men who have appreciated my outlook and have said, 'I don't usually like writing by women, but I like this.' If they can read about strong female characters and accept them, I hope that when they meet such people in real life they won't find them so threatening. I like a good adventure story too, of course; and frankly a spoonful of sugar helps the medicine go down."

Has her writing been influenced at all by commercial factors?

"No, I have been entirely independent from commercial considerations for most of my writing career. I started writing as a career after I got married to Vernor, when he encouraged me to take it seriously. I would not have had the self-confidence otherwise; he gave me the impetus to actually send my work out. He was working in a stable job as a university professor, so we had comfortable means, and I was lucky enough to be subsidized. Being a writer, your income does fluctuate a lot; I've gotten to the point now where I actually can support myself, but in my first year I only made something like a thousand dollars.

"Part of my trouble is and always has been that I write very slowly. I think it would be impossible for me to pound out a lot of words, just to put bread on the table. I get very anxious if I feel I'm writing because I need money; I find that very detrimental. It's much nicer to have no pressures—anybody can tell you that.

"I'm now having great attacks of anxiety about combining writing with being a mother, and how one is going to interfere with the other. It's important to me to have fair amounts of time when I can be quiet and think, in order to write. I can see I'm going to have to hire a baby-sitter just so I can write to get money to pay the baby-sitter."

Throughout all of our conversation, she seems to have taken care not to say anything that might upset anyone. "I don't like to offend people," she remarks. "And I hate it when they offend me. Life is difficult enough. So I'd just as soon not put my most personal opinions in print with my name on them."

She adds, however, that, *off the record*, she has all kinds of strong, outspoken opinions. Hearing this, I suddenly wonder if—is it possible?—deep within this seemingly gentle soul there boils a stinking cauldron of malice, and late at night she slips into a secret cellar, slices gingerbread replicas of her colleagues into tiny pieces with an X-acto knife, and feeds them to her pet buzzard.

But no. When I turn off the tape recorder and she tells me her private opinions, they turn out to be quite mild-mannered and moderate—*X*'s books have too strident a feminist message for her taste, or *Y* is a male editor who seldom publishes stories by women, and so forth.

So I have to report that what everyone says is true. So far as I can tell, Joan Vinge really *is* a nice person.

BIBLIOGRAPHICAL NOTES

Joan Vinge's first novel was *The Outcasts of Heaven Belt* (1978), which depicts in detail the emotional and technical difficulties of asteroid colonists whose resources are running out. Highly realistic and (inevitably) rather claustrophobic, it is a valuable view of the limits to life in space. The same scenario recurs in her novella *Legacy* (1978), collected in one volume under that title together with a novella by Steven G. Spruill.

Vinge's second novel, *The Snow Queen* (1980), portrays a planetary monarch who clones herself and names the clone as her successor, in an attempt to evade her cultural code mandating transfer of power when her planet's climate goes through a slow periodic change. Mythic, romantic, and fantasy-flavored, the story is strengthened by its substantial scientific rationale.

PHOTO BY CHARLES PLATT

Harry Harrison

The young high-tech hero, armed against adversity with pocket calculator, soldering iron, and a set of socket wrenches, seems so quaint these days. His language is too technical. His little lectures on physics and engineering strain the attention span of readers reared on the rhythms of TV commercials and videogames. Science fiction should have computers in it, and fancy gadgets and so forth . . . but we don't really need to know how all that stuff *works*, do we? And we certainly don't want to know about its inconvenient real-life limitations. Thrust aside the time-consuming complexities of that computer bombsight, Luke; shut your eyes and go with the flow of the Force. It's more dependable than Yankee ingenuity, and so much simpler than scientific method.

Technologically accurate adventure fiction isn't dead yet, of course—semi-comatose, it still survives, notably in the pages of *Analog* magazine, its birthplace. But Robert Heinlein, the garrulous guardian who nurtured it to maturity, abandoned the form years ago. Many other writers also left it, seeking other areas of greater ambition, social relevance, and literary pretension.

And why not? The rewards for accurately researched science fiction were always small. You had to stay scientifically up-to-date, you were paid a pittance, and serious critics ignored you. No matter how well you did it, you were still writing category fiction of few literary virtues.

If you took extra trouble to get the science right, that was largely between you and your conscience—*The New York Times Book Review* certainly wouldn't notice.

So it is that Harry Harrison has been relatively rarely reviewed, revered, or even remembered by critics. For Harrison has stayed steadfastly within the technologically oriented, action-packed school. That he has exploited its potential more sensitively and resourcefully than most of his contemporaries has often been overlooked.

Of his twenty-nine novels, he remains best known for *Deathworld* and *The Stainless Steel Rat*, both of which grew into series; and for his most ambitious book *Make Room! Make Room!* which was debased into the movie *Soylent Green*. He has been writing science fiction for more than thirty years: methodically, persistently—and uneconomically, for much of that time. Science fiction in the 1980s can be lucrative for some, including those who, like Harrison, manage to keep their earlier books in print. But back in the 1950s and 1960s, there were only two ways to make a decent living: by turning out large quantities very fast and (usually) rather sloppily, or by treating science fiction as a labor of love and earning a living by writing other stuff on the side.

For many years, Harrison chose that second option.

"I spent ten years writing Flash Gordon, to stay alive," he recalls. "The syndicated strip. Every daily and Sunday for ten years, from 1958 to 1968, every one of those scripts was mine. I also ghost-wrote a lot of stuff. I ghosted comics for Leslie Charteris for years. I wrote for confession magazines; I did 'I was an Iron Lung Baby.' I did men's adventures such as 'I Went Down in my Submarine,' right through 1957, for a nickel a word—maximum!

"But my science-fiction novels have always been novels that I wanted to write. Every single book. That's what's great about science fiction; you can write a book for fun, and have it published.

"The *Stainless Steel Rat* books I almost write for money. I sign the contract and think, 'Not another one.' But once I start writing I sit there laughing like a drain and enjoying myself."

Harrison talks in restless, staccato bursts, moving the conversation along as fast as the action in some of his novels. He's a mix of contradictions: raconteur and drinking buddy, yet secretly shy; aggressive yet a diehard liberal and hardcore pacifist. He advocates ground-breaking experiments in fiction, at the same time that his own writing stays true to time-honored techniques. He made his career as a writer, but for the first ten years he worked as an artist:

"I went to art school, I found working in art really tremendous. I did classical painting—easel painting—but then I went into commercial art because I knew I'd never make a living at fine-art painting. I wasn't that good. But I was pretty first-rate as a comic artist. I broke into comics with Wallace Wood. We were in art school together and we penciled and inked together, early stuff. Horror was very big then, Bill Gaines was doing horror comics, we were doing westerns for him, some horror for him.

"Then I illustrated science-fiction magazines. I illustrated for *Galaxy*, I did some book jackets for Gnome Press, I did that mostly for a hobby, I got ten dollars for a drawing, was still making a living off comics. I got to know all the science-fiction writers because I was Harry the Artist, doing all this. Then I was packaging comics, editing comics, when the *putsch* came, when the comics went from 680 to 200 titles a month, a lot of artists were walking the streets. It was the end of the world.

"So I started editing pulp magazines. I did *Rocket Stories* and *Sea Stories* and *Private Eye*, and Lester del Rey was doing *Science Fiction Adventures* for the same company, he got fired and I took over the magazine. I think I sold my first story around then, in 1951, to Damon Knight; I said, 'What do you think of this story, Damon?' And he gave me a hundred dollars for it.

"But I was still doing other stuff, in New York, to earn a living. I was writing confessions stories, anything, freelance. Bruce Elliott was an old friend of mine, I used to give him work when I was an editor, he'd give me work when he was an editor; in the old days you had to pass work around, there wasn't much work so you gave it to your friends. *Nepotism ruled OK*, you know? I had to get out. I didn't want to be art director—if you're art director you have to read all the crap in the magazine. And I was tired of writing it, so I got about two hundred dollars, gave up my job, my wife Joan gave up her job, we had an old Ford Anglia, took that to Mexico, put the baby in the back, one year old. Never came back to New York except on visits."

Harrison has traveled a lot, since then, living all over Europe and writing an average of one science-fiction novel a year. His first, *Deathworld*, was a deliberate attempt to write a story of non-stop danger and action. It was an instant classic and he followed it with several more in the same vein.

"I did *Deathworld* about seven or eight times in various ways. Once I got the formula right I disguised it with different kinds of titles. *Deathworld* had worked, I knew I could make money off that formula.

"But in the end I had to get out of the routine, so I wrote *Bill, the Galactic Hero*."

This, Harrison's comic novel satirizing many of the storytelling traditions of science fiction, was rejected by Berkley, the first publisher Harrison submitted it to.

"I gave Damon Knight, who was reading for Berkley Books, a couple of chapters and an outline with some vague idea of where it would go, and thought he'd give me like $1,500, $750 of that on signing the contract. But when it came in he bounced it, saying, 'It's an OK book but you made a mistake, it's an action novel, go through it and take out the jokes.'" Harrison rolls his eyes in despair at the memory. "So I submitted it to Doubleday, and they bought it. But it was very heart-stopping for a while, there; I feared all along that I'd written a book that no one wanted, and for a while it seemed I was right, no one wanted it. I got so shocked by that that I went back to doing *Deathworld* again, or something like it, and built up slowly, to the work it would take to get *Make Room! Make Room!* done."

In that novel, written at a time when few people took overpopulation very seriously, Harrison projected as carefully and thoroughly as possible the future effects of an uncontrolled birth rate. The job took five years, and he has not attempted anything as challenging since.

However, even his lighter novels are scrupulous in their use of science and technology, and are sufficiently factually accurate to placate the most nit-picking engineer. Also, there is often an underlying political or social message.

Where this is concerned, Harrison seems to be the only high-tech science-fiction writer who espouses a left-wing ideology as opposed to the conservatism of others such as Heinlein, Pournelle, Niven, or Bova.

"Well, most engineers *are* pretty right-wing. But being right-wing is just a native American fashion. We always had it. We've also had native American socialism. We almost had a socialist president—Eugene Debs was two million votes from being elected president. That's what frightened the far right in America, who gave us what we have now, no liberal press, no liberal thought, and a disaster like the present president. Oh, you'll say there are a few liberal outlets around, but say you live in the small town of Asshole, Texas. You get a Hearst paper in the morning, a Hearst paper at night, a Hearst TV station, and if that's not enough you can read *Time* and *Newsweek*. What do you know about nine-tenths of the world? Americans are just as uninformed as *Pravda* readers in Russia, from the opposite point of view. We have freedom in this country, no one's denying that, but freedom of information is something else altogether. When you're getting nothing but one political attitude all your life, you have no real freedom of choice. And you wonder why they elected Reagan?"

Harrison himself has now settled outside of his native America, in Ireland. "I very rarely go to science-fiction conventions, I never do the big hoo hoo and the big ha ha, and they don't know that I'm alive, that little clique that wins those bought-and-paid-for prizes like the Hugo and Nebula. I'm not part of it; *Skyfall*, a book of mine that sold a quarter of a million copies—they printed about 350,000 and actually sold a quarter of a million—never received one nomination for a Hugo or a Nebula. So I have a strong suspicion that someone's buying and someone's reading, but someone else altogether is nominating.

"The Hugo and Nebula mean a lot as far as money goes, if you mention them on a book cover. But one award, I won't tell you which, I really have seen won by ballot-box stuffing. But we really don't want to go into print about Nebulas and Hugos do we? I mean are they important in the world? They're no different from, say, the Oscars, which are also bought and paid for—they must be, if really rotten pictures like *The Deer Hunter* win and good pictures are ignored. Something rotten always wins awards; which is why Brian Aldiss and I founded the Campbell award, which is voted by a handful of people who have critical, writing, or editing experience, enjoy science fiction, and also have experience of literature outside of science fiction."

I mention that some people regard the Campbell award as being cliquish.

"It's no more cliquish than a Nobel Prize. We have one judge in Sweden, two in England, one in Ireland, one in Germany, three or four in the United States, and for six months we correspond intensely, and then we use the Australian system to vote. Where's the clique? If anything it's the direct opposite. What does Tom Shippey have in common with Jim Gunn? And Kingsley Amis is a new judge. That's a clique? Come on now."

Judges of the Campbell Award have also been criticized for picking books which editor John W. Campbell, after whom the award was named, would have found unreadably modern. It seems odd that Harrison, who sold most of his early work to Campbell's magazine, should continue to write straightforward storytelling himself, at the same time that he advocates breaking the old storytelling rules. Of the "new wave" of the sixties, he remarks:

"I could never write that kind of thing. I couldn't afford to write it. I am a slow writer, which means I have to be a commercial writer, because if I'm only doing one book a year I can't afford to have that book not sell. So as a writer I have a specifically defined area that I can work in. As a reader and an editor I have a much larger one."

And as a reader, his tastes are not satisfied by much of the science fiction currently being published.

"I think it's pretty rotten for the most part. Badly written, completely derivative, digging out old plots—rewriting Edgar Rice Burroughs if it's possible. And this whole new move to fantasy; it's so easy to write fantasy. You're not really writing science fiction when you take a world so far in the future that it's completely isolated from everything we know.

"I love female writers, I always try to anthologize women who write, some really fantastic people like Kate Wilhelm and Kit Reed and Sonya Dorman, but they don't write enough, so instead we have what I can only describe as the 'tears and Tampax' school of science fiction, prizes for dreamsnakes and dragons, that kind of stuff. You've read it, or at least you've held it in your hand. Have you ever read one? All the way through? Hmm, strong fellow! Did you enjoy every word of it? Well, tell me later, off the record, eh?

"Not too long ago I was on television in Britain with four or five writers, one of whom shall be nameless, and people were saying how wonderful he was and I was sitting there very quiet. Then someone read the jacket copy of his book and it said, 'More ideas than in six other science-fiction novels.' And I said—'Yes, *all* the ideas *taken from* six other science-fiction novels.' So now he's not talking to me anymore. But you know you get a little fed up after a while. You pick up a book and you read the first chapter, and you know what's going to happen. The writer's fairly incompetent, can't handle the English language at all. Juvenile, puerile, repetitious—and ninety-five percent are that way."

Does he think that there must be good manuscripts that are not being bought by editors for some reason?

"*Everything's* being bought. That's the worst part of it. I was so glad when science fiction expanded, I thought there'd be so much more printed and a residual amount of good stuff would be there. But now it's expanded, it turns out nothing residual is any good. The new writers coming in don't seem to know how to write at all. And by new writers I don't mean people like Tom Disch, who is still referred to as 'new' even though he's been around for fifteen years. Who's come along since him? Very few of any consequence."

I ask what Harrison's own ambitions were, when he was a new writer himself, starting out. Looking back, he seems to come to the conclusion that ambition never really came into the picture. It was more a matter of surviving on a day-to-day basis.

"I was born in Stamford, Connecticut, in 1925. When I was two years old I moved to New York. My father was a printer, stone broke during the Depression, moving house in midnight flits every three months, beans-and-tea, all that kind of thing.

"My generation was a draftee generation. We knew the second we turned eighteen, we'd be in the army. I went in in 1943, and we didn't even know if we'd win the war or not. So we never looked ahead; you'd fart around in school, try to chase girls, couldn't get near them in those days. And you saw it coming, a sort of a feeling of doom, you never really thought where you were going to go, except stay alive; get through high school and a week later you're in the army.

"I came out of the army, I was happy to be alive, but it was a tremendous thing to readjust to civilian life. It wasn't a matter of ambition, it was just staying alive again. People forget, you know, the shell-shock from the war. A lot of guys became alcoholics, couldn't readjust. You're shaped by the army, that horrible, stupid institution. I couldn't even read; I worked down to the *Daily News*, there was nothing I could read that was more complicated, and then one day I found I couldn't even read that. Well, if you're in an emotional position where you can't read the *Daily News*, you've got trouble, buddy!

"I worked out of it, you know, drank a bit more, the usual solutions you go through. Nobody could afford shrinks in those days. I went to art school, became a comics artist. That field was pretty cheap, though, so it was still a matter of staying alive. But I experienced the joys of reading science fiction, and meeting the writers and the artists and the editors in the field, the bunch of drunkards.

"I never had any big ambitions except to stay alive as an artist rather than have a job. I loathed jobs. Mild aims. Staying alive with a family is enough, without high-flown literary ambitions. Yes, you want your novels to be accepted, you want Book of the Month Club. But also, being a science-fiction writer, you're always being knocked down, you're in plenty of hubris, let me tell you. My novel *Captive Universe* went through three editors at Book of the Month Club. One of them loved the book; the other said 'Yeah, we'll take it I guess'; and the last one said, 'It's science fiction, we can't take it.' Two months later they took *The Andromeda Strain*, packaged as being 'not science fiction.' You get enough experiences like that, you expect no justice, you know.

"I've written books that tried to get out of the field. Like *The Technicolor Time Machine*, which almost got out of it. Every fourth or fifth book I take a deep breath and write one that can bridge—and no one notices it. With *Make Room! Make Room!* I tried to get out, and Doubleday said 'No, Harry, if we do it as a straight novel we'll sell three hundred copies.' They wouldn't have promoted it or anything. I sold it to the films years later by accident. There was a lawyer who wanted to buy it, and once he bought it he sold it to MGM for a dollar—he was fronting for MGM all the time. They don't want to give the author anything. That's the history of film. You think publishing is ruthless; try those swine out there in Hollywood. You have to be just like they are, go for the throat, tear it out, show no mercy!

"Someone once sent me a clipping from some magazine, an interview with George Lucas, saying, 'I grew up reading science fiction, I really was a fan of science fiction, but I didn't like things written by people like Heinlein or Bradbury, I thought Harry Harrison was my god, and I enjoyed everything he wrote.' That kind of thing. I thought, 'Well! Why the hell didn't you write to me and have me do a god damned script for you, you know, if *that's* what you feel, *old son*, I'd be very happy to come over and make some money from this rotten field.' Oh, there's no justice in this field. But I earn a living in it, I live abroad, I have all my novels in print in English, all thirty of them, and in twenty-one other languages as well. I get a lot of reversions of rights and sell them again, my kids are growing up, the financial pressures get less. I was screwed blind a couple of times, we've all been screwed blind by publishers, but they can't screw me anymore. Films screwed me once but can't screw me again. And I'm making a living at it, I'm not going to suffer over it, you know, I'm not going to fall into the syndrome of another of our friends who spends his time worrying about money he didn't earn. Eat, drink, and be merry."

BIBLIOGRAPHICAL NOTES

Harry Harrison's *Deathworld* series commenced with the novel of that title (1960), describing the struggle to tame a planet whose virulently dangerous life forms evolve rapidly in reaction to hostile thoughts from human colonists. *Deathworld 2* (1964) and *Deathworld 3* (1968) depict further adventures.

The Stainless Steel Rat (1961) was the first of a series that still continues, featuring an arch criminal turned interstellar cop. The tone is intentionally light, with the accent on action and invention.

Bill, the Galactic Hero (1965) went further into outright comedy, including some satire of science-fictional sacred cows such as Asimov and Heinlein.

Make Room! Make Room! (1966) was, by contrast, an entirely serious and impassioned warning against overpopulation, and remains possibly the best-researched novel dealing with that theme. The content was considerably degraded when remade as the movie *Soylent Green*.

More recently, *Skyfall* (1976) is a disaster novel, aimed partly at a non-science-fiction audience, and *Tunnel Through the Deeps* (1972) postulates an alternate world in which the British Empire won out in the American revolution, and a tunnel link is built across the Atlantic.

PHOTO BY AMY MEADOW

Donald A. Wollheim

The office is like something out of a TV series—*Dallas*, perhaps. It's a Hollywood fantasy of how a New York executive's lair should look.

The decor is muted beige. There are plants in tubs. Fluorescent lights gleam on the chrome trim of the swivel chairs. The only sound is a faint hiss of air conditioning, as the corporation president sits talking on the telephone, behind his large desk facing huge windows of tinted glass. It's a corner office—naturally!—and from up here on the thirty-second floor, there's a classic Manhattan panorama of skyscrapers reaching into the afternoon haze.

The man behind the desk is Donald A. Wollheim, editor-publisher of DAW Books; and, for him, it hasn't always been quite like this.

Think back, for a moment, almost to the dawn of intelligent life in science fiction as we know it. The year: 1934. The magazine: *Wonder Stories*. The editor: pseudoscience visionary Hugo Gernsback. The writer: Wollheim, then a naive nineteen-year-old, selling his first story for the mind-boggling sum of ten U.S. dollars.

The story is published. But the check never comes.

Wollheim grows suspicious. He locates other authors and learns Gernsback hasn't paid them, either. He hires a lawyer on behalf of all the writers. Gernsback finally settles out of court for a lump sum of seventy-five dollars, of which Wollheim's lawyer takes ten.

A low-budget beginning; with more to follow.

Wollheim becomes an editor himself at a succession of grubby, cheesy adventure magazines—the kind with ads at the back for muscle-building techniques, the Rosicrucians, and elevator shoes. One of these magazines is so cheap, its editorial budget is literally zero. But Wollheim perseveres.

He joins Avon Books, in the 1940s, when it's a fledgling enterprise specializing in sexed-up detective novels and general low-grade sleaze—the type of books that have to be sold fast, before the paper turns brown and spontaneously disintegrates. As editor, Wollheim works for "the kind of man who boasts he's never read a book in his life. He'd judge a book by riffling through the pages; if he didn't see anything salacious, he wouldn't buy it. He thought that that was how people bought books at newsstands." Wollheim sticks it out at Avon for five miserable years.

Then he establishes Ace Books with publisher A. A. Wyn. Ace is never a high-class operation, but they put out more science fiction than anyone else, and give a lot of unknown writers their first chance in the field.

But—A. A. Wyn dies in 1968 and his estate sells Ace to a Wall Street conglomerate. They decide to expand the business; so with shrewd commercial acumen they hire a man whose entire experience has been in manufacturing pumps. Within three years, Ace is almost bankrupt.

Wollheim bails out. He starts DAW Books—as his own boss, this time. He signs with New American Library, one of the biggest established paperback houses, to use their printing and distribution. But he retains complete editorial and financial control of his business. He moves into that plush corner office on the thirty-second floor at the big black Paramount tower on Fifty-first Street and Broadway.

After forty years of low-budget operations, it looks as if Wollheim is safe at last. But as you might imagine, with a background like that, he is a considerably cautious man. He knows the cheap basis on which science fiction was run for so long. He knows how easy it is to make mistakes and lose all that you've gained.

And so he has run DAW Books, for ten years now, in a very conservative style.

"You don't change a successful formula unless it stops being successful," he tells me. "We do five titles a month, one of which is a reissue, sometimes two. Our sales are excellent. We don't print the number of books that a firm like Pocket Books or New American Library would print, we don't publish millions of copies, but we're successful. We don't engage in gambling; the royalty advances I pay are based upon known facts of the previous sales of the author. We operate very carefully.

"I have the option, if I wish, of going into hardcovers, or trade paperbacks [the large-size paperbacks which many publishers are turning to as hardcovers become unaffordable], or I could expand our line. My co-publishers, New American Library, have always said that they'd be happy to see us do it. But I see no point to getting into a field in which I don't have the figures. I don't believe in changing a successful formula."

I ask him if he can tell me exactly what this formula is.

"If you are an editor whose taste is equal to that of, let's say, seventy-five percent of your potential readers, then you're going to be successful. If you have a rather esoteric taste, and you only reach twenty percent of the possible public, you will not be successful.

"That is not to say whether that taste is right or wrong. But for better or for worse, I happen to have the kind of taste which is the lowest common denominator.

"I'm occasionally wrong; but when I buy a DAW book it represents the kind of book I probably like, and it's the kind of book that I think my readers will like.

"I myself do read other books—there are science-fiction books that I have enjoyed immensely, which I wouldn't publish. Let my competitors do them! But generally speaking, when I publish a book, it's because I like it."

What qualities does he particularly look for?

"I honestly can't answer that. If I enjoy a book, I get into it. I escape into it. And if that happens to me, I feel it's going to happen to my readers.

"If I read a book which I find difficult, despite the fact that it may have bright ideas, then I keep thinking my readers are going to start fidgeting at the same time I start fidgeting."

Paradoxically, despite Wollheim's simple tastes, while he was at Ace Books he bought novels from new writers who went on to become some of the most progressive or even avant-garde in the field. I mention a few names: Samuel R. Delany, Philip K. Dick, Robert Silverberg, Ursula Le Guin, Thomas M. Disch, John Sladek, Michael Moorcock, Brian Aldiss.

"It's true that from the beginning, Delany tended to be very literary; his novels were never clean, straight hacked. So I edited him. But when he got a little famous, and got a little power over editors, he made them publish the books over again in the original versions, you may recall. He was always a writer who was firmly convinced of his own genius, and ended up ramming it down the throats of his editors. I acknowledge him as a fine literateur; but he isn't writing what I want to read, now, and I have a feeling he isn't writing what my readers would want to read.

"There are some writers who can get away with experimenting, and Philip K. Dick is one of them. But I don't see him as being an avant-garde writer. At Ace Books, where we did a good many of his earliest works, people liked them. And Ace was a great company for putting out hack fiction, you know.

"As for Silverberg, in my opinion he has not really changed. He became terribly introverted for a period and wrote very troubled work. He got over his 'hack' period, but he's still able to do that, and I think his present work shows a lot of it. I would still publish Silverberg, if he wanted to write for me. But he doesn't have to write for me, because now he commands very high rates and hardcovers. Even so, I don't see him as changing that much."

I ask Wollheim for his overall perspective on science fiction today.

"I tend to be discouraged about the sheer quantity of books being done by other publishers. Some of these books are junk, and some of the writers are being hideously overpaid, which is distorting their view of the field.

"Some companies have been increasing their lines, but we're in a recession period, and money is tightening up, so I think it's a very strange risk to take. I'm pleased that DAW can simply maintain its line; we could go up to six books a month, but I have no plans to do it. I hesitate because I know that it's costing people an awful lot to buy books these days. They're not thirty-five cents or even fifty cents any more.

"So I think there are a lot of wild things being done by my dear competitors. They're paying some crazy prices to some of the authors; in the case of Frank Herbert or Robert Heinlein, that's obviously worthwhile, but if publishers pay equivalent money for unknown authors, that money is not going to be earned back, which is the sort of thing that causes accountants to say, 'We'll cut out science fiction for next year, it isn't doing well.'"

If it doesn't make good sense for publishers to pay out large sums, why do they do it?

"I've always said that any damn fool can spend money. As long as it's somebody else's money, believe me, it's no problem! The problem is, can an editor hold his job two years later, when the last of the sales figures come in?

"Everybody in this business tends to be working a little bit blind. I have the figures to tell me which DAW Books authors are selling. We have stopped publishing some authors, because I discovered that they didn't have the audience. You'd be surprised at some of their names.

"Then I see these same authors being picked up and published extensively by other companies, and I say to myself, 'Do they know what they're doing? Are they successfully selling the author I can't sell, and, if so, how are they doing it?' I don't know. And the truth is that even the editors, who are only hirelings, usually don't know either. Only the publisher and his accountants know.

"The motivation for paying a lot for a novel should be, of course, to get a well-known, selling writer on your list. If the writer really does sell, then your gamble pays off. But I'm not a gambler by nature."

Does he think that Heinlein's *The Number of the Beast*, for example, ever really earned back the $500,000 that its publisher paid for it?

"Yes, I think it probably has. Apparently the readers who know Heinlein's name are not critical. I think myself that the book is unreadable, but nobody discovers that till they buy it, and Heinlein's gotten away with four or five books, now, which are equally unreadable. Evidently the public can always be stung once more. On a smaller scale, I don't think you can get away with that, but on a larger scale, apparently, you can.

"Still, the history of capitalism is full of that sort of thing. Look how many years Detroit got away with making rotten cars, until the crunch came!

"But, again, an editor is spending somebody else's money, and the 'somebody else' these days is often a giant corporation of which the entire publishing business is one small subsidiary. So if they lose half a million that year, what the hell, they write it off, they're making money at something else. Remember why RCA decided to get rid of

Random House, Ballantine, Knopf, Pantheon, you name it, some of the best publishing imprints in the field? Because it was penny-ante stuff—they could make more money making paper bags! Yes, there's more money in paper-bag manufacture than book publishing. Check it out some day. Publishing is a tiny field compared with the billion-dollar corporate industries that dominate the world."

How does he feel about the trend toward fantasy as a separate category?

"The increase in fantasy is attributable to the tremendous success of the Tolkien novels, which caused publishers to say to their editors, 'Let's do books like these.' And it's much easier to write outright fairy-tale fantasy than it is to write a story which is going to be credible to somebody who is even remotely science-oriented."

What about the trend toward science fiction that doesn't have any real science in it?

"We now say in physics that we are uncertain about the absoluteness of any scientific law. We discovered that everything is not beautifully mechanical, as it seemed in the 1920s, so that almost anything is now possible. This theory that there could be innumerable alternate parallel worlds, for instance. There is so much vagueness today in physics, that the basis of science fiction can be easily transferred into fantasy. And of course we also have this general concept that humanity is going to go out into the universe and colonize ten thousand planets. Then if they somehow lose contact with each other we'll reach a situation where every planet is an island, so that any world can be a fairy-tale world. Middle Earth can be circling some other star. Who knows the difference? Why bother to explain it?"

I suggest that this is an invitation for authors to become lazy.

"I think you're right. Of course it is. You get a lot of people coming into the field today who are not deeply grounded in science and don't really care for it much. Science has become kind of difficult for the average person to follow too easily. So science fiction has its average-type works, its potboilers, its hacks, as well as its bright spots. But on the whole science fiction tends to have more bright spots than any other category fiction. Because every work is an attempt to do something unique. So even hack work comes out with an occasional bright idea or a new twist."

As an editor-publisher who used to be a writer himself, I ask Wollheim how he feels about writers who claim that publishers are ripping them off in various ways—by paying royalties late, drawing up scurrilous book-publishing contracts, and so on.

"The writer's viewpoint is completely divorced from some of the realities of the publishing field. One of the things that some of them have been stressing is that money earned on sales of an author's book is not paid to the author for many months. That is, if the book earned a lot of money in January, the author's not going to get it until September. The theory is that publishers are taking these millions of dollars and investing them to make eight months' solid interest.

"Well that sounds terrible, but from the publisher's end of the field, this just isn't so. The publishers just don't have that money. It comes in in dribs and drabs, they never have it to sock away in the bank. Every time the royalty payment period comes around, twice a year, you'll find a lot of publishers running to the bank to *borrow* money, in order to pay authors their royalties."

Does Wollheim think that the Science Fiction Writers of America, a kind of union group, has done anything constructive?

"I think it's a lot of hogwash, mostly. I think the Nebula Awards that they give are a lot of hokum. It has all the characteristics of a fan organization: backstabbing, internal rivalries, all this nonsense."

They have a "model contract" that they suggest should be adopted by publishers, to give authors a fairer deal.

"I don't like it. A contract is basically a partnership agreement in which the publisher says to the author, 'Let us go hand in hand as partners on this. You have written a book, we will put up our money to print, distribute, and sell it, and we'll divide the profits.' To take the viewpoint that the publisher is only a commercial operation and the author is simply a character selling a product, and wants a guaranteed payment, is one-sided.

"But the thing that counts is this. In the seven or eight years since that model contract was produced, nobody that I have bought a book from has ever proposed or submitted it to me. So the model contract is just another figment of their imagination.

"Another point that writers never think about is that, at any particular time, a publisher is out a great amount of money on the books he has paid for. If he pays an author $5,000 or $20,000 or half a million, that's money he's loaned out to an author. It's supposed to be earned back by the sales of the book, but that won't happen for one, two, or three years.

"Right now—this is July—I'm scheduling the books I'll be publishing in April next year. These books have been bought from the authors, who have been paid. Now if you figure four new books a month, on which money has been paid out, and keep adding that up, you realize there's a great sum involved there. Plus the fact that I've actually committed myself to books a year or more *beyond* next April.

"This means that, at any one time, I have a tremendous amount of money invested in authors, which is not earning me one penny. It's a free loan to authors! And sometimes the authors don't produce—don't even bother to write the book. And you're never going to get it back from them; there's no sense in suing, which is something publishers soon learn. What has an author got? He's got the roof over his head, and he's lucky if he has that. So you can't collect your money back.

"If you're a major paperback house doing twenty titles a month, you may be out at any one moment from five to ten million dollars. And as fast as you make it back, you have to keep buying new books. It isn't a matter of scheming publishers riding around in their Rolls Royces. Forget it!"

I ask how much capital it would take, these days, to start a totally new, independent paperback publishing company.

"You'd need at least a million or two million dollars, which you couldn't raise, because of the present interest rates and things like that. It would be almost impossible.

"My own intent when I started DAW Books was to be an entirely independent corporation, and raise our own capital, but you can't even think of going into business without a distributor. So what we first did was go around and make contact with distributors and discuss it with them.

"We saw several without getting any acceptance. They usually had several paperback lines they were already handling. Then I tried New American Library, which had just created its own marketing and sales, distributing system. Their attitude was that I could come with them in any way I wanted. I could have been an employee of NAL, I could have created a division of NAL, or I was offered the possibility of co-publishing.

"Co-publishing turned out to be the most practical. I am an entirely independent company; they finance our production; our sales, marketing, and promotion are all handled by them; I buy my own books, my contract is my own and not theirs; the situation has worked out marvelously. The profits, after we pay off our debts for production, are split between us, and it's been profitable for both sides.

"You'll notice I have a corner office, here. One of the four. This is how NAL regards us—as one of the four pillars on which their organization rests. I'm serious!"

Did he ever imagine he'd wind up in such a comfortable position?

"I started out in the deep depression, when nobody had any money. I met a man who wanted me to put out a magazine, even though he hadn't any money for the editorial budget. We had a group of would-be writers that wanted to get into print so badly, they'd write even if they didn't get paid for it.

"In those days science fiction was a very, very small field. Anybody who read science fiction was pretty hard up to find anybody else who did, unless you joined a club, and a club in those days would be ten or twelve people, no more. So there was always that embattled feeling: we were this little group of crackpots that ran around and believed that people were going to fly to the moon."

Wollheim's New York science-fiction society, the Futurians, was formed in 1938. It included members such as Frederik Pohl and Damon Knight.

"We've never really gone our separate ways. There's an affinity. A lot of us are competitors, now, and we've learned to be careful of each other, but I guess we feel a sort of family relationship. You know, 'Hello cousin,' after all these years.

"I find that fans today still have pretty much the same approach as we did then. I can talk to somebody of eighteen or twenty-two and still feel that they're thinking the way we used to think. Even though science fiction is a big business, these days, its fans still have a little bit of that defensive, in-group attitude—a superiority complex which probably comes out of feeling rejected from the everyday world."

Unlike the other Futurians, Wollheim has never strayed from New York City.

"We live in Queens. I was born in New York, and my parents are native New Yorkers, too, so—this is the way it is. I'm familiar with the city. Sometimes it scares the hell out of me, but I'm familiar with it."

He's a cheerful, matter-of-fact businessman—more like the manager of a manufacturing company than most people's image of a book editor. Nor does he have any affectations; in fact his casually frank manner doesn't really match the office he's in.

He looks younger than his sixty-seven years, but at the same time wears a perpetually harassed expression, as if he won't be happy till all the chores are done and his desk has been cleared. In line with his conservatism about spending money and taking risks, he's a hard worker. His wife handles some of the DAW Books publicity, and his daughter now reads unsolicited manuscripts that come in from unknown authors, but Wollheim still handles the rest of the tasks himself—unlike the president of any other publishing house that I can think of. I ask him if he ever plans to retire.

"When I worked at Ace, I was doing up to twenty titles a month, buying them, blurbing them, reading them, contracting for them, the whole bag. Here, I do only five titles a month, one of them a reissue, so this to me *is* a retirement job. We are able actually to take off one week a month, if I feel like it.

"I hope my daughter will take over, if I ever have to quit. But as far as I'm concerned, this is as much as I ever plan to retire."

BIBLIOGRAPHICAL NOTES

Although primarily an editor throughout most of his career, Donald A. Wollheim has written many science-fiction novels, most recently *To Venus! To Venus!* (1970), *Destiny's Orbit* (1962), and *Destination: Saturn* (1967), all under the pseudonym David Grinnell, the third of these titles written in collaboration with Lin Carter.

He wrote prolifically under the Grinnell name in the 1950s, most of the books being planetary adventures; and under his own name he created the "Mike Mars, Astronaut" series of eight books for children (1961–64), dramatizing the space program with thoroughly researched background material courtesy of NASA.

Also under his own name, he has written a book about science fiction, *The Universe Makers* (1971).

As an anthologist he has edited about seventy short story collections, including *The Pocket Book of Science Fiction* (1943). In collaboration with Arthur Saha, he continues to compile the annual *World's Best SF* anthology, a series which he began in 1965, when editor at Ace Books.

Edward L. Ferman

The little two-lane highway snakes up a valley smothered in green. Rounded hillsides, thick with trees, loom hazy in the summer heat. Once in a while there's a glimpse of the Housatonic River splashing over mossy rocks, or a wooden "ANTIQUES" sign comes into view, followed by a little wooden house with old furniture standing out on the lawn. And then the vegetation closes in again, so dense and rich that you can actually smell the sap.

Another highway sign: "Cornwall, incorporated 1740." The road divides, there's a little old rusty cannon on a triangle of grass, a rock shop, a pottery store, the Hitch Post Country Motel (with an American flag outside), the Cornwall volunteer fire department, the National Iron Bank, the Cornwall Bridge Package store, and that's it—that's all there is of downtown Cornwall, Connecticut.

Turn right and continue up alongside a little stream named Furnace Brook, into the hills; turn right again, and there's a fine Victorian house hidden among the trees. *The Magazine of Fantasy and Science Fiction* is edited and published in this country retreat.

F&SF, as most people call it, is such a basic resource in the science-fiction field that readers and writers almost take it for granted. In the decades since 1950, it has never missed its monthly schedule, despite ominous changes in magazine publishing. Science-fiction magazines used to be at the focus of the field, where all the important writers made their debuts and built their reputations. Now, despite successes such as *Omni* and *Isaac Asimov's Science Fiction Magazine*, the magazine market has gotten smaller, and many have collapsed. Since Ferman has been *F&SF*'s editor and publisher for more than sixteen years—longer than any other editor currently in the business—I ask him for his overview.

"So far as the quality of writing is concerned, in the manuscripts I receive, I think standards are as high as they have ever been—or higher. What concerns me is a decline in literacy which may be occurring in the people who are *reading* science fiction.

"I don't know if you saw our June issue, but we published a survey of our readership, based on the returns from 10,000 questionnaires that we'd sent out.

"The one thing that really worries me is that there's been a drastic change in age distribution. Ten years ago, twenty-three percent of our readers were under eighteen, and fifty-three percent were under thirty. Now, only *five* percent are under eighteen. I have to wonder if that means that teenagers aren't reading any more. And I've gotten some letters from people who think that this is indeed true. Sherry Gottlieb, for instance, who owns A Change of Hobbit, the science-fiction bookstore in Los Angeles, wrote in saying she'd noticed that hardly any of her customers are teenagers, now, whereas they used to be mainly high school and college kids. I suppose the kids are all playing videogames, or at the movies, or whatever they do these days. They're not reading science fiction."

Ferman is talking to me in his office on the top, attic floor of the grand old house where he lives and works. He sits behind an antique desk, beside a window looking out onto a wide lawn and tall willow trees. From a room downstairs comes the faint noise of a Selectric typewriter, as his wife and another woman handle correspondence and subscriptions. Then the typing stops and once again there's serene silence.

I ask how the magazine business itself has changed in the past decade or two.

"We always used to be distributed by the American News Company. But they went out of business, which left nothing but a series of independent wholesalers, who essentially found themselves with a monopoly of each area of the country. If you wanted to distribute your magazine in Chicago, say, there was only one wholesaler. And that's still pretty much the case. So, with no competition. . . . " He shrugs and grimaces.

"Meanwhile, at the same time, the small newsstands and corner stationery stores across the country have been going out of business, and their place has been taken by big drug stores and supermarket chains. That's where most magazines are sold now, and these big chains have what they call 'restricted lists': they only want magazines that sell a lot of copies. They want teenage romances or men's magazines or women's magazines. They don't want small magazines, so it's hard to get in.

"We used to sell seventy-five percent of our copies by newsstand, the rest by subscription, and now it's completely reversed itself. It hasn't killed us, because we've concentrated more on subscription promotion and now have almost 50,000 subscribers. But having a big subscription list requires a lot more effort on our part than selling copies on the newsstand, where the national distributor takes care of collecting the money and sends us one big check every month. The one big check is now a very small check."

Edward Ferman doesn't sound gloomy as he describes these problems, even though they've been serious enough to threaten the existence of his publishing operation. In fact he laughs as he mentions the hassles and blunders, as if he refuses to let business worries become the center of his life. I get the impression that he feels a good game of tennis, for instance, is more worthwhile on the cosmic scale of things than sitting fretting over sales figures.

He's a neatly dressed, amiable man, who must be the most civilized—let's not mince words!—the most *normal-looking* male science-fiction editor I've ever met. But then, he's never been a gung-ho science-fiction fanatic like the rest. He didn't enter the field because he was obsessed with it; he fell into it through circumstance.

"My father bought Mercury Press in the 1950s. They had already begun publishing *Fantasy and Science Fiction*, in 1949. So that's how I became connected with the magazine. Purely through nepotism! I grew up with publishing around the house, but not with *Fantasy and Science Fiction*, particularly—that was just one thing they were publishing. They were also doing *Ellery Queen's Mystery Magazine* and *The American Mercury*, which gave Mercury Press its name, and at that time was a very prestigious journal like *The Atlantic* or *Harper's* is today.

"I went to college and majored in English and economics, which turned out to be the right thing to do, in that it set me up to be both an editor and a publisher. I had a feeling, I guess, in the back of my mind, that I wanted to go into publishing. I was not particularly a reader of fantasy or science fiction—except for the books that everyone's read, like *Stranger in a Strange Land*—so initially I went to work for a textbook publisher, Prentice-Hall, editing boring high school textbooks. Textbook publishing was slow, and dull, and picky, so I moved on from that to Dunn and Bradstreet, where I wrote reports on floor-covering companies and ridiculous things like that.

"When Avram Davidson became editor of *F&SF* around 1961, my father said I should come in and learn the business, as assistant publisher and assistant editor.

"Then Avram wanted to move to Mexico and continue editing the magazine from there. Well, we liked him, so we tried it. We used to mail out the manuscripts to Mexico each week, and he'd mail them back, they'd arrive all ragged and smelly—it just barely worked. In the end he quit and I took over, and in 1969 we decided to move out of New York City to the country. And since then it's worked very well."

I ask if Mercury Press still owns any other magazines.

"No. We've *started* several, but—they've been terrible failures!" He sits back in his chair and laughs cheerfully.

"You may remember *Venture* science fiction, which we tried twice, once in the 1950s and once in the 1960s. It was almost successful—but, uh, not quite. Then in the 1960s we did a nostalgia magazine, for three issues. It was called *P.S.*, which was a *stupid* title." He laughs again. "We should have called it *Nostalgia*, but that seemed too *simple* somehow. So we had a long drunken evening trying to come up with a title for this thing. It was a terrible bomb, but it was a good magazine, and we had a terrifically devoted readership—of about 2,500.

"Then we did an occult-supernatural type magazine, like *Fate*, called *Inner Space*. We did one issue of that—which was also a dud.

"There's one other thing we've tried, which is our book-publishing program. The idea was—" He stops himself with a chuckle. "Let's be positive about this. The idea *is*, it still is, to co-publish with Charles Scribner's Sons a small line of science-fiction hardcover books that will be representative of the sort of thing that *F&SF* publishes. I want to publish writers who have just begun getting known, and writers of first novels. Since there aren't many hardcover publishers doing this kind of thing any more, I'm hoping to come up with some very fine books. I still think in the long run it will work out. These are not great times as far as the book business goes; I sense that everybody's kind of pulling back a little, and being very careful, and in a way we are too. But if nobody publishes any first novels, the field is heading for trouble. I'd really like to see some of these people published in hardcover and available in libraries.

"I think I'm a little more enthusiastic than Scribner's are at this point, in that I want to get started even though we may not have the perfect book. They have to approve it, though, because we're splitting the costs fifty-fifty. This all came about, incidentally, through a Scribner's editor who lives up here in Cornwall. I'd known him for years. We just decided to get together and try it."

In view of his own publishing experience, does he think it's possible, at this point, to start a new science-fiction magazine?

"I think magazine publishing is very risky and pretty complicated, so whenever I see any announcement of a new magazine I tend to assume it's going to be a failure." He shrugs. "Most magazines *do fail*. On the other hand, most of the new science-fiction magazines that failed in the last ten or fifteen years were published by people who lacked experience. *Isaac Asimov's Science Fiction Magazine* is successful, or at least has been so far, because it was published by Davis Publications. It's no better than, say, David Hartwell's magazine *Cosmos* was, but it's survived because it's published by a real professional guy who knows exactly what he's doing."

Was Ferman surprised by the success of *Omni*?

"I was absolutely flabbergasted. In fact I'm still not convinced it *is* a success. I've been told that it is, but on the other hand, they would probably go on publishing it, even if it wasn't. So who knows?"

Omni has tried to attract the best science-fiction stories by paying writers as much as a dollar a word—ten times what Ferman can afford. And yet the stories that Ferman publishes are the ones that win prizes. I ask how this can be so.

"Comparing us to *Omni* isn't quite fair, because they don't publish as much fiction as we do. But it is true that more of our stories have won awards over the years than those in other magazines. I think all editors are looking for the same thing: a really well-plotted, entertaining story, which is also beautifully written. There aren't many of these available, so we have to make compromises. Most editors will compromise on the writing quality, but I prefer to say—and this has always been the tradition of this magazine—that I'll publish a story that isn't strikingly original or strongly plotted, provided it is well written.

"This magazine was originally conceived as being somewhat more literary than the others in the field. Which is not to say that it's terribly literary—it isn't! But it's more literary than the *others*. And there's no point in changing something that's worked for us."

Ferman himself has now won an award as Best Editor of 1981. But, of course, he refuses to take this seriously.

"'Best Editor' has always struck me as a totally ridiculous award. First of all, how can any reader know who the best editor is? Why should they have any sense of it? It's just a stupid award, I've always objected to it, and now that I've finally won it I guess I can say so! The only people who really have any idea who the best editor is are some writers and some other editors."

When he chooses stories, does he buy what he likes personally, or what he thinks his readers will like?

"I don't read everything that comes in, of course. Ann Jordan reads the material from people we don't know, and that's between seventy-five and a hundred manuscripts a week, no matter what. It's amazing, the way those manuscripts just keep on coming in. They never stop, and there have always been the same amount, in all the years I've worked on the magazine.

"She passes on to me anything she thinks is good, plus I receive maybe ten or fifteen stories a week that are from professionals or agents. And in general I just buy what I like. I like to read well-written pieces, I don't like to read real crap like Arthur Hailey, you know? On the other hand, I don't normally like terribly demanding or obscure types of fiction. I guess I have middle-class tastes in fiction. Well—" He laughs. "*Upper* middle class, maybe."

Although his magazine has "fantasy" in its title, it never seems to publish the kind of sword-and-sorcery that's so popular right now.

"I tried to read one or two of those books. I couldn't get through them. *Sword of Shanarrah*? Have I got the title right? Awful book. Once you've read one, why bother reading the others? It seems to me they're all basically the same."

Does he have any idea why that kind of fantasy is selling so well?

"I think people in general are much more credulous than they used to be. They're willing to believe almost anything, so writers are giving them what they want, I suppose, and editors have become much less skeptical or rigorous about weeding things out that don't make any sense. I guess people really *want* to believe in flying saucers and poltergeists."

F&SF has always published a good number of stories by women. Does Ferman feel there's any difference between their work and the stories that men write?

"Only to the extent that some of them are obviously concerned with the women's movement, and that concern finds its way, naturally, into their fiction. I'm willing to publish an occasional piece like that because, after all, everybody makes their concerns known in their fiction on occasion, and it doesn't bother me too much.

"I must say that in contemporary literature, the women's movement has gotten so strong, it's taken over so much, I find much of the mainstream fiction written by women really unreadable. If you think it's bad in science fiction, you haven't read people like Marge Piercy! She makes me so mad. Those books are just not meant for men to read. It's a pity, because a lot of women write much better than the men do."

What does he read for recreation?

"I hardly ever read science fiction aside from what I have to read, and the occasional novel from writers whose work I've always liked. For pleasure, I read people like John Updike, Malamud, Cheever, John Fowles. I read detective fiction by people like Donald Westlake, Dick Francis, John D. MacDonald. And straight suspense thrillers. The quality of the writing there is very variable; I can't read Robert Ludlum, for instance. But John Farris is pretty good.

"I tend to read a lot of books around the fringes of science fiction, too, to see what they're doing. That's where Stephen King started.

"And then I read some nonfiction. Some political books like the Kissinger memoirs; I'm interested in politics, maybe a little more than average. I'm active in the Democratic Party here, and used to serve on the planning and zoning commission until I lost an election. I'm a democrat and this is a republican town."

So Ferman's life seems to revolve much more around the small town of Cornwall than the small world of science fiction.

"I like most science-fiction people, they're fun to talk with—though my first contacts with them were kind of intimidating. My first experience was at some science-fiction convention while I was in college, and it seemed like a totally wild, out-of-control scene. My father introduced me and my date to Asimov, who, instead of shaking my date's hand, shook her *left breast*.

"I still go to one or two science-fiction events each year. But if a whole group of science-fiction writers were my best friends, I might feel I had to buy any crap they'd send me, so I prefer to keep business and social separate. Even though I'm working out of my home, here, I start work in the morning around nine-thirty and I generally finish around five or so, and I don't usually work in the evenings, or on weekends."

From this I suspect that Ferman feels no need to be remembered as an editor who devoted his life to science fiction and molded it in his image.

"No, I'm not that kind of mover and shaker. There've been very few of them: Campbell, or maybe Damon Knight. All I intend to do is keep publishing this magazine and, I hope, build up the circulation a little bit so that it's profitable enough to pay the authors a little more, and maybe someday get enough money to have an editor replace me so I can just be the publisher. You see, I'm basically a pretty lazy guy, so I'm content to work just six or eight hours a day."

I suspect that he's exaggerating a little, but even allowing for this, and for his persistent modesty, it's clear that to him science fiction is a job, not an obsession. Perhaps it's easier for him to maintain such a rational air of detachment when he lives in such a remote, peaceful, New England location.

We go outside to his car, which is a dusty black Volvo, looking just as conventional and unobtrusive as he does. He takes me on a short tour of the local tourist attractions. "Don't miss that tree up ahead," he says, as we enter a nearby pine forest. "That's the local landmark. You might say it's the Statue of Liberty of Cornwall, Connecticut. See how it's actually *growing out of the top of that big rock*?"

I marvel at this wonder of nature, and ask how the local residents refer to it.

"Oh," he says, "we call it the Tree on the Rock."

A little farther on, he points out a house where James Thurber used to live. Cornwall was once a center for contributors to *The New Yorker*; some artists and writers still remain, but it has now become an area for New York lawyers and businessmen who maintain homes here that they use only on weekends and vacations.

Our tour ends at the local post office, a white barn with a gray roof, two minutes' walk from Ferman's house. "One of the best things about our location," he claims.

"I hope this interview was some use," he adds, before I leave. "I did warn you at the outset, that I didn't think I was an ideal subject."

More modesty. And yet, someone with such a detached and sensible outlook on the importance of science fiction in real life could hardly be expected to see things any other way.

BIBLIOGRAPHICAL NOTES

Edward Ferman has edited several book-length anthologies of stories that originally appeared in *F&SF*. The most recent is *The Best from Fantasy and Science Fiction: 24th Series* (1982).

In collaboration with Barry Malzberg, he co-edited *Final Stage* (1974), a memorable collection of new short stories.

Kit Reed

There has been, I must admit, a tendency for some of the writers in this book to lament their lives of humiliation, deprivation, and obscurity in science fiction. They're underpaid, they don't get seriously reviewed in the places that count, their editors want them to write action stories for kids instead of serious literature for adults—and, to be fair, much of this is true.

But let's look for a minute at someone in the so-called literary mainstream.

Kit Reed has written two science-fiction novels, and a lot of science-fiction stories, but she's never been trapped in that category. On the contrary, she's produced ten books that weren't categorized at all, and she sold them all to serious, respectable hardcover publishers. Plus she's had a Guggenheim fellowship (1964–65) and a five-year grant from the Abraham Woursell Foundation, and she was a Rockefeller fellow in Aspen (1976)—exactly the kind of classy credentials that science-fiction writers dream of, as they grovel in the ghetto gutters, cursing their fate.

It turns out, however, that life can be just as difficult outside science fiction as in it.

"Sometimes," Kit Reed says, "I look at what I'm doing and I don't know whether I have a career or a very expensive hobby. I know that if I went into high school teaching, full-time, I would make half again as much as I do from writing, because a career in the 'mainstream' world, which is where I have spent most of my efforts, doesn't earn that much money.

"I have taught writing here at Wesleyan, and I had a student whose first and second novels were both bought by Farrar, Straus, and Giroux," (one of the more prestigious New York hardcover publishers), "and he's done very well, but I was pro-rating his income over the five-year period and I realized he's making something like three to four thousand dollars a year. And this is a guy who is a literary *success*!

"Right now, the mainstream fiction market is getting more and more constricting, whereas category fiction seems very healthy to me."

Kit Reed lives in Middletown, Connecticut, on the edge of Wesleyan University. She shares a big, comfortably informal old house with her husband Joseph Reed, who also teaches at Wesleyan and is an exhibited artist.

Her first science-fiction novel, *Armed Camps*, pictured an apocalyptic near-future United States in which the simplistic solutions of militarism and pacifism turn out to be equally inadequate. Her second, recent science-fiction novel, *Magic Time*, takes the idea of Disneyland one step further—to a park where fantasy becomes reality, and some visitors become unwitting participants who are not allowed out. The set-up epitomizes the way in which technology can and is subsuming life; and the characters cope with personal problems that relate to those in the everyday world.

Both novels manage to combine subtlety and adventure. Add to them the two excellent short story collections, and it seems strange that Kit Reed hasn't made a bigger impression in science fiction.

Armed Camps appeared in 1969, *Magic Time* in 1980. I ask why there was such a long gap between the two.

"I felt for a long time that I didn't want to write a science-fiction novel at all. I like science fiction's off-the-wall quality, and the suspension of disbelief, and the idea that anything can happen. But it only seemed worth departing from our so-called reality for purposes of a short story. I didn't want to send my mind off to some alternative system for the length of time that it would take to write a novel.

"I long since quit reading science fiction, for the same kind of reason. It all has to do with what I feel is—real? Real problems, anyway. I don't mean real problems like world hunger; but so much of science fiction is so *unreal*, it seems unimportant to me.

"I've seen too many people who have escaped into genre fiction as a way of avoiding any of the real things about living and writing. The minute you put two characters on a planet and get busy with the hardware and the scenery and all the rest of it, you have caught the interest of a certain kind of reader, when you wouldn't have caught his interest if your characters were living right here and now in a split-level, where you might have to look a little more closely into what their souls are like and what problems they might have. There are all kinds of problems to be solved and ways to live. I don't think books can tell you how to live, but on the other hand, I don't think they should tell you that you don't have to think about it.

"Escapism, to me, is when you present a central character who makes the reader feel transformed into someone big and strong and tough, who can go out and subdue everybody and not be stopped by anybody. Unendurable pleasure, indefinitely prolonged. Sword-and sorcery seems to me the purest form of it: pure wish fulfilment. But fiction is not a place for wish fulfilment, or for escape; the writer should be trying to figure real things out, not trying to get away from them."

This sounds like a moral position, and I think that many of her stories do have an implicitly moral tone—a sense of absolutes, anyway, and of right and wrong. This does not mean that the stories are sanctimonious—on the contrary, they're witty and entertaining. Often, though, the characters are concerned with analyzing the essence of a situation and making an ethically correct decision.

"In the course of what I'm writing," she says, "I'm usually trying to figure something out. The characters and I discover the solution together. In many of the stories, people figure out how to go on living after something disturbing happens."

She's an energetic, animated woman who speaks so quickly it sounds as if the words are getting in the way of what she has to say. She seems formidably intelligent and organized, and she insists on thinking positively.

"As you schlep along through life, you learn more and more about grace under pressure, and all the rest of it, and you realize that there is no real reason to appear to be miserable, no matter what's happening to you. It's kind of a noblesse oblige thing. You make the best show of life that you can. The show must go on.

"I'm not implying that I have a miserable life. What I'm suggesting is that, as two of the characters in *Magic Time* discover in the course of that book, it's a case of recognizing that whatever happens to you, whether it's good or bad, you're going to live another day, unless you get hit by a truck, so you might as well do it with as much style as possible.

"I was in the newspaper business for five years. In the fifth year we had our first child. I worked up until the last week. At that point I think I had sold my first three stories to *Fantasy and Science Fiction*, and then I had the baby, which meant that I was home all day, because at that time the ethic was that you stayed home and did it yourself, you didn't attempt to keep working. So suddenly I had all this spare time—which people with children are infuriated to hear me say, but indeed, I was home, so the fiction suddenly took off, because now it had all my working concentration.

"Women who, for whatever reasons, are unable to manage their families, just hate to hear that I was able to do more writing once I had kids. But my career as a writer of fiction didn't really begin until then, around 1959.

"My experience would also infuriate a great many women in that, as a writer, I was being subsidized. I was learning to be a writer while my husband was paying my rent.

"Would I have done any more if I'd had no children and had been single? Probably not. I think you're never going to be any better than you're going to be; whatever you say got in your way is only your excuse for not having been any better than you were.

"I've been in rebellion since I was about fifteen, but it's been a fairly selective rebellion, basically a productive one. I was never afraid to go anywhere, say anything, or do anything, simply because I grew up in a protected environment.

"My mother was a Southern lady, and Southern ladies don't work. Then I was educated for much of my life by nuns. I went to parochial schools, then to two years in a public high school, and then to Georgetown Visitation Convent in Washington and from there to Notre Dame in Baltimore. So out of sixteen years of education, fourteen were by sisters of various kinds.

"At the college level, the nuns had been freed to live the life of the mind. Of course, there were other sisters behind the scenes, scrubbing and doing the wash, but you didn't know about that, and they probably didn't think about it too much either. As a result, the assumption was that you could do what you wanted with your life.

"Also I suppose I did have this kind of brash quality, maybe because I was an only child, though I don't think that was it. It just never *occurred* to me that I couldn't do what I wanted."

So, she says, she never experienced the conflicts and prejudices that most women talk about, when she took on a "man's job" in the outside world.

"I didn't know anything about sexism. Nobody had told me. I started in the newspaper business on *The St. Petersburg Times* in Florida, and the newsroom was filled with women, because this was a very enlightened paper with enlightened hiring policies. Then I went to *The New Haven Register*, and was kind of surprised that there was only one other woman in the newsroom, but it still didn't cross my mind that I was someplace where I might not be welcome or that there would be problems with it.

"When I started writing science fiction, my name was adrogynous, and for about ten minutes, at least, nobody knew I was a girl. But Kit Reed just happens to be my name."

I ask how she got interested in science fiction in the first place.

"I'd begun by reading the *Oz* books as a kid, and had a certain taste for fiction that departed from reality. Later on it was John Collier, and Roald Dahl. I fell from that into reading science fiction, up until my late twenties. During that period I began writing stories which I sent to the science-fiction magazines.

"Then I received an astonishing rejection letter from, I think, H. L. Gold at *Galaxy*, who said I was too good a writer to waste my time on the likes of his magazine, and why didn't I get serious. By that time I had, anyway, begun to write stories which were supposedly for mainstream magazines, and I had gotten into the first novel, which was a mainstream novel. So what might have been a pure science-fiction career was aborted—but at the same time I went on writing some stories that departed from reality, and the only people that would buy them were science-fiction editors."

So she divided herself between science fiction and contemporary literature, and became impossible to categorize.

"I'm not a woman writer, I'm not a Catholic writer, I'm not a science-fiction writer, and I'm not a Southern writer, even though these are all things which I've done.

"I refuse to write always about the same thing, which is probably why I'm not richer or more famous. Some of my mainline fiction is funny, some of it is elegiac, some of it is psychological. This is how I keep from getting bored, but I suppose it's also what keeps people from remembering who I am. I have this fantasy that some publisher at some point will say, 'My God, this work is all by one person, we really ought to publish all of this person!' But Farrar, Straus, and Giroux, for instance, were only interested in the second and third mainstream novels, they were not at all interested in the science-fiction short story collections. That wasn't their idea of what I was."

Does she have fantasies of writing best sellers?

"I would love to write for money, but when I was first learning to write short stories I would occasionally try to write a *Ladies Home Journal* story, for instance, and it would turn to schlock under my hands. You know, if you are not convinced by what you are doing, it is no good. If I could write like Jacqueline Susann, and be convinced by it, I would do it. But I have this problem, which is that I *can't* be convinced by it.

"There was one occasion in which a fit took me and in three weeks I wrote a novel which is now being published in paperback under a pseudonym. It's about this virus which turns women into homicidal maniacs who kill only men. It was great writing it, just like reading, it was so fast, I did twenty-five pages a day. But it took longer to sell than it should have, because it was inadvertently funny. For instance, there's a woman who has had the virus and has turned into a homicidal maniac—and I somehow can't resist mentioning that she's wearing fuzzy bedroom slippers. That's my problem."

Does she get frustrated and baffled when New York publishers don't share her humor, or her interest in doing a lot of widely different things?

"When you publish your first novel, your assumption is, 'This will be published and I will become famous.' Then you see it not happen, and you become aware of two or three hard facts of life. By the time the second novel is published, you realize which reviews have to appear where, in order for the book to make it, and pretty soon you meet people who tell you even more unpleasant things about publishing.

"When you're a patient who's been told that you have some terrible disease, you get very interested in what the disease is, and you want to know every detail about it, and whether there's a possible cure. Similarly, writers develop an interest in publishing, and feel they have to learn a lot about it, in order to survive.

"It would probably be much nicer just to sit up here in blissful ignorance, and think that everything was fine, and not know that the publishing business was going to rack and ruin and hell in a handbasket. But I know a lot of editors who are scared, and I know quite a few editors who have lost their jobs. I think when editors feel in danger of losing their jobs their approach to whatever you may have written is bound to be affected. They're not looking at your work in and of itself, they're looking at it and wondering how it will affect their careers—will they get fired if they publish this book?

"I think at the moment things are really tough, and it's really scary. So, given the tenor of the business, my plan at the moment is simply—survival at any cost! I'm currently at the stage where I'm sort of casting around to decide what to write next. I'm trying to decide whether I want to write science-fiction stories for a while, until I decide what is going to be the next novel. Or do I want to write mainline stories, do I want to do both, do I want to write something that would *be* both—which would be the most interesting thing for me.

"When or what the next novel will be, I don't know."

BIBLIOGRAPHICAL NOTES

Kit Reed's first science-fiction novel, *Armed Camps* (1969), depicts a near-future United States, under military dictatorship, involved in a seemingly endless war. Told from the alternating viewpoints of a left-wing young woman and a militaristic young man, the story demonstrates the inability of either to resolve the situation.

Kit Reed's second science-fiction novel, *Magic Time* (1981), is a multiple-viewpoint adventure that takes place within a futuristic amusement park. Trapped inside the fantasy environment, citizens find themselves compelled to act out adventure roles for the benefit of an unseen audience; to some extent this is a metaphor for human behavior in modern life.

Her two short story collections are *Mr. Da V. and Other Stories* (1967) and *Other Stories and: The Attack of the Giant Baby* (1981).

Her non-science fiction includes *Mother Isn't Dead She's Only Sleeping* (1961), *At War as Children* (1964), *The Better Part* (1967), *The Cry of the Daughter* (1971), *Tiger Rag* (1973), *Captain Grownup* (1976), and *The Ballad of T. Rantula* (1979).

James Tiptree, Jr.

In 1967, a woman named Alice Sheldon began writing stories under the name James Tiptree, Jr. She kept her real identity secret from everyone in the world, except her husband. She established a P.O. box and a bank account for "Tiptree," and she hid behind that name for ten years, while her remarkable stories attracted all kinds of acclaim and awards. Had it not been for some detective work by a science-fiction fan, she would still be hiding from us now.

Pseudonyms are common enough, of course. Sometimes a writer wants a more glamorous name, or uses different bylines for different categories of fiction. Either way, it's seldom a big secret. Even writers who seek privacy will usually stop short of becoming totally anonymous.

But Alice Sheldon is not like most other writers.

She and her husband live a few miles outside Washington, D.C., close to the headquarters of the CIA, where both of them used to work. Perhaps it's only natural for a one-time agency employee to want to write anonymously. As I journey to interview Alice Sheldon at her home, I wonder if this is the whole explanation, or if there were deeper motives behind the male name. Even now, five years after her identity became known, she has never been interviewed in person.

She turns out to be a strikingly beautiful woman. Only a slight trace of gray at the edges of her curly rufus hair betrays that she might now be over sixty. She has compassionate eyes, and a quick smile; her manner is forthright, with a touch of elegance. She stands with a scrupulously correct military posture, which somehow suggests a refusal to recognize weakness or adversity.

Together with her husband, whose diffident manner and bushy white beard conceal a sharp mind and wit, she shows me around their home, which they designed themselves. It gives the sense of being outdoors, inside; there are large open spaces, large panels of glass, a floor of polished concrete (aesthetic in its simple practicality), a wood-burning stove, and a big pond of multicolored fish. She shows me how to feed a carp so that it nibbles my fingers.

We walk out into a garden full of exotic flowers and trees. Raccoons live in the woods beyond the lawn; she likes to treat them to dogfood and peanut-buttered crackers. In the pines and willows, birds of blue and scarlet call to one another.

As we exchange the smalltalk of strangers, I sense she is discreetly weighing me up. In addition to working for the CIA, she was a behavioral psychologist. Her fiction has been sometimes playful, sometimes formidably perceptive, and I have a suspicion that the same is true of her.

As if to confirm it, she casually mentions some obscure events in my own past history. She's *checked up on me* somehow, to even the score between interviewer and interviewee. When I ask where she discovered the details, she just laughs teasingly and changes the subject.

Changing the subject turns out to be one of her greatest talents. A casual comment about goldfish provokes a little lecture on the mechanism of growth-suppressing hormones. Mention of horses inspires a dissertation on the equitation seat and the cruelty of Arab harnesses. By the time we start the actual interview, I've come to realize that these anecdotes are a form of evasion: She's shy of talking about herself, and switches instinctively to any other topic. And then she stops and apologizes, and tries to control her own waywardness. She wants to do the interview properly, because she is, I think, a woman with a strong sense of duty—as becomes obvious after our in-person conversation is over. She writes me letters, she asks for the tape transcript and returns it covered in amendments, she sends me transcripts of subsequent interviews with other people, and I record three more conversations with her over the phone.

Writing this now, I'm faced with 103 pages (25,000 words) of my own tape transcripts, plus an equal quantity of other transcripts and written material from her, including muddy Xeroxes, letters in tiny, neat handwriting on exuberantly colorful stationery, endearing little postcards, a haphazard bibliography—everything annotated with extra remarks in the margins and on slips of paper taped at the bottoms of pages, as if she became more and more obsessed with the task of telling this story truly and completely.

The trouble is, Alice Sheldon's remarkable life is too big for a profile. As she has described it herself, rather modestly in the third person, for *Contemporary Authors*:

"She found herself interacting with . . . lepers, black royalty in lion skins, white royalty in tweeds, Arab slaves, functional saints and madmen in power, poets, killers, collared eunuchs, world-famous actors with head colds, blacks who ate their enemies and a white who had eaten his friends; and above all, women; chattel-women deliberately starved, deformed, blinded, and enslaved; women in nuns' habits saving the world; an Englishwoman in bloomers riding out from her castle at the head of her personal Moslem army; women, from the routinely tortured, obscenely mutilated slave-wives of the 'advanced' Kikuyu, to the free, propertied Sumatran matriarchs who ran the economy and brought 600 years of peaceful prosperity to the Menang-Kabaui; all these were known before she had a friend or playmate of her own age."

She was the daughter of Herbert Edwin Bradley, an attorney and explorer, and Mary Wilhelmina Hastings Bradley, a writer who taught herself everything from foreign languages to big-game hunting. With them, she saw more of the world by the time she was ten than most of us will ever see.

"Mother and Father dreamed about Africa when they were in their own youths. They became enamored of Carl Akeley, an ornery, cantankerous man, but a multi-faceted genius—one wing in the American Museum of Natural History in New York City is named after him, and devoted to him. His final expedition was in search of the black gorillas of the mountains of Uganda; Father had made a little money in real estate, and said he would finance Akeley if Akeley would take him plus two scientists from Princeton. Somehow, the two scientists turned into me and Mother.

"We walked 2700 miles across Africa, and had 250 porters, carrying sixty-pound loads, because that's what it takes to maintain you for a one-year safari, living on the country. No radios or planes or any means of rescue existed then; all roads, phones, and electricity ended at the coast; and in the interior there were no maps, towns, or landmarks, only foot trails made by the slavers.

"In a sense I was badly brought up, because, by the age of five, if I dropped something I was quite accustomed to clap my hands and have six large, naked cannibals spring to attention and pick it up for me. And I considered it quite normal to have thirty natives watch me having my hair brushed every morning. My hair was so strange, almost white, they weren't quite sure if I was a child or some kind of goddess.

"Mother wrote thirty-five books, including five about Africa. She was the first to state in print, 'Gorillas are tame, delightful creatures, and we've had lunch sitting within ten feet of a troupe of them.'"

Alice Sheldon goes to one of many shelves of books in the converted sun porch at the back of the house, where she works amid piles of papers and overdue mail stacked in big plastic trays. One tray is labeled "For God's sake read these and answer them!"

She pulls out one of her mother's books: *Alice in Jungle Land*. "This one she wrote about me. In has my line drawings in it, and photographs—there's me, riding a baby elephant. I had crêpe-de-chine bloomers on, and they made me ride the bloody thing.

"Once, I ran away; I got into a good patch of elephant grass, where I made a secret house by crushing the grass down. Mother led a search after me and hauled me back out. You know, being hauled out of my James Tiptree retreat, when everyone found out who I was and I had to go back to being Alice Sheldon, was a similar feeling. I guess I cried, if it doesn't sound too soapy.

"I really don't like people paying attention to me. It probably comes from the experience of growing up in Africa, with my parents and their adult companions; I had the feeling of being on a microscope plate, with these six enormous eyepieces goggling down at me. I was my parents' precious child, and I was never left alone, because they'd lost the other nine through miscarriages—they had an Rh problem. I was a classic example of the 'Hartley Coleridge Bind,' which makes children of high achievers so lucrative to psychotherapists."

She felt obliged to equal the achievements of her remarkable mother. "She was a small, red-haired, blue-eyed person, the kind you help through doors, and then discover she can carry a Springfield rifle and walk forty-five miles hunting elephants, and do it again the next day while her first day's partner is resting up in bed, and then do it the next day, and the day after that. Even as a child, without meaning to, you compete."

At the same time, she tried to meet the expectations of her father—who, she learned later, had always wanted a son. "Every time I did anything boy-like, like going into the Army, Father approved deeply."

To these family pressures were added some traumatic traveling experiences. In India: "I remember the streets of Calcutta, which I saw at age nine. As we went for some morning sweet cake, we'd step over dying people with dying babies in their arms, each living their whole lives on one square yard of sidewalk."

In Africa: "The first people I ever saw dead had been accused of witchcraft or thievery. The belief in witchcraft is the curse of African society; it gives free rein to all the paranoid impulses. These two people had first been tortured, and then crucified, on horrible little bushes stuck through their vitals, and flies were crawling over them. At age nine or ten, this makes an impression.

"One effect of this kind of thing," she continues with a smile, as if to downplay it, "is that I have been very gullible and naive all my life. I knew, as facts, so many weird things, that I would believe anything. I had seen people burning their grandmothers on the steppes of the Ganges, so I was honestly a little surprised that when my grandmother died, they buried her in a grave in a cemetery, instead of burning her on the steppes of the Chicago river."

By the time she was twelve, "I had just about had it. I didn't realize that my parents, in the name of love, had dumped their accumulated nervous tensions onto me. I got razor blades and put them in the back of a five-pound history book, and brought it down, sawed and sawed—I was so stupid, I tried this side first." She shows the top side of her wrist, where even now there are thin white scars. "But," she adds quickly, not wanting to suggest that she was courting sympathy or creating a fuss, "I must add, there wasn't any hurrah. I came to, cleaned up the mess, and went to class."

To escape the parental influence, she asked to go to a Swiss school. "I had an unpleasant tendency to be smart, because that was something Mother and Father praised. I didn't know how to talk or act around people of my own age. I was always the youngest, and I never had the sense to be unobtrusive. My little hand would always shoot up if I knew the answer, and the more desperate I got, the cleverer I acted. Like a rat, when the little food pellets give out—he still goes on punching that same button."

And so she was ostracized by the other kids. "I was lonesome and did a great deal of experimenting with getting killed. I would go down to the railroad track, and see how close I could stand when the train to Geneva went through. Every night I would stand closer, and one night something just brushed me, like a feather, except of course it was going past at about a hundred miles an hour."

Later, at Sarah Lawrence college, she still found it hard to fit in. "I was known as 'That Girl' and nobody would room with me. I wasn't in the art club, for example, although by this time I was a selling painter."

She found a strange consolation in the indifference of the universe. "I was a great one for running off from parties and finding a local cemetery or lawn, where I would lie down—even if there was snow on the ground—and look up at the stars. I'd think, 'There's Sirius, and Sirius looks on all things, and *Sirius doesn't care*.' My life, my death—Sirius was utterly indifferent. And that was so comforting; the cold indifference of those stars, I actually felt it, all down my front."

She married for the first time while still at Sarah Lawrence. "I was made into a debutante, and I thought that meant I was on the slave block, so I married the first boy that asked me, three days later. I'd seen him for seven hours. He'd been seated on my left at the party, he was certified as a poet and a gentleman by the president of Princeton, so I ran off and married him in Waukegan. Broke my mother's heart, because she'd given me the most expensive debutante party ever seen, in the middle of the depression, and had intended a grand tour to follow, culminating in my presentation at the English court, to the King, with three feathers on my head. Anyway, I married this beautiful but absolute idiot—what they hadn't mentioned in the documentation was that he was maintaining half the whores in Trenton and was an alcoholic."

She got divorced in 1938. Having published graphic art in *The New Yorker*, she worked to refine her painting in oils, and exhibited and sold her work in Washington, D.C. and Chicago. Then, in 1942, she enlisted in the U.S. Army and was "the first woman ever put through Air Force Intelligence School at Harrisburg, with thirty-five men who had nothing better to do than watch me." She became a photo-intelligence officer and started work "literally, in the cellar at the Pentagon," interpreting high-altitude photographs of the Far East for use in bombing sorties.

In 1945, she joined the Air Staff Post-Hostilities Project, devised by its commander, Colonel Huntington D. Sheldon, who had been Deputy Chief of Air Intelligence in the European Theatre. His aim was to seize and bring back to the U.S. as much German secret scientific research and personnel as possible, including atomic physicists, the first operational jet aircraft, and rocket technology. Without his initiative, most of this knowledge and material would have been lost to the Soviet occupation of East Germany.

Alice Hastings Bradley married Huntington D. Sheldon in a French mayor's office, very shortly after she had begun working in his project. They remain married to this day, a very strikingly close and devoted couple.

After the war, she and he left the military and ran their own small business for a while. But in 1952, "They'd been after Ting, and after him, to come back to Washington and help start what was then not yet formed: the CIA. All we'd had till then was the OSS, full of aged cowboys who wanted to do it like we did it in Dusseldorf. Ting finally joined the CIA at supergrade level; I was at mere technical level, helping to start up their photo-intelligence capability, which was then evaluating captured German air photography of the U.S.S.R.

"It was an awfully hectic life. Since the Russians are always doing something at two in the morning our time, that blasted loud-ringing telephone would go off, and I'd hear Ting murmuring in the pillow, 'I guess you'd better get the President on this one, John. All right, we'll put the watch staff together.' And then he'd be up and dressing and on his way. And then I would be on my way at eight in the morning to *my* rather harassing job.

"After we had the department set up and running, I got bored with it. So I played games on the clandestine side for a bit."

Wondering if she means that she did actual espionage work, I ask if she was sent out of the country.

"No, no, I was just—on the clandestine side." For the first time, she seems shy of speaking. "I stayed in the United States. Mostly I was being trained."

I ask if she's allowed to say what she was actually doing.

"No. Except that it was not James Bondish, really. It probably would have eventuated into a little James Bondism, but. . . ."

Was she commissioning people to go out and get information? Or was she just interpreting results?

"Neither. I was working up files on people. That's the clandestine side; the overt side does all the interpretation and evaluation. That's why the Bay of Pigs happened, because the clandestine side took control, got out from under, because Allen Dulles was the clandestine type, and totally end-ran the evaluation process, which was saying 'No such effort can succeed.'

"My photo-intelligence work had been a clean, harmless contest of skills. No one had been blackmailed or coerced, or even endangered. It had no more moral ambiguity than looking over the neighbor's fence and counting his laundry. But the clandestine side, dealing in assassinations and military operations, actually strikes me as wholly inappropriate to intelligence work, and its long-range effect tends to discredit the nation that employs it with anything less than superhuman care."

So for a little while she was actually out in the field—wherever 'the field' was.

"Well, I—I was around." She laughs. "But after I got started there, I realized that what I wanted to learn was not intelligence of the military sort, in which I include our civilian agency. I wanted to find out secrets that were in *nobody's* head. I wanted to do basic science.

"When I had finished being an artist, I was left with many questions about perception: Why is a spot of orange up in the left-hand corner very good, when a spot of blue wouldn't be? What *is* the perceptual evaluative mechanism? I developed the modest aim of knowing more about visual perception than anybody in the world, before I was dead."

So at this point she went back to college?

"At this point, I said, 'The hell with it.' I left a safe open one night. Twenty minutes later, I checked it, and caught it. But I'd never done that before in my life, and I said, 'My innards are telling me something.' So I wrote a two-line letter of resignation, and ran away from *everybody*. I used the techniques the CIA had taught me, and in half a day I had a false name, a false bank account, a false social-security card, and had rented an apartment and moved in. I was somebody else."

I comment that this reminds me of the retreat she built as a child in the elephant grass.

"Yes, very much. I wanted to think. So I thought, then I got back in touch with my husband, and we thought together, and decided we could really work things out.

"To do what I wanted to do, I needed a doctorate in experimental psychology. I was in my late forties, but I was helped into a predoctoral fellowship at the National Institute of Health, the only snag being that I had to get straight A's. You can be young and stupid, or old and smart; I was old, so I had to be smart. I did get a lot of honors—I graduated summa cum laude, and I had a Ph.D. magna cum laude. My husband was an incredible emotional and practical help through all of this, so deeply supportive, I couldn't have done any of it without him. I don't think I'd even be *alive* now, without him.

"I dragged out the predoctoral fellowship, long after I finished my Ph.D. exams, so that I could do four years of solid research, and I'll tell you, there is no greater thrill I've ever had than to stand bare-faced in front of Nature and say, 'I think this is the way your creations work; tell me, am I right?' And Nature grumblingly and reluctantly makes you do—as I did—thirteen different paradigms of the god damned experiment before you get the thing without any uncontrolled variables, and then finally says, in answer to your question, a clear-cut 'Yes.' That is the most thrilling moment I have ever had in my whole life."

The experiment that she devised was to debunk an item of orthodox wisdom which held that, because laboratory rats will cluster around anything new that is put in their cage, animals must be generally attracted to novelty. Alice Sheldon had observed for herself that wild animals *avoided* novelty; her experiment finally established that animals in a safe, familiar enviornment will go to the novel stimulus, while animals in an unsafe environment prefer things that they know. "This sounds like common sens—which is typical of many behavioral findings that take months or years to prove under strict experimental control."

But behind the experiment was her interest in human perceptions. Why, for example, does the public first shun a painter's work, and then decide that his paintings are worth millions, after he has died a pauper?

Sadly, she was unable to continue her research. "As a new Ph.D. I had to teach monster classes of education students who could barely count their toes." She applied herself to the task with her usual sense of duty. "I tried and I tried. The teaching was emotionally draining. I also had to renew my grant, and grantsmanship is a terrible job. I saw no way to do research again in the next five years, and I just burned out. I was too old. I had to quit for health reasons, which caused me great sadness for two or three years."

But by this time she had sold some science fiction. The first four stories had been written, in a fit of defiant bravado, during her Ph.D. exams.

"We had a torture rite at G.W. You took five exams, one every forty-eight hours, each lasting a whole day, on a different field of psychology. One boy lost all his wisdom teeth, another broke out in blood all over his shirt front, other people had less spectacular troubles. I wrote my first science-fiction story."

She had been reading science fiction since she was ten years old. "I always felt a mystic glow about being a science-fiction writer. I've had a story in *The New Yorker*, and I used to write a page of art criticism every week in the *Chicago Sun*, but to be published in that cruddy little blotting-paper magazine sent shivers up and down my spine. People reading *my* story—I still don't believe it, you know? As the rich man's mistress said, 'Even if it is only carbon crystallized under immense pressure and heat—*I want it!*'"

And yet she chose to publish all her fiction behind the most closely-guarded pseudonym. This, of course, was consistent with her desire to retreat and not be observed; 'James Tiptree' was yet another patch of elephant grass to hide in.

But why did she choose a *male* name? At first, she ducks this question.

"I thought, well, the editor will send this stuff back, so I'd better use a false name, and then I can try the next story with a different name, so he won't remember having rejected me."

When pressed, she goes further.

"A male name seemed like good camouflage. I had the feeling that a man would slip by less observed. I've had too many experiences in my life of being the first woman in some damned occupation; even when I wasn't the first woman, I was part of a group of first women."

And finally, when I *really* press her on the subject:

"I simply saw the name on some jam pots. Ting was with me; I said, 'James Tiptree' and he says—'Junior!' It was done so quickly, without conscious thought; but I suppose I couldn't have avoided having the thought—although I don't remember it—that the editor would take my stories more seriously."

She was sincerely astonished when all her first stories were accepted. She started taking her writing more seriously, and developed deeper themes, which were sometimes complicated slightly by her posing as a man. "I was faced with all these mysterious male drives and conventions that I didn't share, but I squeaked around that by making the male narrator old in most cases. The country of the old was the country of the dead, to most of my readers, who figure life ends about forty, so anything I ascribed to an older man, they would believe. Also, the glandular systems of older men and women are more alike. Being older myself, I naturally tended to use universal motives, as in that story 'Mother in the Sky with Diamonds,' where a man is trying to save his wretched old mother from a heartless tyranny.

"However, men have so pre-empted the area of human experience that when you write about universal motives, you are assumed to be writing like a man. And so when my identity was revealed, some people said it proved that a woman could write like a man. Now, in the first place, this assumes that I was *trying* to write like a man, which was the last thing I was trying to do. I was writing like myself, with the exception of deliberate male details here and there. Other critics talked about my 'narrative drive' as being a male writing style, but narrative drive is simply intensity, and a desire not to bore. It has never been confined to men. Take one of the first women utterers that we know about: Cassandra. *She* was never accused of a lack of narrative drive. She was just a little before her time, which is often what women's crimes consist of."

"James Tiptree" soon started attracting attention as a new writer of exceptional power and skill, and letters began arriving at the P.O. box, offering praise—and asking awkward questions. Alice Sheldon was characteristically scrupulous in her replies. "Everything I said to everybody was true, with the exception of the gender implied in the signature. I never *stated* I was a man." And to avoid lying, she gave "Tiptree" her own life history—which was her undoing. In 1977 Jeffrey D. Smith, a fan of the Tiptree stories (and now a close friend), saw an obituary of Alice Sheldon's mother in a Chicago newspaper. The details were too close to the known facts of "Tiptree's" mother to be a coincidence; and so Alice Sheldon was unmasked.

"The feminist world was excited because, merely by having existed unchallenged for ten years, 'Tiptree' had shot the stuffing out of male stereotypes of women writers. At the same time, the more vulnerable males decided that 'Tiptree' had been much overrated. They sullenly retired to practice patronizing smiles."

I ask her if there were any other feminist reactions.

"Ursula Le Guin said it was sort of embarrassing to have kicked me out of the feminist letter that was going around a few years previously. They'd asked me please to leave because, as a man, 'Tiptree' just didn't have the basic sympathy! Also I had started talking about mothers, which none of them liked to talk about. I'm not a mother myself—I was prevented from being a mother by a healthy case of peritonitis which I contracted in the middle of the Mojave Desert one August. But I have great respect for mothers, and a serious interest in the whole subject."

I ask her if she was influenced by any science fiction in particular, when she began writing.

"When you say that, what passes before my mind is simply a marvellous pageant, all mixed up and jumbled together. Sturgeon, especially, and the early Philip K. Dick, and Damon Knight, were big influences. Frederik Pohl helped me enormously. The early Barry Malzberg I like very much; I corresponded with him when I was a man. And the very freaky stuff—I liked things that I couldn't do. Some of your British people. The Vermillion Sands chap—Ballard. And Moorcock, except that I began to realize that some of his work was stunty; the Cornelius stories never rang true.

"Then of course there's that great neglected work, *Bill, the Galactic Hero* by Harry Harrison. What a rodomontade. It's almost *Dr. Strangelove*. Of course, you see, I'm a frustrated comedian, and a really good black comedy, I eat up. My own early stories, the shallow belly laughs, I esteem rather more than my critics do—a good laugh is rare. Not to be sneered at.

"When I started writing, I felt as if I were peeling away layers of myself, like an onion. I started getting pretty close to the really inside layers, and I felt I'd peeled myself down to the empty core. I wrote 'Slow Music,' which reads like a funeral march, a goodbye. And I meant it that way. I thought I was through, and, typically, I was going to kill myself.

"But then it seemed as though there was a little more of me after all. I found another onion."

Most recently she has produced some grim and powerful stories, and a gently lyrical series in which the closely-observed natural beauty of the Quintana Roo territory of Mexico is infused with a mystical sense of Mayan history. Alice Sheldon herself maintains a small house in that part of the world.

After a hiatus brought about by severe health problems that necessitated open-heart surgery, she has now resumed work on a new novel. She seems reluctant to say very much about the book, but remarks that "it's going to represent a great leap forward in my own writing discipline."

Unsurprisingly, in view of her artistic background, almost all her work is vividly visual. And her interest in behavioral psychology shows itself in many stories where a large social truth is acted out on a small-scale human level—much as an experiment in psychology will demonstrate a law of species behavior.

Her characters are often fiercely independent, and forced to fend for themselves; yet her stories lack right-wing libertarian flavor of the "rugged individualist" school of modern science fiction. I ask if, in fact, she identifies with any political philosophy.

"Around the late 1930s, I can't tell you how much time we wasted defining our differences with Stalinist communism, and Trotskyite communism—I'm sort of burned out on the subject. Only some benevolent dryad kept me from joining a John Reed club; once you do that, you're stamped as a communist front member forever.

"I'm an anarchist if anything. But I figure that the changes we're going to see in our time are going to be brought about more by reactions to external circumstances than by groups of people working *for* one system or another. Most likely is the dropping of the Bomb; short of that, there's ecological devastation, or an economic upheaval in the West. It's not that I have a feeling of helplessness; I think the individual can do a great deal in the world. You're not old enough to remember the real movement toward fascism that there was in this country, but George Dudley Pelley, just before the Second World War, had 10,000 armed men, called Silver Shirts, drilling in New Jersey. I joined Friends of Democracy right after the war, a little counter-espionage organization. We used to enroll in hate groups, send away for their literature. They were reasonably discreet to start with, but then they'd send these incredible, mad brochures advocating the sterilization of all Jews and cripples. We traced the movements of people from group to group—they never could resist listing all their founding fathers on their letterheads. I came to the conclusion that there was about a ten percent hardcore paranoid component in this country: those whose natural idea of government, whether impassioned or lethargic, was fascism. I still do believe that; they smolder there like an ember. Reagan started out from a point further toward the middle, but he attracted in his following, of course, a lot of what is politely called the extreme right. He gave the whole thing an impetus and a nourishing ambience, and I think the far right has probably done a good bit of recruiting."

Is she as skeptical of authority in real life as she is in her fiction?

"Yes. Power corrupts, absolute power corrupts absolutely, and as Eric Hoffer said, an absolute religion engenders the most absolute cruelties. Look at the wars in Ireland. But much as I loathe Roman Catholicism as an authoritarian religion, Islam is worse. Mohammed has no compassion, no understanding that man might require forgiveness for anything. He taught that women have no souls. He was a military leader who didn't have even the breadth of spirit that *Eisenhower* had.

"I was brought up on the knowledge that the Inquisition had burned alive two of my great-great-great grandfathers, for the crime of possessing a Bible. They wanted to read the thing in their own hands, without the intermediary of a priest. Man's humanity to man, I do not believe in; women only have the degree of freedom we have now because of these very artificial social circumstances; kindness to the weak does not hold when the war of all against all starts. Our freedoms and privileges will be the first to go. And, as in the case of Rome, the fall of the kingdom will be blamed on our liberties."

I remark that this sounds unmitigatedly pessimistic.

"God simply hasn't come down and told me, 'You will save yourselves.' If we don't actually kill ourselves off, I think we'll end up as a sort of Calcutta. That's what an exponential birth rate means on a finite surface. There are simply too many people."

I still object that she seems to lack faith in our ability to solve problems and change.

"Man does not change his behavior; he adapts to the results of it. This is, to me, the most grisly truth I learned from psychology. It's often the only predictor you need in any given situation, especially for groups, and often for single people. Man believes that, whatever the situation is, it's going to continue. For instance, because science has helped us in the past, we assume it will continue to do so.

"Being a lifelong atheist, I have had to work out a structure of basic values for myself. My premise is that we like a value which we essentially represent; to a giraffe, for instance, a long neck is *good*; life loves life. Life is a denial of entropy; it's a striking manifestation of *negative* entropy. So I believe it can be shown that things with a high degree of organization, meaning a low degree of entropy, seem good to us. For example, Nazism is a highly entropic form, and democracy is far more complex. An altruistic act is more complex than a selfish one; you can carry these concepts quite a ways, to show that most things we feel to be 'good' in the New Testament sense, and sensible, involve a more organized structure of action. To me, Lucifer is positive entropy, runaway breakdown of the system, the war of all against all, which I think will, unfortunately, recur."

Stated so briefly, her philosophy may seem facile. But it demonstrates her belief that human values can be deduced systematically. Her search for this kind of truth, and her heightened awareness of good and evil, recur throughout her fiction and her descriptions of her life.

Perhaps it's in the nature of an experimental psychologist to invent a scale against which human values can be measured. Perhaps a far-left anarchist who has worked at a high level in the CIA will inevitably end up preoccupied with morals and motives. Perhaps any child exposed to countless bizarre cultures will search, as an adult, for a bedrock of truth amid all the chaos; and any precocious adolescent misfit, lacking the intuitive ability to fit in, will turn to logic as a tool to cope with quirks of human behavior.

I don't presume to draw these conclusions myself; I think Alice Sheldon has already hinted at them for me. I suspect, in fact, that she picked out beforehand the anecdotes that would provide the best insight into her own character: the story of her little secret home in the elephant grass (which she described right at the start of our very first interview), and her description of finding solace when she would lie alone in a cemetery and contemplate the indifference of the universe. Below her, the exanimate; above her, the inanimate. Dead people and distant stars impose no demands, no perplexing social mores.

I think this makes it discreetly clear that her desire for anonymity, and her exaggerated, naive responses to people's demands, are interlinked. Again and again, she has portrayed herself over-reacting clumsily to what she thought people wanted: from her awkward attempts as a young child to please the adults, to her marriage to the first man who asked her, to her self-inflicted exhaustion as a teacher, coping with the needs of students and sacrificing her career as a psychologist in the process.

Before I met Alice Sheldon, I assumed that her reclusiveness was comparable to that of some other writers I had encountered. By making themselves inaccessible, they impose a little test of dedication on anyone who wants to talk to them. Their act of aloofness is really a power-play, and a hard-to-get courtship ritual.

I now understand that, for Alice Sheldon, this was not the case at all. While it lasted, her anonymity was a form of self-preservation—protection from those endlessly perplexing, undeniable social demands.

And now, of course, I'm guilty of eroding her privacy further, with my demands as an interviewer—to which, as usual, she responded with mad excesses of conscientiousness. All I can do at this point is close with what seems to me her most eloquent statement on the subject.

"When I was at Sarah Lawrence college, I used to do all my work at night and leave it on the professor's desk in the morning, like the elves. I'd still like to do that, to be able to write stories on old leaves, or something, and have them flutter down through an editor's window, with nobody knowing who did it.

"All that's gone, now. All that wonderful anonymity."

Note: the first interview with Alice Sheldon, from which some of this profile is derived, was conducted with Shawna Mc.Carthy (editor of *Isaac Asimov's Science Fiction Magazine*), who arranged the meeting.

BIBLIOGRAPHICAL NOTES

With the exception of a short story in *The New Yorker*, ("The Lucky Ones," 1946), all of Alice Sheldon's fiction has been published under the name James Tiptree, Jr., or Raccoona Sheldon, the latter being used for five later stories when she felt she needed to be able to write from an overtly female perspective.

Her one novel published to date, *Up the Walls of the World* (1978), ambitiously links unexpected effects of government research into ESP with an alien world inhabited by flying telepathic beings, about to be wiped out by a vast, lonely creature devouring planets that lie in its path.

Her short stories have won several Hugo and Nebula awards, and are collected in *Ten Thousand Light Years from Home* (1973); *Warm Worlds and Otherwise* (1975), with an introduction by Robert Silverberg ridiculing what was then a rumor that "Tiptree" could be female; and *Out of the Everywhere* (1981), which includes her prize-winning "The Screwfly Solution," in which aliens impose on us the kind of pest-control techniques that we use against insects. This collection also includes two stories not previously published elsewhere.

The Fiction of James Tiptree, Jr. (1977), by Gardner Dozois, is a study of her work which Alice Sheldon feels is particularly perceptive, even though it was written before her identity was known.

Stephen King

He brings out a stack of fat, lurid paperbacks. "Look at this. Look what I just went out and bought." He holds one up and growls with heavy melodrama: "*They Thirst!* by Robert McCammon." He shakes his head, as if in regret. "I'm afraid I'm going to love this book. I've got a real taste for crap. I'll probably like it better than this one, *Blood Rubies*." He picks up another paperback. "But I'll probably like *this* one best of all. *Judgment Day* by Nick Sharman. I'll bet at some point somebody will get killed in a bathtub, and they'll turn black, and somebody else's fingers are going to *plunge into their writhing flesh*." He grins cheerfully.

I suppose this is the kind of thing you expect from Stephen King, especially if you've read *Danse Macabre*, his book about himself and horror fiction, in which he plays up his popular tastes and avoids any hint of academic literary criticism—even though he has the background to write it, if he should choose to.

But he chooses not to. He makes it clear that, regardless of his success and his money, he still goes out and buys books and gets off on cheap thrills like any other horror fan. He presents himself as an everyday American, just like the ones he writes about so compellingly and so sensitively in his own novels.

But there's the catch, of course. No matter how hard he tries to be a regular guy, his rather special writing talent is still there to prove that he's anything but average. And when I talk of talent, I do not merely mean his flair for shocking people. His novella "Apt Pupil" in the *Different Seasons* collection makes it clear, if there was ever any doubt, that he can write fine prose of subtlety and precision. Personally, I think he's the best popular novelist we have, when it comes to capturing everyday life, truly understanding American character, and building a structure of modern myths on this foundation of gut-level reality. In his verisimilitude and in his fantasies, he expresses the essence of our times.

He might receive more praise from serious critics if he would spoil his books by making them more ponderous, less dramatic, more pretentious, and less fun. But he seems constitutionally opposed to any hint of snob-appeal, in his fiction and likewise in his life-style. He continues to live in Maine, and shuns the New York cocktail-party continuum that has served as a breeding ground for so many other effete literary reputations.

"One of the reasons I don't want to live in New York," he says, "is that I see it as a kind of literary party with these dickey birds that crawl all over you saying, 'Hey, come on out and let's have a few beers down at the Lion's Head.' Or, 'Let's pop over to my apartment, and we'll do a few lines, and we'll talk about books.' But we won't *write* books, because we'll be doing lines and having a few beers at the Lion's Head.

"What writers really talk about is not art, anyway, but money. They want to know, 'What's your contract like? What kind of advertising budget are you getting?' I have always perceived the worst enemy of the writer to be the guys around him."

So he stays in Bangor, a town that still has some rough-and-ready, frontier feel to it, and he has a grand old house, with steps up to a big front porch with white pillars, and two turrets, one circular, one square—a rambling mansion which, inside, turns out to be furnished with almost anonymously contemporary American taste: nothing cheap, but nothing ostentatious, either.

King is tall, hunches his shoulders slightly as if shy of showing his height, and speaks more readily about reading or writing than about himself. His face is very expressive, switching quickly from mischievous dimples to a hint of melancholy. He sits out with us on the back porch, drinking beer, dressed in an old T-shirt and threadbare pink corduroy pants, while his kids play in the garden. He seems happy to be surrounded by family, and he chats in a deliberately relaxed fashion to myself and Douglas Winter (who arranged this interview and will write his own version of it in a forthcoming book about King).

"Most people think that because I write horror, I must be weird," King tells us. "If they meet me, they take this kind of careful approach, like, 'Are you all right? You're not going to bite me, or anything like that?' A lot of times I feel that I'm disappointing them, in that I seem very mild-mannered and not very threatening. If only I had a little more of the Boris Karloff or Bela Lugosi charm, or something—even Christopher Lee!

"Of course, the other myth is that I must lead a very glamorous life, on the Riviera and all that. Well, it's a nice house, and a comfortable life, but it's not like something out of Rosemary Rogers. It's not the *glitterati*."

Someone as famous as Stephen King, of course, has already been interviewed endlessly, to the point where you might expect that he has nothing new to say. He has also written about himself in his book *Danse Macabre*. So I suppose some readers will be wondering why I wanted to include him here, especially since he's not even a science-fiction writer. Cynics will assume that I'm merely using his well-known name to help sell my book.

In fact, King's other interviews (and I've read a dozen of them) barely scratch the surface, and *Danse Macabre* is shy of self-analysis. The interview that I present here is much more revealing, and it also happens to sum up many of the themes in the two *Dream Makers* books, which is why I'm featuring it as a finale. As I've said above, I regard Stephen King as our preeminent modern myth-maker, or Dream Maker, if you will. He probably has more science fiction in print than most people realize; and he certainly has opinions on the subject.

"I've been at a couple of science-fiction conventions," he says, "and those people were out in a fucking *void*. There were people there who were literally separated from reality. Fundamentally, it seemed to me that they all felt alien, and maybe that is why they like science fiction. When you have people who belong to this Society for the Preservation of Creative Anachronisms, or whatever it is [a group that acts out medieval fantasies in full costume], I mean, those guys have blown their cogs! They're *gone*! If they didn't have people looking out for them, some of them would be committed."

He leans forward and adds, in self-parodying, confidential style, "A lot of them are *fat*, too. Have you ever noticed that at science-fiction conventions? There's always some dude that comes sort of boiling off the elevator, he's wearing Bib overalls, and he's nine feet wide. The floor shakes!

"I was never part of a fan network. I never had that kind of a support system. I grew up in a little town called Durham, which is about 150 miles from here. In a city, you find other people that are like you and like the same things. Then you get all this talk, talk, talk at club meetings, or conventions, and it's a dangerous thing. Everybody begins to reinforce everybody else, and starts to write about everybody else's characters. You develop a mythos. Whenever anybody develops a mythos, that means that the last ounce of creativity has expired somewhere. Like—Lin Carter forever!" He laughs.

He used to read science fiction, but not so much now.

"If I look at the first page and I see a lot of italics and sentences like, 'He chevvied his hamscammer and frotted over to Billegum'—I don't want to read a book where I have to learn a whole new vocabulary. So many people in the science-fiction field—I don't want to name names—are not very good writers. They're forgiven for writing awkwardly, or unoriginally, or a little bit boringly, because it's science fiction.

"But just because you work in a genre, you shouldn't be allowed to write poor prose. You shouldn't be allowed to say, 'I can write this kind of prose because, in the context of science fiction, it's great writing.'"

Perhaps science-fiction readers will resent this kind of criticism from the man who's already confessed his weakness for books like *They Thirst*. But I suspect King of being a very analytical reader, even while he's claiming a craving for cheap thrills.

When he first started writing, he wrote science fiction.

"I think I must have been seven or eight. I was sick, just constantly sick, with the same thing I've got now—bronchitis. There was one year I didn't go to school, I just lay there in bed and wrote a lot of stories. I was very aware of how bad I was, so sometimes I would copy other people's stories, till someone told me, 'Oh, Stevie, that's *wrong*! You can go to *jail* for that!'

"I started to submit stuff when I was about twelve, to magazines like *Fantastic* or *Fantasy and Science Fiction*. These stories had the trappings of science fiction, they were set in outer space, but they were really horror stories. One of the few good ones was about an asteroid miner who discovered a pink cube, and all this stuff started to come out of the cube and drive him back further and further into his little space hut, breaching the airlocks one after the other. And the thing got him in the end. All the science-fiction magazines sent it back, because they knew goddamn well there was no science in it, there were no aliens trying to communicate using psionic talents, or anything like that. There was just this big pink thing that was going to eat someone, and it ate him.

"I used to imitate everything that I liked. I would have short stories where I started off sounding like Ray Bradbury and ended up sounding like Clark Ashton Smith. Or even worse, they would start off as James Cain and end as H. P. Lovecraft. I was just silly putty. And still today, there will be reviews that say, 'The kindest thing we can say about Steve King is that he doesn't have much of a style.' I never have, and I know that. But I think that there's a lot of critical interest in writing that's pretty, rather than writing that's serviceable, and I'm more interested in stripping down. I don't want people to see my face in the book at all."

In fact he seems to go out of his way to write in the most popular, colloquial style, as if anything else would run the risk of seeming pretentious. For some reason that I can't pin down, pretentiousness bothers him a lot. It's the one topic that he is evidently reluctant to talk about.

"When someone tries to make a 'thing' out of being a writer, that's bad enough," he says. "What's even worse is if people call you an *Author*, and you let them do that. That's terrible!

"In college I would go around with a John D. MacDonald book, or a collection of short stories by Robert Bloch, and some asshole would always say, 'Why are you reading that?' And I'd say, 'Hey, this man is a great writer.' And in fact MacDonald has written a novel called *The End of the Night* which I would argue is one of the great American novels of the twentieth century. It ranks with *Death of a Salesman*; it ranks with *An American Tragedy*.

"But people would see the picture on the front, a Gold Medal paperback with some lady with her cakes falling out of her blouse, and they would say, 'It's garbage.' So I'd say, 'Have you read anything by this guy?' 'No, all I gotta do is look at that book, and I know.' Which was my first experience with critics, in this case my teachers at college.

"I always liked that kind of fiction, and that's what I always wanted to write. There ought to be a middle ground, where you can do it with some nobility, instead of either a) being a schlockmeister or b) saying 'Hey, everybody's just *saying* that I'm only a popular writer. They don't understand how sensitive my soul is.' There ought to be a place in the middle where you can say, 'I'm trying to do the best I can with what I've got, and create things that are at least as honest as what any craftsman would make.'

In his novella "The Body," in the *Different Seasons* collection, King includes what appears to be one of his own very early short stories—and mocks its slightly self-important strivings as being "painfully sophomoric. . . . Could anything be more *serious*? More *lit'ry*?"—as if that is the ultimate embarrassment.

"The Body" also depicts a seemingly autobiographical childhood among lower-middle-class, dead-end kids: an almost anti-literary background, where there would have been no place for anyone who indulged in affectations.

"In the family that I came from," he says, "there was a high premium on keeping yourself to yourself. I hung out with the kids, I worked on cars, I played sports—I had to play football, because I was big. If you didn't play football, and you were big, that meant you were a fucking faggot, right? Inside, I felt different and unhappy a lot of times. But I kept that part of myself to myself. I never wanted to let anybody get at it. I figured that they'd steal it, if they knew what I thought about this or that or the other thing. It wasn't the same thing as being embarrassed about it, so much as wanting to keep it and sort of work it out for myself.

"I could write, and that was the way I defined myself, even as a kid. Maybe I couldn't put one past the centerfielder, and maybe all I was good for in football was left tackle. You know, I used to get cleat marks up my back. But I could write, and that is still how I define myself, and that's a danger, because you tie up your self-image, your masculinity, whatever, in being able to do this, which means that if you lose it, you have nothing left.

"After *Carrie* was published, my wife Tabby got very exasperated with me, saying, 'You've made all this money, you are a success, let's spend some of it.' But I was insecure inside, for a long time, saying, 'Look, I don't trust this. Nobody can do this. You can't do this twice or three times.' My idea was, the success would never happen again, so I should trickle the money out. Maybe the kids would be eating Cheerios and peanut butter for dinner, but—that's okay! Let them! I'll be *writing*."

And then, as if feeling that all this is beginning to sound too serious, he adds:

"I've always regarded being a writer as a twitch, like being able to do this." (He wiggles his thumb, which is double-jointed.) "It so happens that *that*"—he wiggles it again—"doesn't make any money. But the ability or the desire to write everything down is that same kind of a twitch."

I ask him if, like some other writers, he feels he is writing for a particular person.

"I think that there might be. I really think it's myself; but there does seem to be a target that this stuff pours out toward. I am always interested in this idea that a lot of fiction writers write for their fathers, because their fathers are gone." (King's own father left the family when he was an infant.) "I don't know if there is anything to that or not. But there is that feeling of it going out toward a point, when it's the best."

This seems to be as complete a statement about the creative process as anyone could ask for, so we tackle the next topic, which has to be the obvious one: horror novels. What does he feel is the most important element in horror?

"Character. You have got to love the people in the story, because there is no horror without love and without feeling. Horror is the contrasting emotion to our understanding of all the things that are good and normal.

"If you can't bring on characters that people believe and accept as part of the normal spectrum, then you can't write horror. This is a problem that a lot of the supermarket novels have: you don't believe the people, and therefore you don't believe the horror, and you're not scared."

So King's work is almost always about everyday characters in everyday settings with which the reader can identify fully. For some people, though, his work can become a little *too* real.

"I got a really strong reaction to the 'Apt Pupil' story in *Different Seasons*. My publisher called and protested. I said, 'Well, do you think it's anti-Semitic?' Because it's about a Nazi war criminal, and he begins to spout all the old bullshit, once the kid in the story gets him going. But that wasn't the problem. It was too *real*. If the same story had been set in outer space, it would have been okay, because then you'd have had that comforting layer of 'This is just make-believe, so we can dismiss it.'

"So they were very disturbed by the piece, and I thought to myself,

'Gee, I've done it again. I've written something that has really gotten under someone's skin.' And I do like that. I like the feeling that I reached right between somebody's legs"—he makes a graphic, grabbing motion—"like that. There has always been that primitive impulse as part of my writing."

The renewed popularity of horror is still relatively recent, of course. Some writers in *Dream Makers II* have complained that their work won't fit the fiction categories, and suffers as a result. King's answer, as things worked out, was to develop a new fiction category to fit his work. He knows how things would have been if he'd been writing at a different time.

"In the 1950s, they would have gotten the manuscript of *'Salem's Lot* and they would have cut it in half and published it as a 'Crime Club' title, and I would have made fifteen hundred dollars. There's a novel by Richard Matheson, *A Stir of Echoes*, published as a 'Crime Club' in the 1950s. Nobody would touch it. But now they can call it a 'horror novel' and it's commercial. And the critics buy that completely. The critics will buy almost anything that a publicist puts in front of them."

At first, he seems reluctant to complain about criticism that he's received. Yet there are obviously some hard feelings.

"Some critics seem to feel that something very popular can't really be good, because that low common denominator is represented by people like Sidney Sheldon, Jacqueline Susann, people who are not good.

"But I'm convinced that most of the critics who review popular fiction have no understanding of it as a whole. They don't seem to have a grounding in it. They seem almost illiterate in some fields. There's so much popular fiction that nobody even sees, because it doesn't hit the *Times* best seller list. There are books that are not best sellers, that *are* popular fiction, that are wonderful novels, wonderful stories. There's a guy named Don Robertson; I think he's one of the most interesting writers in the country. There's a horror writer that even people in the field haven't read; he wrote *The Beguiled* and his name is Thomas Culenin, and he's an interesting writer. A Southern gothicist. I mentioned him in *Danse Macabre*. And nobody has ever reviewed a novel by Michael McDowell in the critical press, that I know of, and I think he's one of the top-drawer novelists in the country right now. There is nobody writing any better books in paperback-original than he is; but he's not reviewed.

"I'm not much on the cult of personality, but if you work hard on a book, you hate to see it dismissed in three or four paragraphs, or not reviewed at all. I haven't had a book reviewed in *The New York Times* Sunday book review since *The Stand*, and that review was about three paragraphs long, and I'm morally certain that the guy didn't read the book, or did a skim job.

"After a while, if you live long enough, by the time you're so old that you've begun to parody yourself or have actually begun to degenerate as a writer, and you and your contemporaries have all had your strokes and your heart attacks, *then* people start reviewing you well—mostly because you've survived the demolition derby. That's when you get good reviews: after you've done your important work."

He adds that some critics seem to resent his books simply because publishers pay so much for them. So he's sold his next novel, *Christine*, for a *one-dollar* advance. In due course, it will earn royalties as a percentage of the cover price of each book sold; but there's no money up front for critics to complain about, and he'll be paid only in proportion to the number of people who actually buy the novel.

I feel he'd rather trust the judgment of an average book-buyer than that of a critic—or even an editor, for that matter.

"A lot of hardcover editors seem to me to have very Ivy League sensibilities. It used to be that at least they would bring out decent novels, even if those novels didn't sell much more than 2,000 copies. But now they're all saying"—he goes into a snobbish accent—"'Well, all right, we must publish these awful potboilers, so we'll choose them.' And they pick out the worst, most awful, abysmal books to push. I'm not talking about best sellers—I'm talking about the ones that are pushed really hard and do *not* become best sellers. There was one by a guy named William Kinsolving called *Born with the Century*. It has got to be one of the most dreadful pieces of trash. It makes *Princess Daisy* look like *War and Peace*. And yet somebody thought it would be a big money-maker, because they don't have any understanding of popular taste—the understanding that we would have from what we pick out on the newsstands. These editors don't go to the newsstands. Ask a hardcover editor what he's read and in most cases he'll say, 'Well, I've been working my way through Henry James for the fifth time, and otherwise I don't have time to read anything but manuscripts.'

"The truth is that the level of taste, in the general body of people who read in this country, is a little bit higher than most hardcover editors, in their ignorance, are willing to admit. The real bad stuff won't sell. But the American public *will* respond to quality popular literature. For instance, *Watership Down* was a big best seller."

It might seem that someone as successful as Stephen King would no longer have any difficulties dealing with editors, so far as his own work is concerned. And yet success creates new problems of its own.

"I like to write three drafts: a first, a second, and what I think of as the editorial draft, when I sit down and take an editor's criticism and work it through in my own mind, and put the whole book through the typewriter again, and repolish the other stuff as well. But as the successes have mushroomed, it's been tougher and tougher for me to get my editors to give me time to do that third draft. What I'm really afraid of now is that one of them will say, 'I think this is great,' just because it fits the publication schedule. Every year, I'm on a faster and faster track. I'm supposed to get proofs of *Different Seasons* today. It's a 600-page book, but Viking wants the proofs read in five days, so they can take advantage of co-op advertising between the paperback house, themselves, and the movie company that's releasing *Creepshow*. They're going to have Bernie Wrightson's *Creepshow* comic book, and the hardcover of *Different Seasons*, and the paperback of *Cujo*, in 3,200 dump bins, not only in bookstores but Shop 'n' Saves or something. So therefore I am supposed to read the proofs in five days. Now, what if we let a bunch of dumb errors go through? It isn't a matter of creativity, or trying to do the best book possible, that's governing things right now—it's advertising. And that scares the hell out of me, because we'll fuck up real good one of these days, and then people can say, 'Steve King writes for money,' and at that point *they will be right*.

"In the case of the last couple of books that Viking has done, the hardcover sales have been enormous. There've been like 385,000 copies in hardcover. So we're talking about a gross which would be $13.95 times 385,000. This is important enough so that, at this point, I think that if there was any change suggested to me that I didn't want, all I would need to say would be, 'No. I won't do that.' And it would never be a question of their withdrawing my contract, would it? They'd just finally say, 'Well, okay then, don't do it that way.' Which means, in effect, that if I'm willing to be really intransigent, there'll be no editing at all."

Some writers might see this as an ideal position of power. But King recognizes the dangers of no longer being subject to any editorial feedback.

"It's a terrible position to be in. I think I just have to resolve to take editing, even if I think the changes are wrong. To do otherwise is to become a monster and claim that I'm doing it right, and I don't need any criticism, editorial help, or guidance. And I can't do that.

"On the other hand, I say to myself, 'Well, the things that I do are the things that have made me a success.' And if somebody wants to tamper with that, maybe they're wrong."

The writer-editor relationship has been a recurring theme in both volumes of *Dream Makers*, as I have tried to show how compromises occur between what a writer wants, and what an editor thinks the readers will want. Stephen King, of course, no longer needs to worry too much about having his work rejected, or having to tailor his books to suit the needs of the market— he *is* the market, or at least a large segment of it. But his comment about allowing himself to be edited demonstrates that, no matter how important a writer becomes, his writing still does not exist in isolation. There is always a subtle interplay; the process by which a book is published still leaves its mark on that book.

And this, of course, has been my concern all along.

In the introduction in the first *Dream Makers* I suggested that if we simply look at a finished novel, and ignore the process by which it was conceived, written, and published in the real world, we're leaving out some of the most pertinent facts about that novel.

Stephen King prefaces his *Different Seasons* collection with the rather modest motto: "It is the tale, not he who tells it." However, as his own profile shows so clearly, the tale *is* he who tells it; and it is also a product of commercial constraints, financial pressures, and other practical factors that poison or fertilize the creative process.

I have tried to pinpoint some of these factors in the profiles I've presented here, as well as portraying for you the Dream Makers whose inspiration and talent will always remain the most important factor of all.

BIBLIOGRAPHICAL NOTES

Carrie (1974), King's first novel, portrays a teenage misfit with telepathic powers, ultimately used to revenge herself at her high-school prom. It was released as a movie in 1976 coincidentally with paperback publication of King's second novel, *'Salem's Lot*. The impact made him a multi-million-selling author.

The Shining (1977) is probably his most popular book so far, describing the plight of a would-be teacher/writer, his wife, and their precognitive five-year-old son, trapped in an empty haunted hotel.

The Stand (1978) is a multiple-viewpoint science-fiction-flavored catastrophe novel in which near-future America is decimated by a virus accidentally released from a laboratory.

In *The Dead Zone* (1979), a man acquires ESP powers that enable him to foresee the future of a deranged political candidate destined to become president and start a nuclear war. King withdrew this novel from the ballot of The World Fantasy Award, stating that it was not fantasy. In fact, most of his work is closer to science fiction than to fantasy, despite its mystical/occult element. Almost all the novels are set in our rational everyday world, and the addition of just a few pages of pseudo-scientific argument would be enough to make them classifiable as "genuine" science fiction.

Different Seasons (1982) seems to suggest, however, that King would prefer to be thought of as a writer of serious contemporary fiction rather than as a writer of horror fiction, science fiction, or any other narrow commercial category.

A Message to the Reader

Many factors have been mentioned that determine which science-fiction books are published. But one fundamental factor has been left out until now: you, the reader.

You have the ultimate power to determine the kinds of books that editors will want to publish. This, in turn, determines the kinds of books that authors will want to write. To take a very simple example: If you and a million others run out and buy the fifth volume in Frank Herbert's *Dune* series, you can bet that the publisher will commission Mr. Herbert to write a sixth volume. On the other hand, if the fifth volume in the series sells hardly any copies and is a financial disaster, the publisher may well suggest to Mr. Herbert that he should write something different next time.

Editors do keep track of book sales, when they're trying to decide what to publish next. They have an obvious interest in giving you, the reader, the books that you want. However, the system doesn't work very well. Some books sell badly simply because they aren't properly distributed, or because salesmen and store owners don't *expect* them to sell—and therefore don't order many copies, or don't display them prominently.

This means that your buying habits, alone, are not a very effective way of telling editors what you want—especially if you aren't buying books because you can't find anything that you like.

How can you communicate more effectively? Easily: by writing letters. Before you dismiss this as being pointless, please believe that editors really do value anything that readers have to say. Editors are often working by instinct and guesswork; they receive very little feedback. A few letters can make a big difference.

To simplify matters, I have listed, below, the editors who choose most of the science-fiction and fantasy novels that are published in America. You'll see that it's a short list of names. The field is controlled by just a handful of people.

If you do send one of them a letter, as I hope you will, try to be specific. There's no point, for instance, in saying you want "more good books." Define exactly what you mean by "good books." And if a publisher has produced something that you liked in the past, mention the title or the author.

Some paperback publishers are not listed here, because they publish little or no science fiction. Dell Books is an example. And many hardcover publishers have been left off the list, because they produce only one or two new science-fiction novels a year.

Note that Playboy Paperbacks, Ace Books and Jove Books are now a part of The Berkley Publishing Group.

Avon Books
Ms. Page Cuddy, Editor-in-Chief
959 Eighth Avenue, New York, NY 10019

Bantam Books
Mr. Lou Aronica, Science-Fiction Editor
666 Fifth Avenue, New York, NY 10019

Berkley, Jove, Playboy, and Ace Books
Ms. Susan Allison, Science Fiction Editor-in-Chief
Ms. Terri Windling, Fantasy Editor
200 Madison Avenue, New York, NY 10016

DAW Books
Mr. Donald A. Wollheim, Editor and Publisher
1633 Broadway, New York, NY 10019

Del Rey Books
Ms. Judy-Lynn del Rey, Science-Fiction Editor
Mr. Lester del Rey, Fantasy Editor
201 East 50th Street, New York, NY 10022

The Donning Book Co. (Starblaze Series)
Mr. Hank Stine, Science-Fiction Editor
5659 Virginia Beach Boulevard, Norfolk, VA 23502

Doubleday & Co.
Mr. Pat LoBrutto, Science-Fiction Editor
245 Park Avenue, New York, NY 10017

Harper & Row
Mr. Marion S. Wyeth, Science-Fiction Editor
10 East 53rd Street, New York, NY 10022

Pocket Books (Timescape Series)
Mr. David Hartwell, Science-Fiction Editor
1230 Sixth Avenue, New York, NY 10020

St. Martin's Press
Mr. Thomas Dunn, Science-Fiction Editor
175 Fifth Avenue, New York, NY 10010

Timescape Books (see Pocket Books)

Tor Books
Mr. James Baen, Science-Fiction Editor
8 West 36th Street, New York, NY 10018

Reference Bibliography

These are some of the magazines and reference books that I used while writing the profiles in *Dream Makers II*.

The Encyclopedia of Science Fiction, edited by Peter Nicholls and John Clute. Granada Publishing, London: 1979. (The most definitive and comprehensive reference work on all aspects of science fiction. Also available as *The Science Fiction Encyclopedia* published by Doubleday in the U.S.)

Anatomy of Wonder (Second Edition), edited by Neil Barron. R. R. Bowker Company, New York: 1981. (Includes critically perceptive summaries of almost all important science-fiction novels, story collections, and books about science fiction.)

Science Fiction Writers, edited by E. F. Bleiler. Charles Scribner's Sons, New York: 1982. (A series of critical essays analyzing the work of most major names in the field.)

A History of the Hugo, Nebula, and International Fantasy Awards, by Donald Franson and Howard De Vore. Misfit Press, Dearborn, Michigan: 1981. (Lists all the people who have ever won the Hugo or Nebula awards. Also lists everyone ever nominated for the Nebula.)

The Futurians, by Damon Knight. John Day, New York: 1977. (Personal reminiscences about a New York clique of writers that included Donald A. Wollheim, among others.)

Jack Vance, edited by Tim Underwood and Chuck Miller. Taplinger Publishing Company, New York: 1980. (A collection of essays about Vance.)

Profiles of the Future, by Arthur C. Clarke. Harper & Row, New York: 1962. (Clarke's classic book of predictive essays.)

The Cosmic Chase, by Richard Hutton. Mentor Books, New York: 1981. (A useful survey of achievements in space.)

"*Our Man in the Future: Arthur C. Clarke*," by Roger Caras. *Science Digest*, March 1982. (Some quotes from an interview with Clarke in Sri Lanka, plus a partial bibliography).

Cosmic Trigger, by Robert Anton Wilson. Pocket Books, New York: 1977. (Wilson's own account of the background to the *Illuminatus!* trilogy.)

"An Interview with Poul Anderson," by Elton T. Elliott. *Science Fiction Review*, Number 25, May 1978. (More bibliographical than my profile, plus some extra political material.)

With William Burroughs, by Victor Bockris. Seaver Books, New York: 1981. (A series of taped conversations between Burroughs and other literary figures.)

The Third Wave, by Alvin Toffler. William Morrow, New York: 1980.

"On Literary Celebrity," by D.M. Thomas. *The New York Times Magazine*, June 13, 1982. (Thomas's informal account of his visits to America and reactions to sudden best seller status.)

SF in Dimension, by Alexei and Cory Panshin. Advent Publishers, Inc., Chicago: 1980. (A book of critical essays on mainly modern science fiction, with special attention to Heinlein, the "new wave," and the future of science fiction.)

Interview Dates

The sequence of chapters in this book is not the sequence in which the writers were interviewed. Instead, I have arranged the profiles according to links of theme and place.

Some of the writers refer to work that was in progress when they were interviewed, or books that they were then planning to write. The interview dates listed below will put such references in proper perspective.

Name	*Date*	*Place*
Jerry Pournelle	September 1981	Studio City, California
Larry Niven	September 1981	Tarzana, California
Christopher Priest	November 1981	London, England
William S. Burroughs	August 1981	New York City
Arthur C. Clarke	April 1982	By phone to Sri Lanka
Alvin Toffler	August 1981	New York City
John Sladek	February 1981	London, England
D.M. Thomas	May 1982	Hereford, England

Keith Roberts	February 1981	Henley, England
Andre Norton	March 1982	Winter Park, Florida
Piers Anthony	March 1982	Inverness, Florida
Keith Laumer	March 1982	Brooksville, Florida
Joe Haldeman	March 1982	Ormond Beach, Florida
Fritz Leiber	March 1982	Boca Raton, Florida
Robert A. Wilson	September 1981	San Francisco, California
Poul Anderson	September 1981	Orinda, California
Jack Vance	September 1981	Oakland, California
Theodore Sturgeon	September 1981	Los Angeles, California
L. Ron Hubbard	May 1982	By mail to California
Joanna Russ	December 1981	By phone to Oregon
Janet Morris	June 1982	By phone to Massachusetts
Joan Vinge	September 1981	Chappaqua, New York
Harry Harrison	April 1981	New York City
Donald Wollheim	July 1981	New York City
Edward L. Ferman	June 1982	Cornwall, Connecticut
Kit Reed	June 1982	Middletown, Connecticut
James Tiptree, Jr.	June 1982	McLean, Virginia
Stephen King	May 1982	Bangor, Maine
Charles Platt	July 1982	New York City

Charles Platt

By Douglas E. Winter

Charles Platt sets up his own tape recorder next to mine. I ask him why, and he responds with the anxious geniality of a man facing root-canal work: "Well, I want my own tape, to hear what I sound like. I'm not used to being on this side of the microphone."

The devil gets his due, it is said, and an interview with the interviewer seems a fitting close to the *Dream Makers* series. Berkley Books agreed when I proposed the encounter, so I find myself sitting across the table from Charles Platt, trying to recapture the first impression I gained of him several years ago, when a call to an anonymous telephone number, in search of *New Worlds* magazine, led me to his door.

After a confused taxi ride through Greenwich Village, I found Platt's apartment nestled in a shadowland alleyway of parallel row-houses, originally built as servants' quarters to an estate long ago vanquished by urban expansion. e. e. cummings once lived here, and the lower-case, cloistered atmosphere of an artists' colony was unmistakable.

At the last row-house, an elderly tenant waved me upstairs as if she knew my destination. My knock was answered by the clank of a security bar. The door rattled inward, and Platt jack-in-the-boxed out of its shadows. An unruly shock of chestnut hair topped his thin face, whose sharp and boyish features were emphasized by mischievous eyes. "Hullo, I'm Charles Platt," he said, and without further ado ushered me in.

At first, I assumed that his apartment was temporary quarters—there was a spartan and decidedly whimsical quality to its furnishings—but later I saw it as a logical extension of his personality. Books lined three walls of the living room, while a stereo and a stack of records (Dave Edmunds and Nick Lowe albums prominent) stood at the fourth. Beneath one bookshelf were boxes and boxes of Weetabix, a British cereal to which Platt is addicted, and which, along with other eccentric foodstuffs, he will carry on his travels—even, on occasion, when invited to dinner. The apartment's principal feature was a word processor (then, still an innovative tool for a writer); its decor was tacky Americana, ranging from a plastic 3-D Jesus plaque to souvenir plates inscribed with verses to Mother.

As this curious mixture of appurtenances suggests, locating Charles Platt may be easier than defining him. If we look to the public record (and by this I mean the charmingly opaque two-line summations on book jackets) we learn that Platt was born in Scotland in 1949 . . . wait, this one says Tehran in 1944 . . . no, here it says a small English village in 1945, the adopted son of Lord Platt. When I ask about the discrepancies, Platt seems more concerned that I should actually own the books in question. "I can never take anything totally seriously," he says, as if the proposition were not self-evident; but the interview proceeds with candor and a fair modicum of seriousness. At one point, he seemingly apologizes, his expression deadpan: "I promised myself that, as an interviewee, I would do those considerate things that make an interviewer's life easier."

With the question of birthdate unresolved, it seems inevitable that we begin at the beginning. Platt was born in London in 1945 (and Lord Platt, a distinguished physician, was his uncle). At age five, his family moved "to the horrible, dull little town of Letchworth, where I went to a peculiarly permissive and progressive school, which gave its students a totally unrealistic view of life. They all expected things to be extremely easy when they left school, because things had been so easy when they were *at* school. Some of them became disillusioned and bitter; others just remained perpetually naive, which is what happened to me."

He describes his childhood as typical of a science-fiction writer. "I was one of those people who read a book a day and believed in it in that peculiarly intense way that real science-fiction fans have. I wasn't terribly popular socially. I was the youngest in my class—didn't enjoy sports. My idea of a recreation would be plotting a three-dimensional graph and cutting out the little templates and stacking them. I was also interested in astronomy—anything which would entail getting away from being beaten up at school."

Writing science fiction was the inevitable next step. "I wrote comic strips when I was about seven or eight, which I tried to sell to my friends at school. This didn't make me very popular or very rich, but I had *big plans*. I tried to sell a few stories when I was eighteen or nineteen, sending them to *New Worlds*, which at that point was a slightly more literate imitation of the American science-fiction magazines."

In 1963 Platt entered university at Cambridge, intending to study economics, but he quickly dropped out and moved to London. "Almost coincidentally, Michael Moorcock took over editorship of *New Worlds*. I sent him my fifth story, which he liked very much and bought—he made it the cover story, which was a nice way to break into print." (Platt prefers to forget that his first professional sale was in 1964, to *New Worlds*'s companion magazine, *Science Fantasy*.) "It also turned out that I was living in an area of London about two blocks from where Moorcock was living, which was very serendipitous." Platt became the designer and later the (unpaid) production manager for *New Worlds*, supporting himself by writing "ridiculous soft-core nonsense." He also played keyboards in several "obscure" rock bands. When Moorcock left *New Worlds* in 1969, Platt took over as editor.

In the late 1960s and early 1970s, *New Worlds* was the focal point for a loose-knit group of writers who brought a brief and startlingly unwelcome "new wave" to science fiction. Platt is still possessed by the idealism of those times: "Largely as a result of *New Worlds*, I discovered literature which lacked the speculative component of science fiction but nevertheless was equally challenging to the imagination. I was woken up to the fact that most science fiction is not terribly well written, and does not offer any great insights into the human psyche—which is something you ignore when you're sixteen years old, because at that age, *you* don't have many insights into the human psyche, either.

"I'd always been interested in anything new or experimental, so the idea of experimenting with fiction was just fascinating. There weren't any rules at school, so why should there be any rules in fiction? It struck me as perverse that some of the older writers felt that you could speculate on almost any topic, but when it came to writing your speculation, you had to stay within very rigid stylistic limits. I think writers should be able to try whatever they like, to extend their imaginations or tastes as far as they will go."

Was there a feeling of manifest destiny among the *New Worlds* writers, of bringing a real change to science fiction?

"No one would have said so, of course, because we didn't want to seem too pretentious; but there was. There was also a sense of 'us-versus-them,' which was prevalent in all the arts and in politics. The 1960s were the first time in history that youth had been given much power in anything, and I was youth at the time. We had *our* music, we had *our* clothes. I wanted us to have *our* literature, too. And *New Worlds* was the focus of what was new in this respect.

"We didn't think that we were going to take over the world, but we did think we could push science fiction in our direction a bit. And to some extent we were right; although I never imagined that this slow slide back into conventionality would occur. I thought that innovation in music and writing was just going to keep on growing outward and upward. It never occurred to me that people would really prefer to go back to the same old stuff, after they'd had a taste of more innovative and challenging material. People read science fiction to be surprised, so why would they prefer something *less* surprising?"

When asked what happened, he shakes his head, honestly bemused. "I don't know. I tend to draw analogies with music. Music is no longer a very potent force, but in the late 1960s a lot of people were drawing energy from it. The Beatles really did inspire people, by taking this crass form of popular music and adding orchestras, doing what they liked, breaking all the rules and getting away with it. And when that all fell to pieces—when that band split up, and Jimi Hendrix died, and Bob Dylan had his motorcycle accident and came back giving us country music—that was incredibly disillusioning.

"Then, of course, the anti-war movement was *successful*, and there's nothing like success to defuse things, because you no longer have anything to fight against. And a lot of people got scared. I think Dylan's retreat from all those angry lyrics of the 1960s was a classic case of someone getting scared by what he had opened up. Also, you know, people become more conservative as they grow older, which is another thing I don't understand. So the decline of innovation in science fiction, I think, was wrapped up with all of that."

Between 1966 and 1970, Platt wrote four science-fiction novels. All are out of print, and none was especially successful, except perhaps for *The Gas*, a post-apocalypse satire written for the renowned publisher of erotica, Olympia Press. Haunted by his failure to have written a critically or commercially successful science-fiction novel, Platt rages against the thought of being judged solely on his early books: "They just sounded fun to write. I never imagined them lingering on years later to embarrass me."

Platt left England in 1970, resettling in New York City. The reasons for his move "are contained in any Beach Boys or Chuck Berry song—you know, 'I wish they all could be California girls,' or 'Hot dogs and hamburgers . . . back in the U.S.A.' All the national cliches turn out to be true. People talk more bluntly over here, are less reserved. It's a country which, until now at any rate, hasn't throttled itself with its own history. It's still willing to change abruptly, and I like change. I also like cities, and I think New York is probably the most visually exciting city to be in. I get recharged just by riding my bike around town."

He traveled extensively through America in the early 1970s, and "wrote some undistinguished novels in order to finance an itinerant lifestyle." In 1972 he was appointed consulting editor, specializing in science fiction, at Avon Books. He compiled their "rediscovery" list of science-fiction classics, and persuaded Avon to publish two new issues of *New Worlds* in book form. He resigned when Avon refused to buy Philip K. Dick's *Flow My Tears, the Policeman Said* because they disliked its title.

Platt has since spent most of his time writing outside of science fiction, producing a versatile assortment of books, including *Outdoor Survival* (a guide for young people), *Sweet Evil* ("a fantasy of Mansonesque decadence"), and three installments of the "Christina" series of erotic novels. He was New York columnist for the *Los Angeles Free Press* (as well as for *The Fetish Times*), taught evening classes at two New York colleges, worked briefly as a magician, and most recently has authored numerous games and utility programs for home computers.

In 1977 he published his best and most serious science-fiction novel, *Twilight of the City*, "using economic theory as a way of building the future scenario." Although he has since published only one science-fiction story, he still sees himself as a science-fiction writer: "It's hard not to. I imagine it's the same if you learn country guitar: No matter what style you adopt after that, you still think in certain guitar-picking patterns. Even though I've done relatively little science-fiction writing,

I still think of myself as a science-fiction writer, because I'm imprinted that way. I still get ideas for science-fiction books. I have ideas for twenty, at least, written down and stored away."

Platt's major writing influences have been "Alfred Bester, the great innovator of the 1950s, and J. G. Ballard, great innovator of the 1960s," as well as the late C. M. Kornbluth and Algis Budrys ("*Michaelmas* was *the* novel of the 1970s"). He remains interested in most forms of experimentation in literature, but holds little hope for a near-term return to it in science fiction.

"American publishing and, to some extent, British publishing have changed so much in the last fifteen years. Then, science fiction was obscure to most publishers, and they let their hireling do whatever he liked; but science fiction is now considered big business if you get the right formula, and thus it is becoming more like television than a small press—those being the opposite ends of the artistic scale. So it's going to be much harder to do anything very surprising."

The problem is compounded, in Platt's view, by the lack of effective criticism of science fiction. "Most of it is inarticulate, and not much of it is very critical. Most of it is saying, 'Oh, here's another fine Gene Wolfe novel. Jolly good. How pleasing it is to see such fine writing.' Well, that is not criticism; that is the sort of response that occurs when one's pleasure centers are inoffensively stimulated.

"It's a miserable job being a critic. You don't get paid much. You have to think at least as hard as if you were writing a short story. Few critics' works are going to be anthologized, so you are really writing something which is almost disposable. So it's not surprising that few good writers bother to write criticism. Why should they? They're much better paid and better loved for writing fiction."

Nevertheless, in recent years, Platt has returned to science fiction primarily as a critic, to tilt at the windmills of its writing and publishing establishments. He assisted in a brief revival of *New Worlds* from 1978 to 1980, financing, editing, and designing one issue himself. In 1980 he began editing and self-publishing *The Patchin Review*, a "little magazine" that "is the only truly radical, skeptical voice within the science-fiction field." The magazine presents serious criticism hand-in-hand with unadulterated gossip and satiric tomfoolery. Platt's editorial tone has led certain writers and critics—not a few of whom have been the subjects of its barbs—to contend that he pursues controversy only for the sake of controversy. He reacts with hurt surprise: "Any area of the arts gets stale unless people try new things. People are not going to try new things if they are constantly congratulated for doing the same old things. I'm not necessarily in favor of newness for its own sake, but I do get bored if there is a conspicuous lack of innovation. Science fiction should be a literature of surprises. We all know each other in this field, with the exception of a very few editors and writers, so naturally we tend to be tactful socially, and even in reviews that are published in professional magazines. This is bad; it leads to complacency, and complacency leads to repetition, low standards, bad habits that are never corrected. So, I think honesty is an antidote. I don't see what's controversial about that.

"Good heavens, this country has freedom of speech written into its constitution. That's another reason I live here. The country I come from does not have that guarantee, so I feel acutely that it's very important to be free to speak your mind. I'm always surprised when other people want to qualify that. They say, 'Freedom of speech, yes, I completely agree—except, of course, in certain circumstances.' And that, to me, is not a trivial difference at all. That is *all* the difference."

His adamance notwithstanding, trouble seems to follow Platt. In pursuit of his vague ideal of honesty (applied selectively, as witness his revisionist approach to his own history), he holds no truck with tact or diplomacy: "You know, without wanting to sound too profound, sometimes the truth seems more important than a friendship." Indeed, a friend of more than ten years' standing became so upset by his *Dream Makers* profile that he threatened to seek an injunction against publication of the first volume. They have not talked to each other since 1980.

What practical effect does he hope his critical efforts will obtain? Where would he like to see science fiction in ten years?

"I'd like there to be less of it. Some politicians scream, 'Get rid of the welfare chiselers.' Well, in my case, I don't object at all to people on welfare, but there are certain writers who are on a kind of 'science-fiction welfare'—they're conceptual parasites, serving no useful function in creative or literary terms. I would like there to be less of such repetitive, derivative writing.

"There is also a great need for good rational fiction, because there is so much anti-rational fiction being published. There has been such a retreat from science, just because some of the things that science achieved turned out to have unpleasant side-effects. We now have people who are against nuclear *anything*, rather than being selective. As far as I'm concerned, having gone this far, science is the only thing that can save us. So it's all the more important, now, to see stories which are proper science fiction rather than whimsical fantasy, myth, or whatever you want to call it.

"It's a matter of doing the job properly; that is to say, of making it rational—as opposed to fantasy, which is not—and writing it well. Just because it often has not been written well does not mean that that's what science fiction is; it just means it has seldom fulfilled its promise."

What about Charles Platt? Where would he like to be, as a writer, in ten years?

"I always wanted to be about ten different things. That's the whole problem. Unfortunately, there's not enough time to do all these things before you die; and, as one passes the age of thirty-five, one stops thinking about how much time has passed and starts thinking about how much time remains."

Platt's renewed ambition is obvious as he discusses his interest in completing a new science-fiction novel by early 1983. "Doing the *Dream Makers* volumes taught me a lot about the methods used by successful writers. And then I began to understand much more about publishing than I ever had. So I now feel I have a much better shot at writing something which will please me, something which will please other people too, and will perhaps be moderately successful."